# SQUADRON

# SUPREME

## CIVIL WAR II

**COLLECTION EDITOR:**
**MARK D. BEAZLEY**

**ASSOCIATE MANAGING EDITOR:**
**KATERI WOODY**

**ASSOCIATE EDITOR:**
**SARAH BRUNSTAD**

**SENIOR EDITOR, SPECIAL PROJECTS:**
**JENNIFER GRÜNWALD**

**VP PRODUCTION & SPECIAL PROJECTS:**
**JEFF YOUNGQUIST**

**SVP PRINT, SALES & MARKETING:**
**DAVID GABRIEL**

**BOOK DESIGNER:**
**JAY BOWEN**

**EDITOR IN CHIEF:**
**AXEL ALONSO**

**CHIEF CREATIVE OFFICER:**
**JOE QUESADA**

**PUBLISHER:**
**DAN BUCKLEY**

**EXECUTIVE PRODUCER:**
**ALAN FINE**

SQUADRON SUPREME VOL. 2: CIVIL WAR II. Contains material originally published in magazine form as SQUADRON SUPREME #6-9. First printing 2016. ISBN# 978-0-7851-9972-4. Published by MARVEL WORLDWIDE, INC., a subsidiary of MARVEL ENTERTAINMENT, LLC. OFFICE OF PUBLICATION: 135 West 50th Street, New York, NY 10020. Copyright © 2016 MARVEL No similarity between any of the names, characters, persons, and/or institutions in th magazine with those of any living or dead person or institution is intended, and any such similarity which may exist is purely coincidental. **Printed in the U.S.A.** ALAN FINE, President, Marvel Entertainment; DAN BUCKLEY, Preside TV, Publishing & Brand Management; JOE QUESADA, Chief Creative Officer; TOM BREVOORT, SVP of Publishing; DAVID BOGART, SVP of Business Affairs & Operations, Publishing & Partnership; C.B. CEBULSKI, VP of Brand Manageme & Development, Asia; DAVID GABRIEL, SVP of Sales & Marketing, Publishing; JEFF YOUNGQUIST, VP of Production & Special Projects; DAN CARR, Executive Director of Publishing Technology; ALEX MORALES, Director of Publishi Operations; SUSAN CRESPI, Production Manager; STAN LEE, Chairman Emeritus. For information regarding advertising in Marvel Comics or on Marvel.com, please contact Vit DeBellis, Integrated Sales Manager, at vdebellis@marv com. For Marvel subscription inquiries, please call 888-511-5480. **Manufactured between 9/23/2016 and 10/31/2016 by LSC COMMUNICATIONS INC., SALEM, VA, USA.**

10 9 8 7 6 5 4 3 2 1

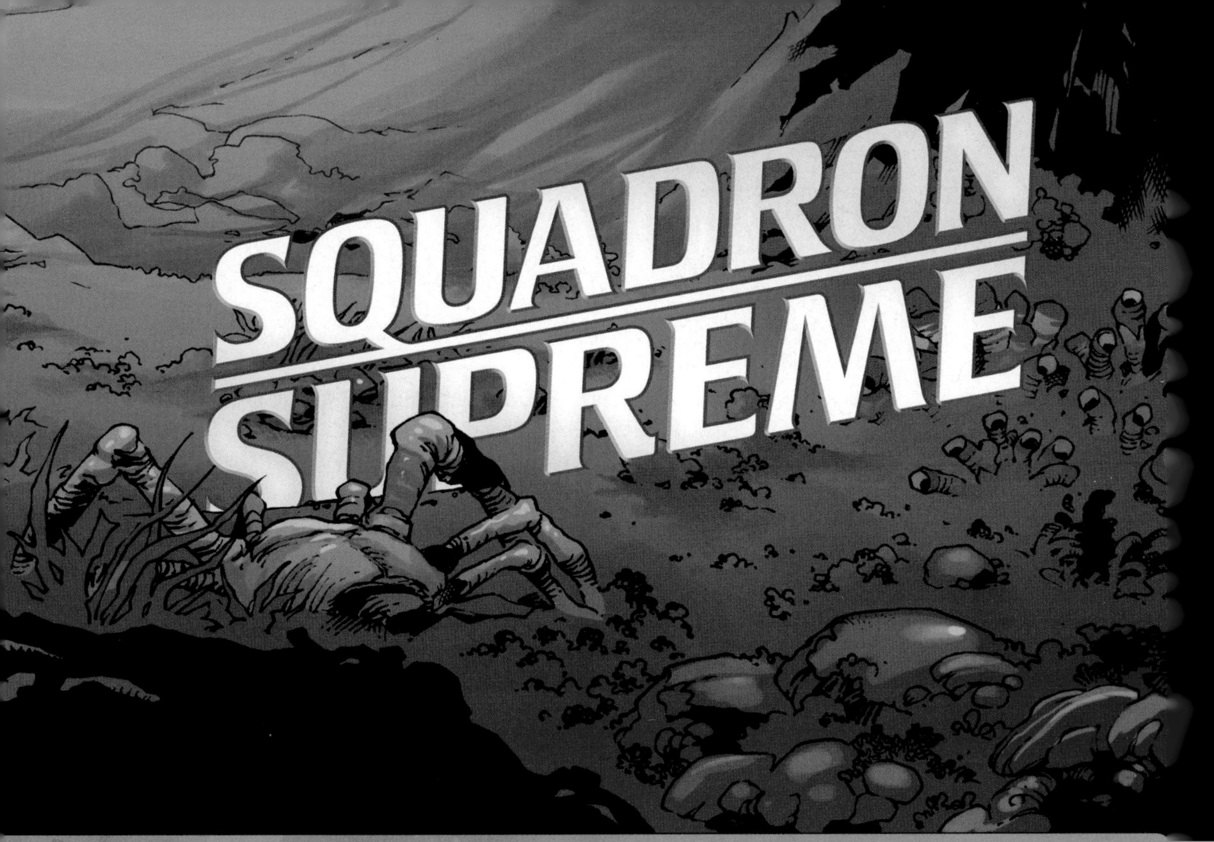
SQUADRON
SUPREME

**JAMES ROBINSON**
WRITER

**#6-8**

**LEONARD KIRK**
& **PAOLO VILLANELLI**
PENCILERS

**PAUL NEARY**
WITH **MARC DEERING** (#7)
INKERS

**FRANK MARTIN** (#6-7),
**GURU-eFX** (#7) &
**CHRIS SOTOMAYOR** (#8)
COLOR ARTISTS

**#9**

MAIN STORY

**ACO**
ARTIST

**MARCELO MAIOLO**
COLOR ARTIST

BACKUP STORY

**LEONARDO ROMERO**
ARTIST

**MAT LOPES**
COLOR ARTIST

**ALEX GARNER**
COVER ARTIST

**VC's TRAVIS LANHAM**
LETTERER

**CHRISTINA HARRINGTON**
ASSISTANT EDITOR

**KATIE KUBERT**
EDITOR

**MARK PANICCIA**
SENIOR EDITOR

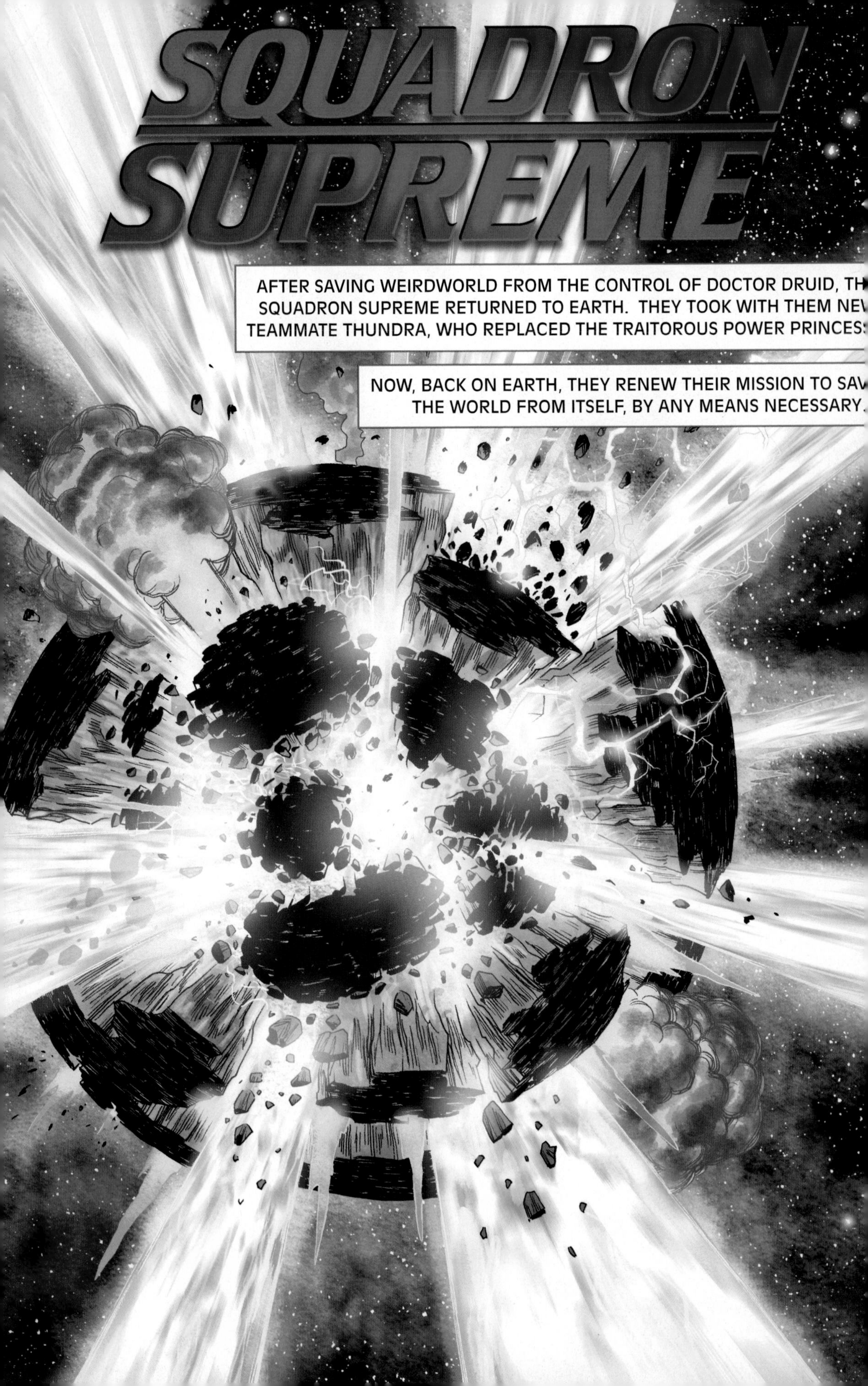
SQUADRON SUPREME
AFTER SAVING WEIRDWORLD FROM THE CONTROL OF DOCTOR DRUID, TH SQUADRON SUPREME RETURNED TO EARTH. THEY TOOK WITH THEM NEV TEAMMATE THUNDRA, WHO REPLACED THE TRAITOROUS POWER PRINCES
NOW, BACK ON EARTH, THEY RENEW THEIR MISSION TO SAV THE WORLD FROM ITSELF, BY ANY MEANS NECESSARY.

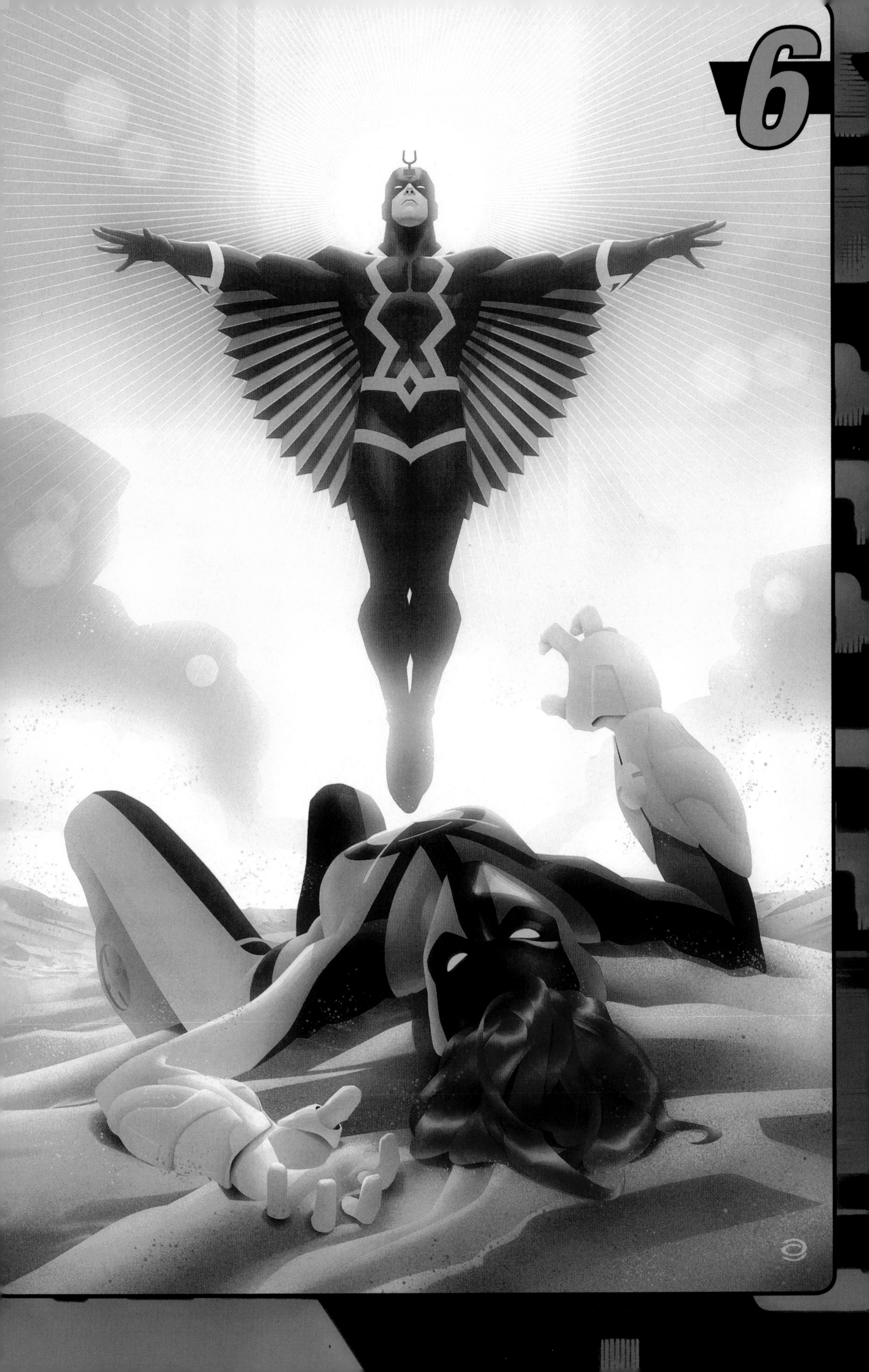
6

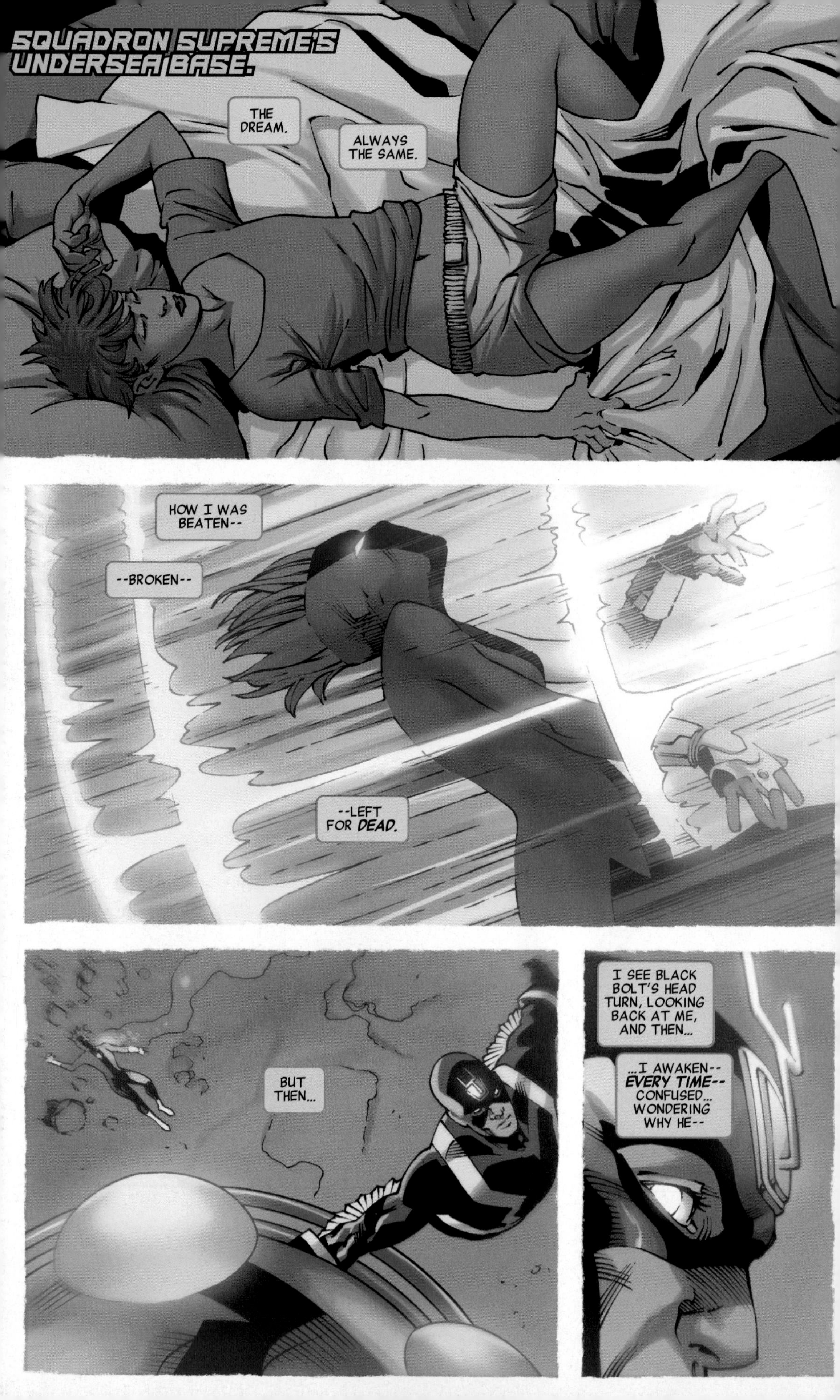
SQUADRON SUPREME'S UNDERSEA BASE.
THE DREAM.
ALWAYS THE SAME.
HOW I WAS BEATEN--
--BROKEN--
--LEFT FOR DEAD.
BUT THEN...
I SEE BLACK BOLT'S HEAD TURN, LOOKING BACK AT ME, AND THEN...
...I AWAKEN-- EVERY TIME-- CONFUSED... WONDERING WHY HE--

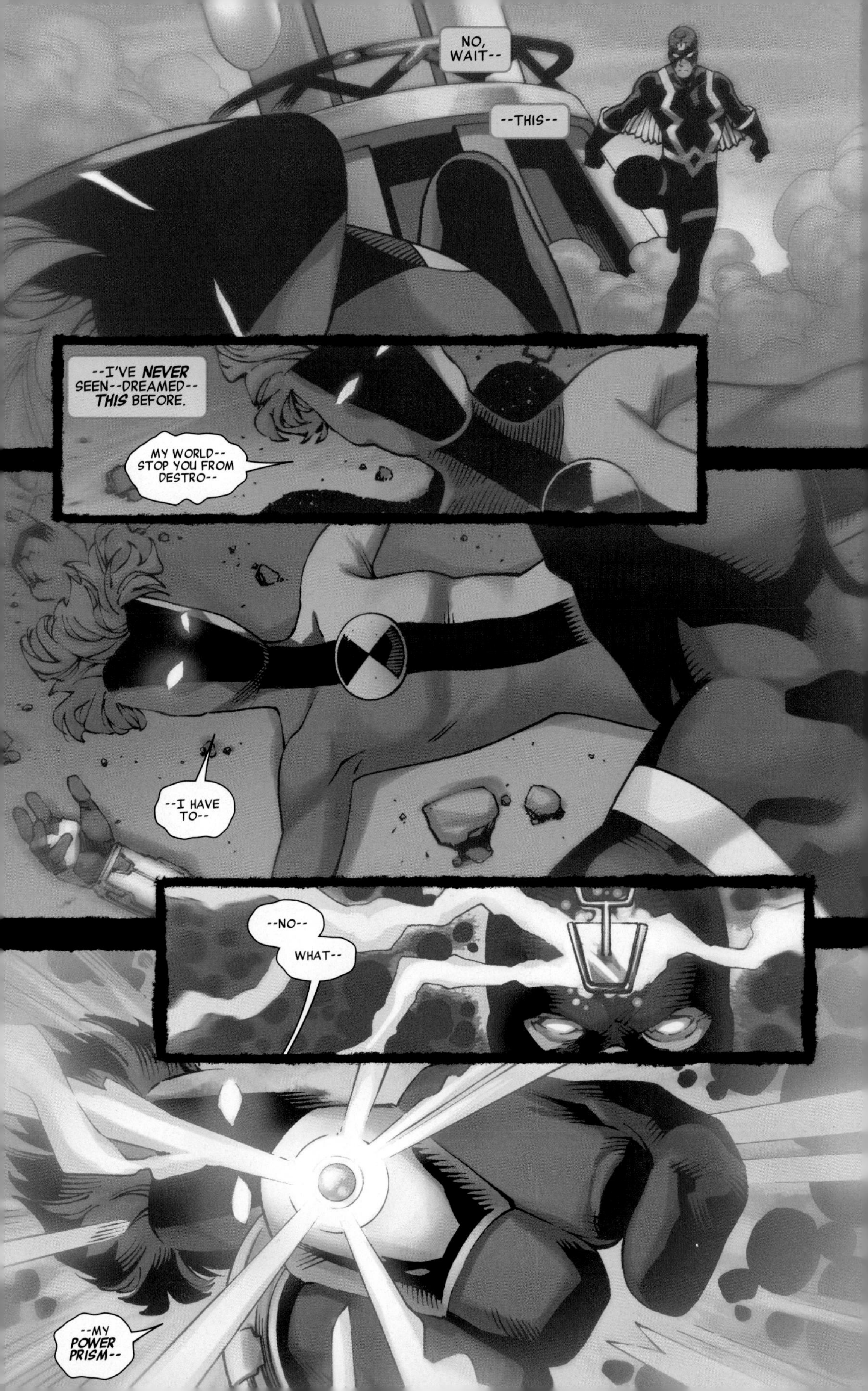
NO, WAIT--
--THIS--
--I'VE NEVER SEEN--DREAMED--THIS BEFORE.
MY WORLD--STOP YOU FROM DESTRO--
--I HAVE TO--
--NO--
WHAT--
--MY POWER PRISM--

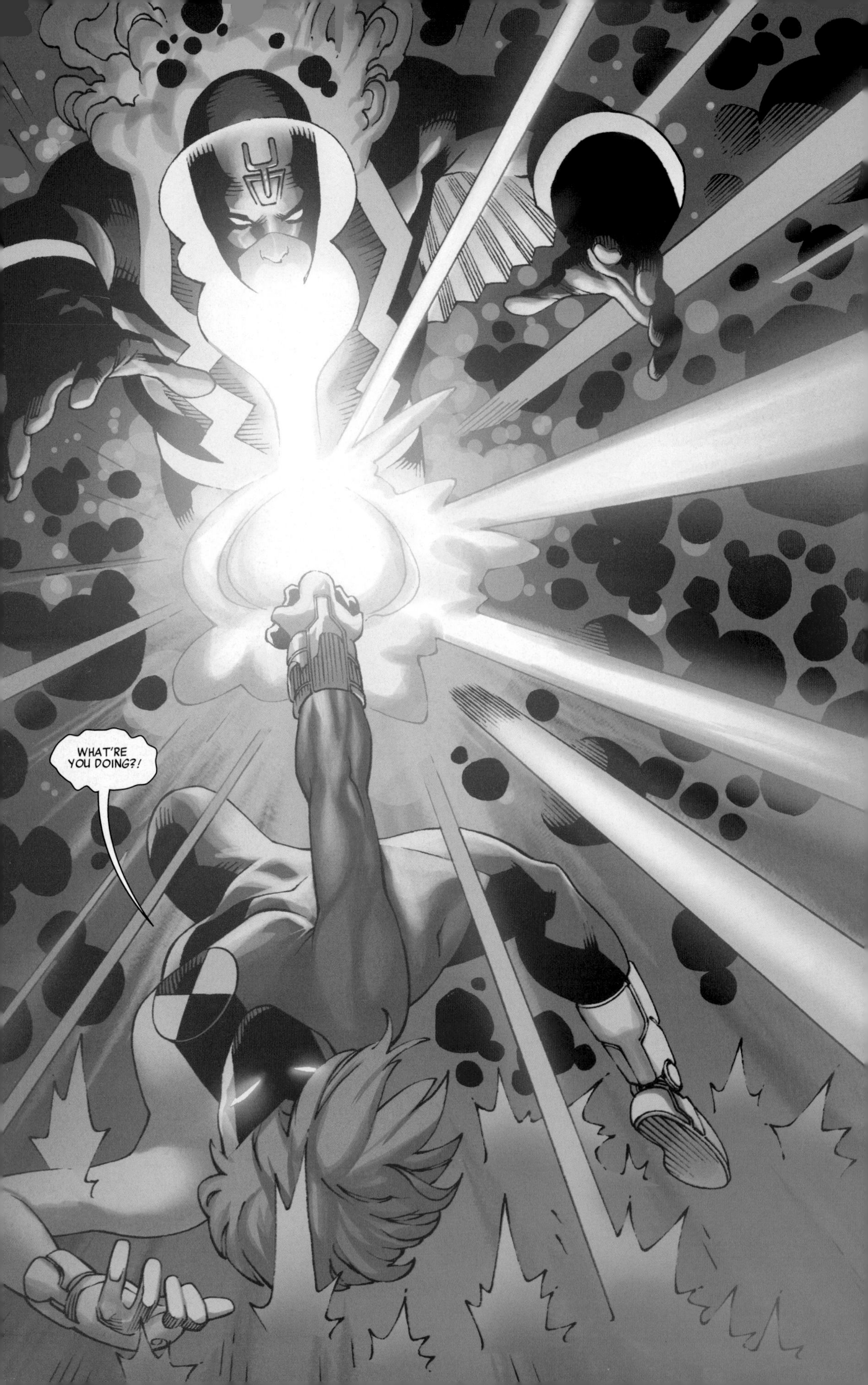
WHAT'RE YOU DOING?!

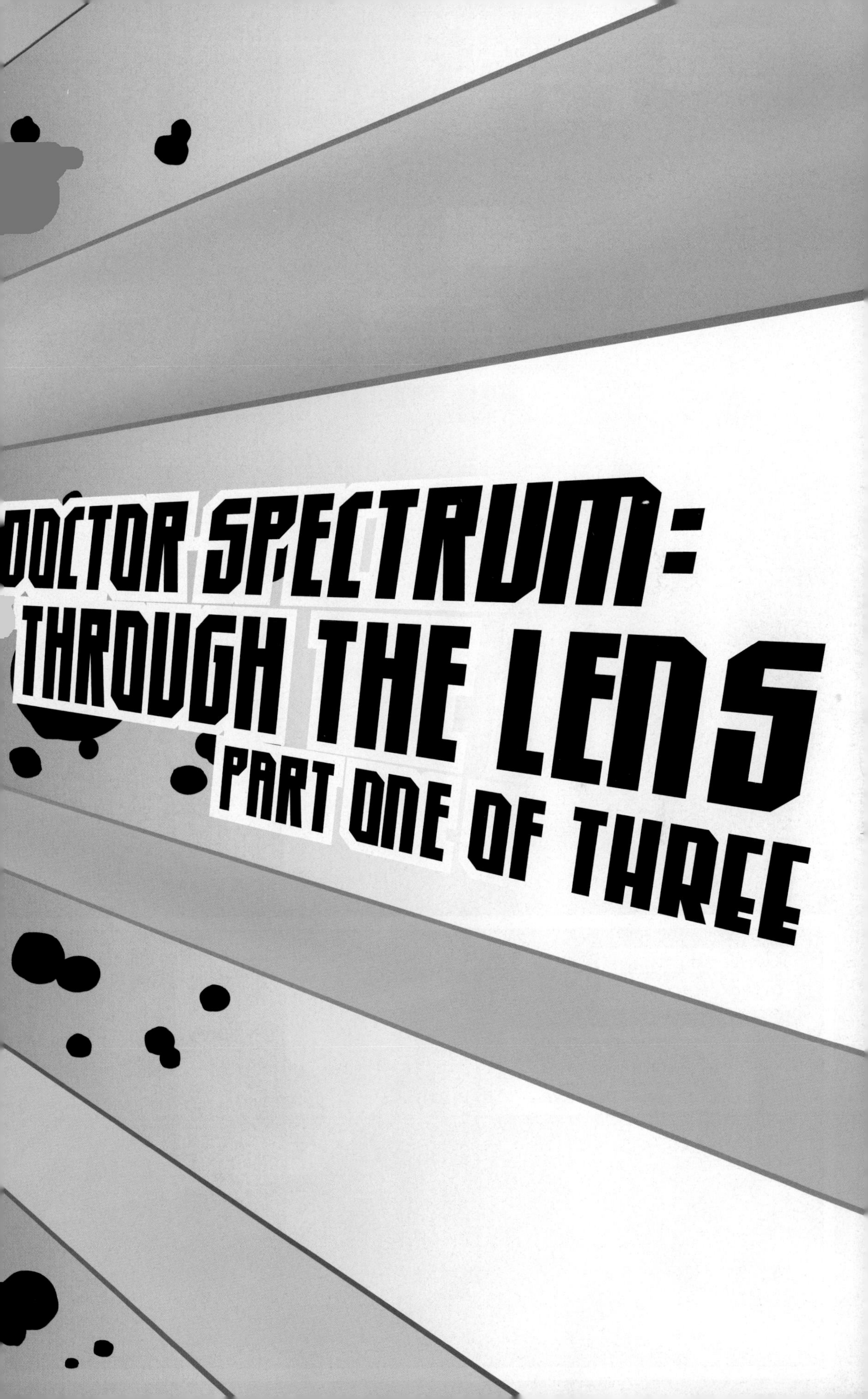
DOCTOR SPECTRUM:
THROUGH THE LENS
PART ONE OF THREE

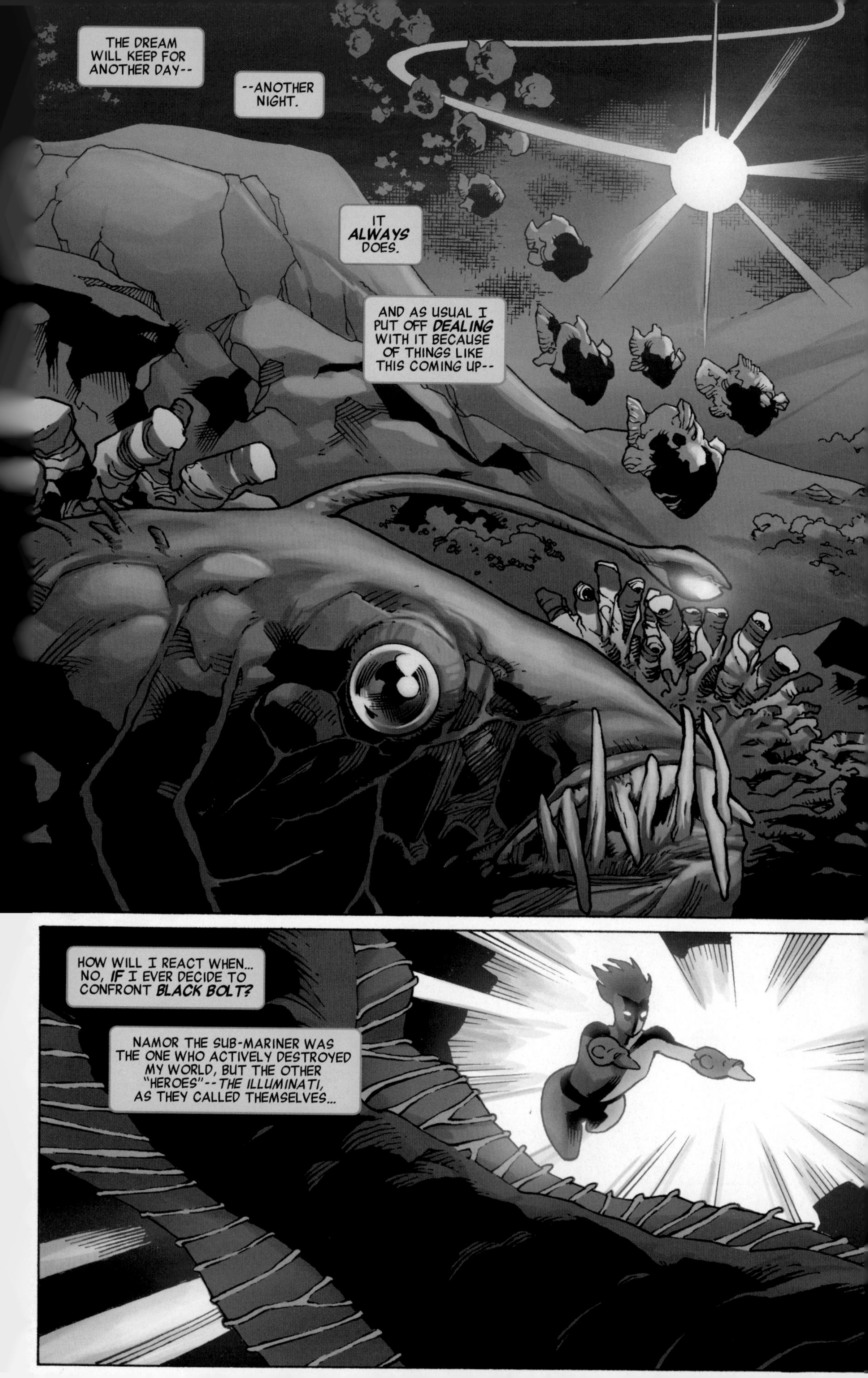
THE DREAM WILL KEEP FOR ANOTHER DAY--
--ANOTHER NIGHT.
IT ALWAYS DOES.
AND AS USUAL I PUT OFF DEALING WITH IT BECAUSE OF THINGS LIKE THIS COMING UP--
HOW WILL I REACT WHEN... NO, IF I EVER DECIDE TO CONFRONT BLACK BOLT?
NAMOR THE SUB-MARINER WAS THE ONE WHO ACTIVELY DESTROYED MY WORLD, BUT THE OTHER "HEROES"--THE ILLUMINATI, AS THEY CALLED THEMSELVES...

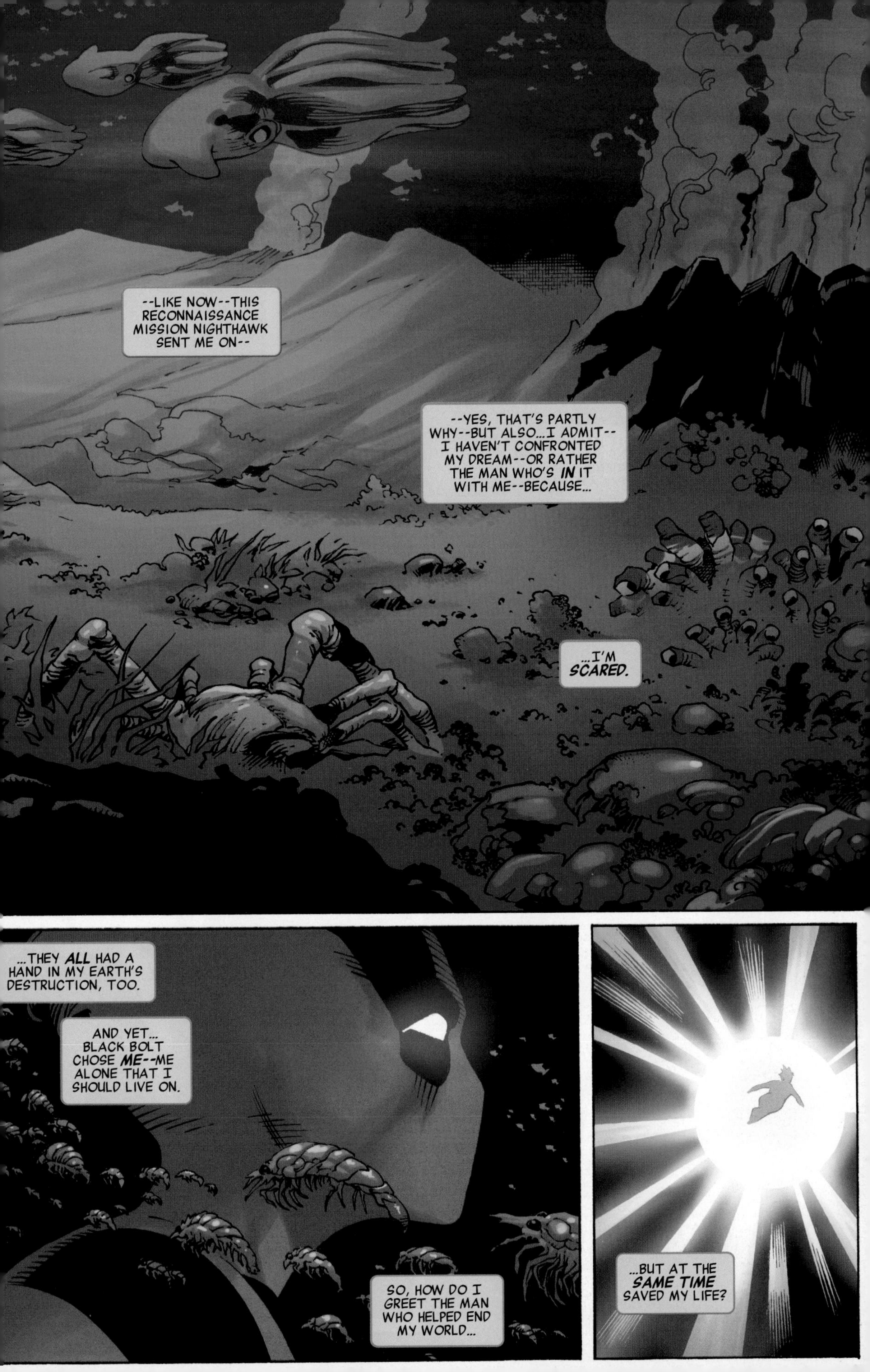
--LIKE NOW--THIS RECONNAISSANCE MISSION NIGHTHAWK SENT ME ON--
--YES, THAT'S PARTLY WHY--BUT ALSO...I ADMIT-- I HAVEN'T CONFRONTED MY DREAM--OR RATHER THE MAN WHO'S *IN* IT WITH ME--BECAUSE...
...I'M *SCARED.*
...THEY *ALL* HAD A HAND IN MY EARTH'S DESTRUCTION, TOO.
AND YET... BLACK BOLT CHOSE *ME*--ME ALONE THAT I SHOULD LIVE ON.
SO, HOW DO I GREET THE MAN WHO HELPED END MY WORLD...
...BUT AT THE *SAME TIME* SAVED MY LIFE?

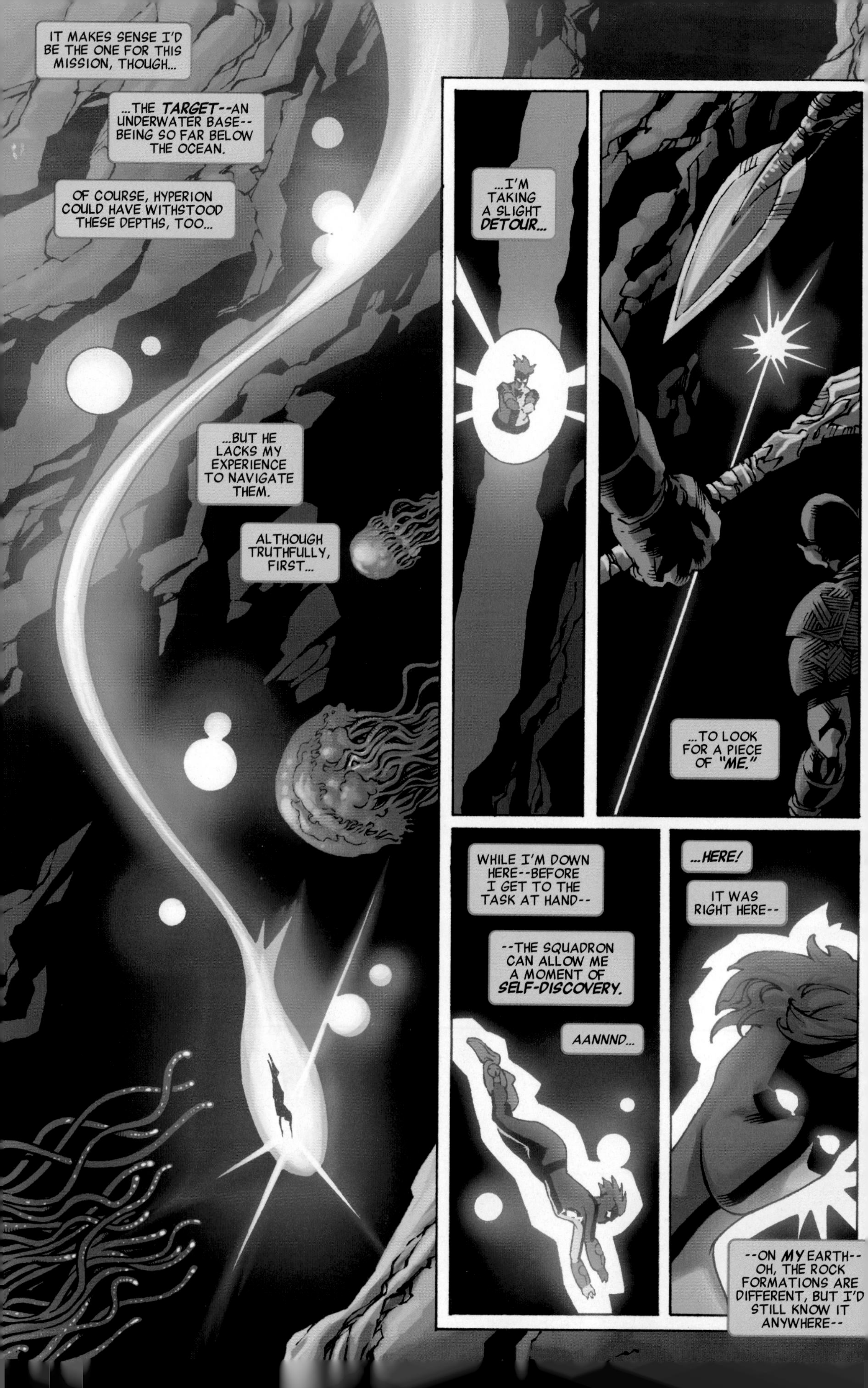
IT MAKES SENSE I'D BE THE ONE FOR THIS MISSION, THOUGH...
...THE TARGET--AN UNDERWATER BASE--BEING SO FAR BELOW THE OCEAN.
OF COURSE, HYPERION COULD HAVE WITHSTOOD THESE DEPTHS, TOO...
...BUT HE LACKS MY EXPERIENCE TO NAVIGATE THEM.
ALTHOUGH TRUTHFULLY, FIRST...
...I'M TAKING A SLIGHT DETOUR...
...TO LOOK FOR A PIECE OF "ME."
WHILE I'M DOWN HERE--BEFORE I GET TO THE TASK AT HAND--
--THE SQUADRON CAN ALLOW ME A MOMENT OF SELF-DISCOVERY.
AANNND...
...HERE!
IT WAS RIGHT HERE--
--ON MY EARTH--OH, THE ROCK FORMATIONS ARE DIFFERENT, BUT I'D STILL KNOW IT ANYWHERE--

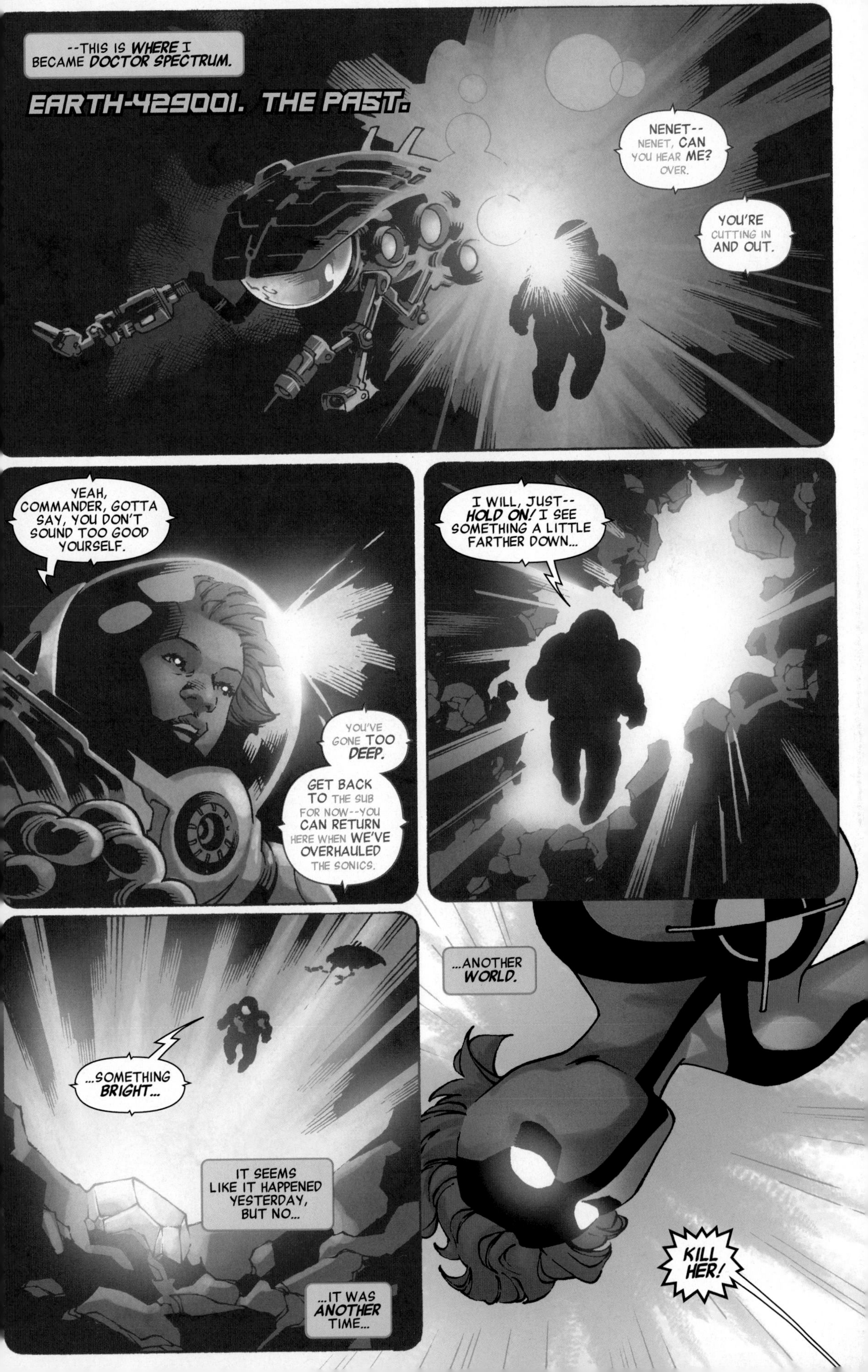
--THIS IS WHERE I BECAME DOCTOR SPECTRUM.
EARTH-429001. THE PAST.
NENET-- NENET, CAN YOU HEAR ME? OVER.
YOU'RE CUTTING IN AND OUT.
YEAH, COMMANDER, GOTTA SAY, YOU DON'T SOUND TOO GOOD YOURSELF.
YOU'VE GONE TOO DEEP.
GET BACK TO THE SUB FOR NOW--YOU CAN RETURN HERE WHEN WE'VE OVERHAULED THE SONICS.
I WILL, JUST-- HOLD ON! I SEE SOMETHING A LITTLE FARTHER DOWN...
...SOMETHING BRIGHT...
IT SEEMS LIKE IT HAPPENED YESTERDAY, BUT NO...
...IT WAS ANOTHER TIME...
...ANOTHER WORLD.
KILL HER!

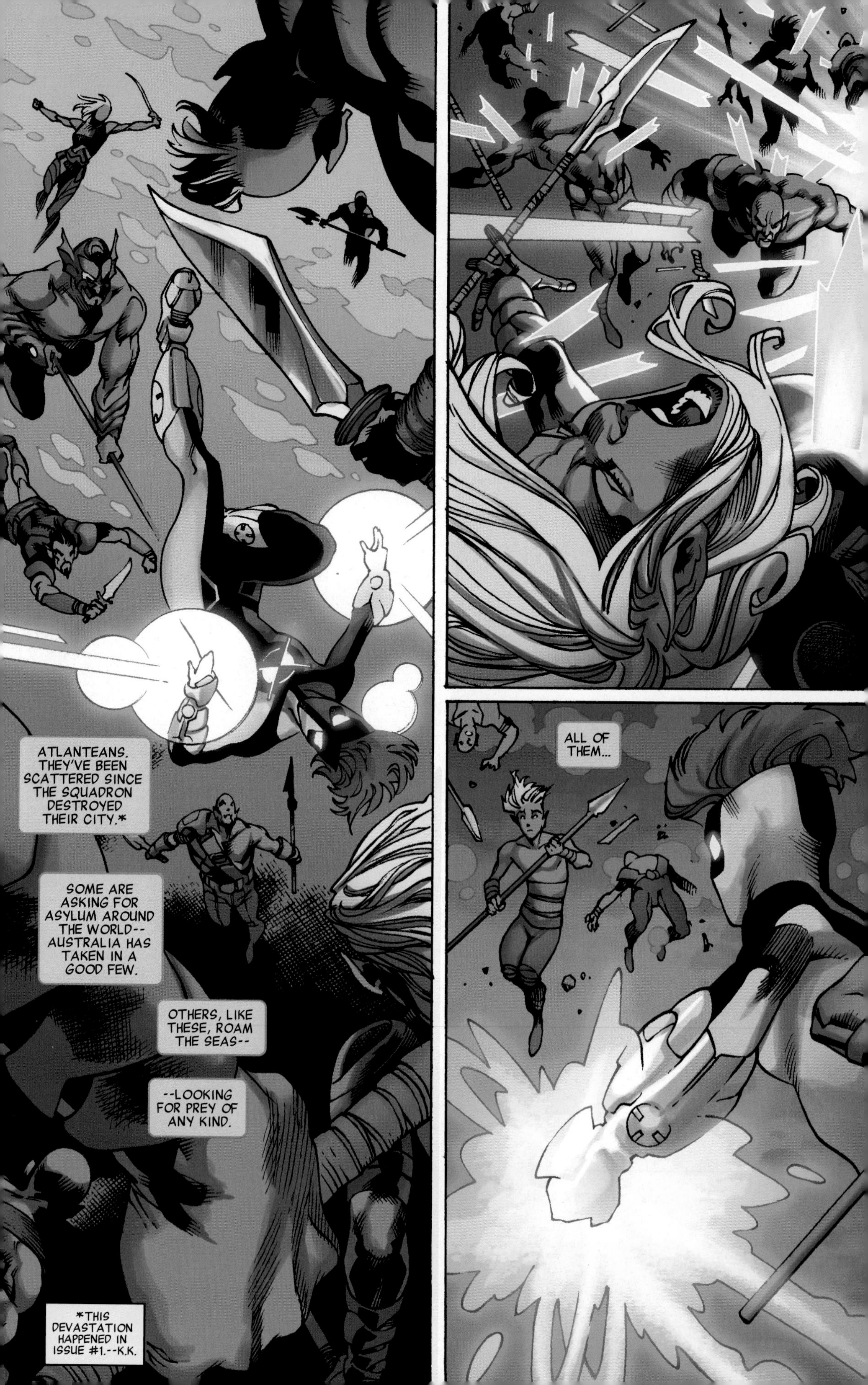
ATLANTEANS. THEY'VE BEEN SCATTERED SINCE THE SQUADRON DESTROYED THEIR CITY.*
SOME ARE ASKING FOR ASYLUM AROUND THE WORLD-- AUSTRALIA HAS TAKEN IN A GOOD FEW.
OTHERS, LIKE THESE, ROAM THE SEAS--
--LOOKING FOR PREY OF ANY KIND.
*THIS DEVASTATION HAPPENED IN ISSUE #1.--K.K.
ALL OF THEM...

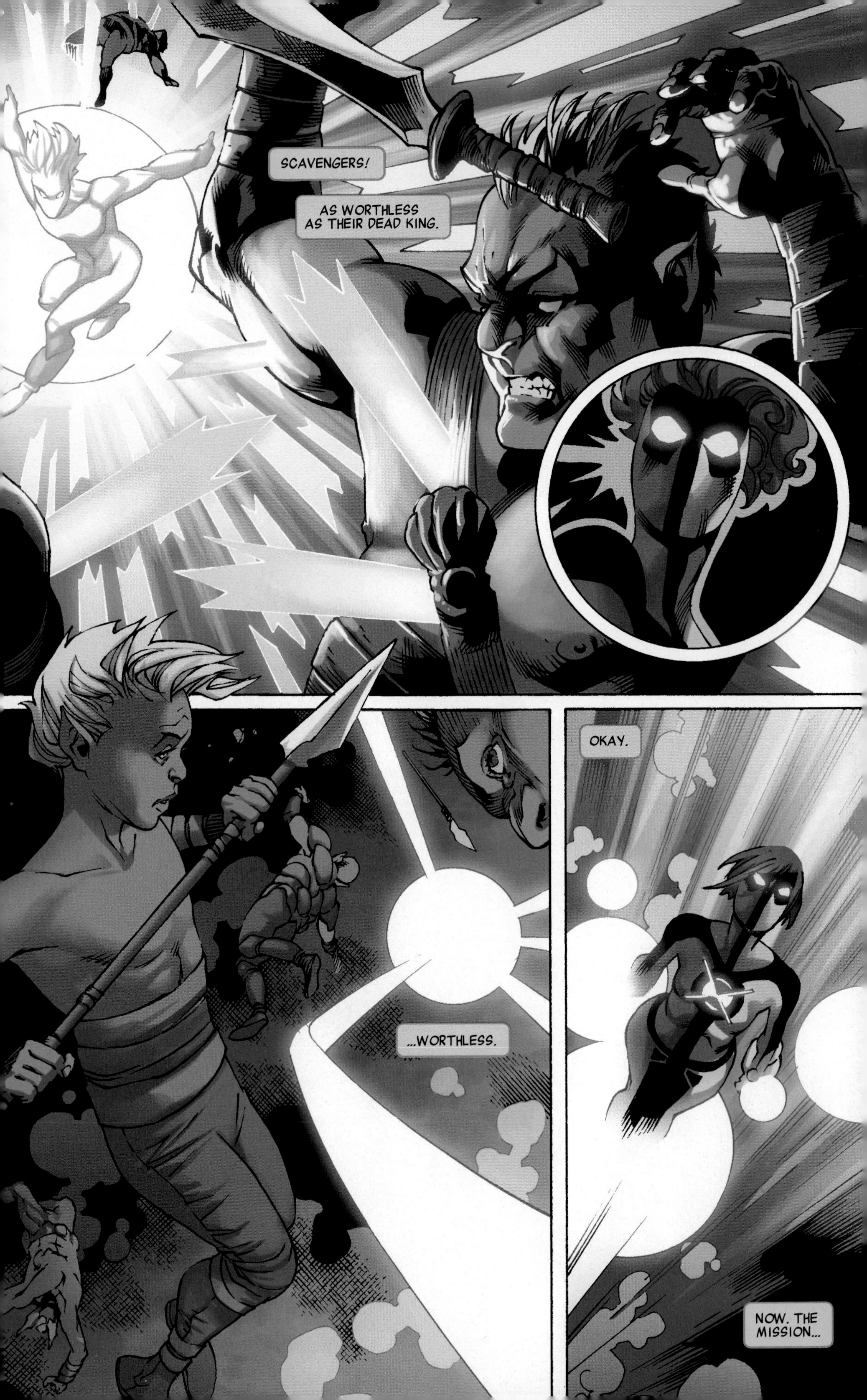
SCAVENGERS!
AS WORTHLESS AS THEIR DEAD KING.
...WORTHLESS.
OKAY.
NOW. THE MISSION...

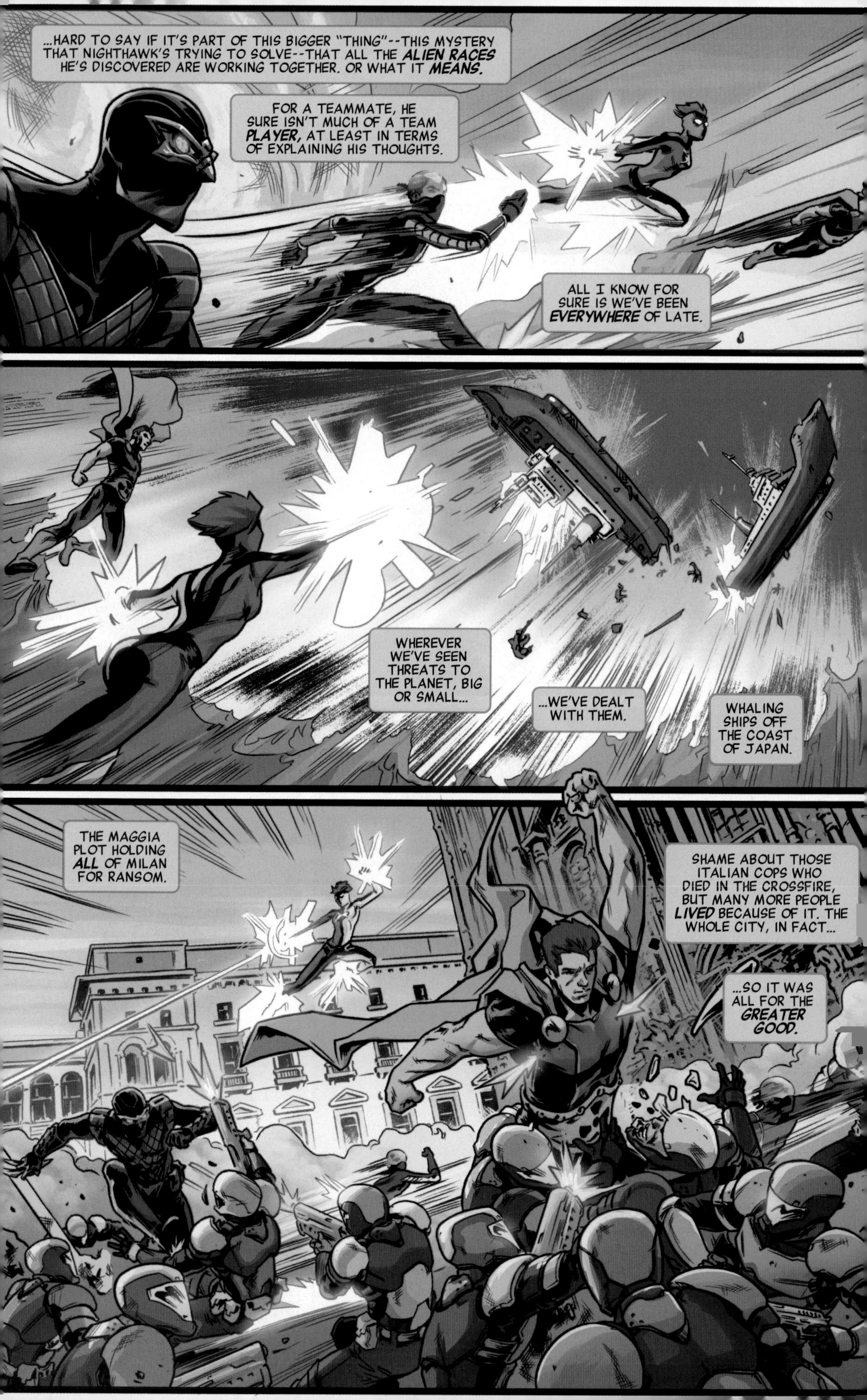
...HARD TO SAY IF IT'S PART OF THIS BIGGER "THING"--THIS MYSTERY THAT NIGHTHAWK'S TRYING TO SOLVE--THAT ALL THE ALIEN RACES HE'S DISCOVERED ARE WORKING TOGETHER. OR WHAT IT MEANS.
FOR A TEAMMATE, HE SURE ISN'T MUCH OF A TEAM PLAYER, AT LEAST IN TERMS OF EXPLAINING HIS THOUGHTS.
ALL I KNOW FOR SURE IS WE'VE BEEN EVERYWHERE OF LATE.
WHEREVER WE'VE SEEN THREATS TO THE PLANET, BIG OR SMALL...
...WE'VE DEALT WITH THEM.
WHALING SHIPS OFF THE COAST OF JAPAN.
THE MAGGIA PLOT HOLDING ALL OF MILAN FOR RANSOM.
SHAME ABOUT THOSE ITALIAN COPS WHO DIED IN THE CROSSFIRE, BUT MANY MORE PEOPLE LIVED BECAUSE OF IT. THE WHOLE CITY, IN FACT...
...SO IT WAS ALL FOR THE GREATER GOOD.

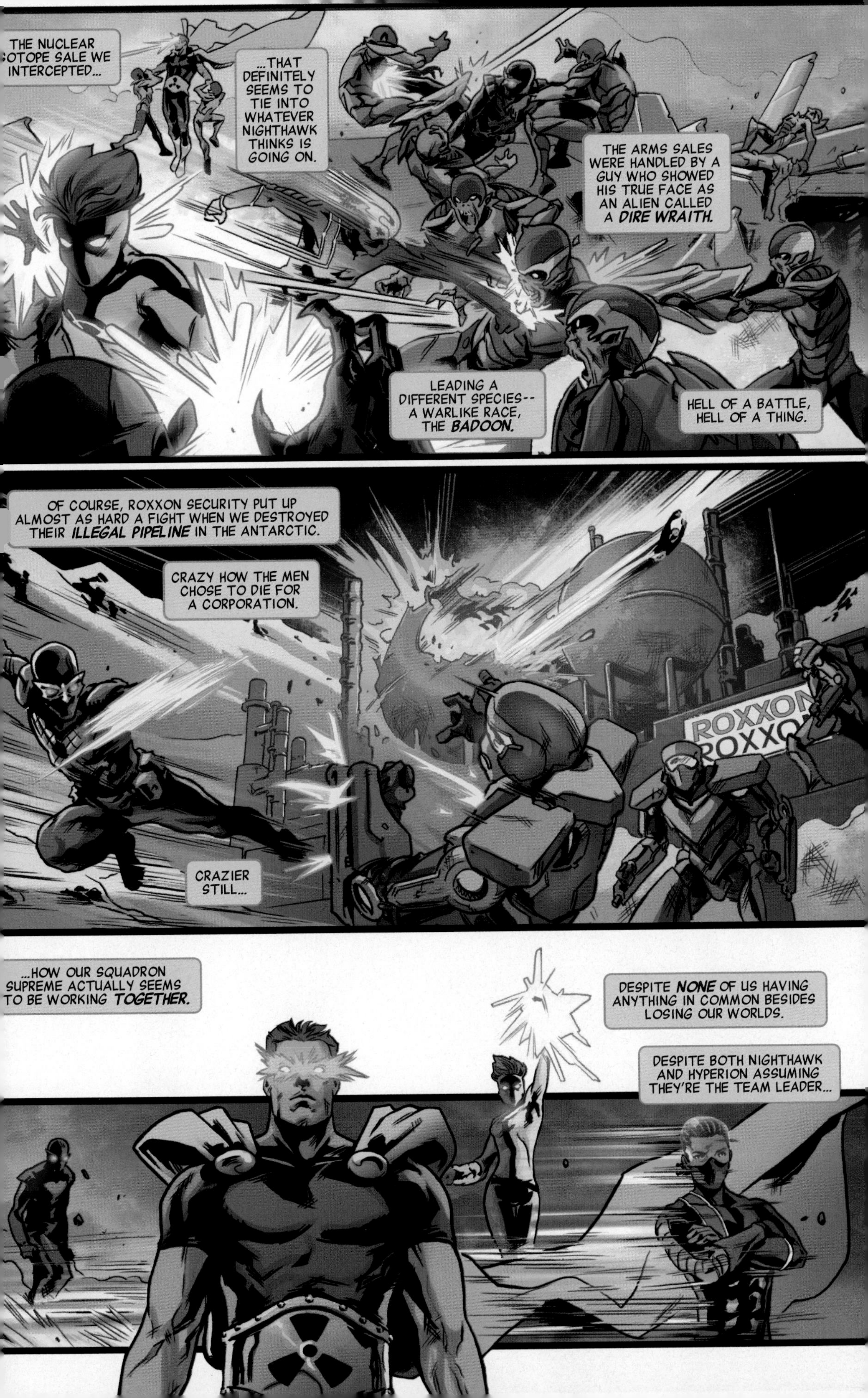
THE NUCLEAR ISOTOPE SALE WE INTERCEPTED...
...THAT DEFINITELY SEEMS TO TIE INTO WHATEVER NIGHTHAWK THINKS IS GOING ON.
THE ARMS SALES WERE HANDLED BY A GUY WHO SHOWED HIS TRUE FACE AS AN ALIEN CALLED A DIRE WRAITH.
LEADING A DIFFERENT SPECIES-- A WARLIKE RACE, THE BADOON.
HELL OF A BATTLE, HELL OF A THING.
OF COURSE, ROXXON SECURITY PUT UP ALMOST AS HARD A FIGHT WHEN WE DESTROYED THEIR ILLEGAL PIPELINE IN THE ANTARCTIC.
CRAZY HOW THE MEN CHOSE TO DIE FOR A CORPORATION.
ROXXON
CRAZIER STILL...
...HOW OUR SQUADRON SUPREME ACTUALLY SEEMS TO BE WORKING TOGETHER.
DESPITE NONE OF US HAVING ANYTHING IN COMMON BESIDES LOSING OUR WORLDS.
DESPITE BOTH NIGHTHAWK AND HYPERION ASSUMING THEY'RE THE TEAM LEADER...

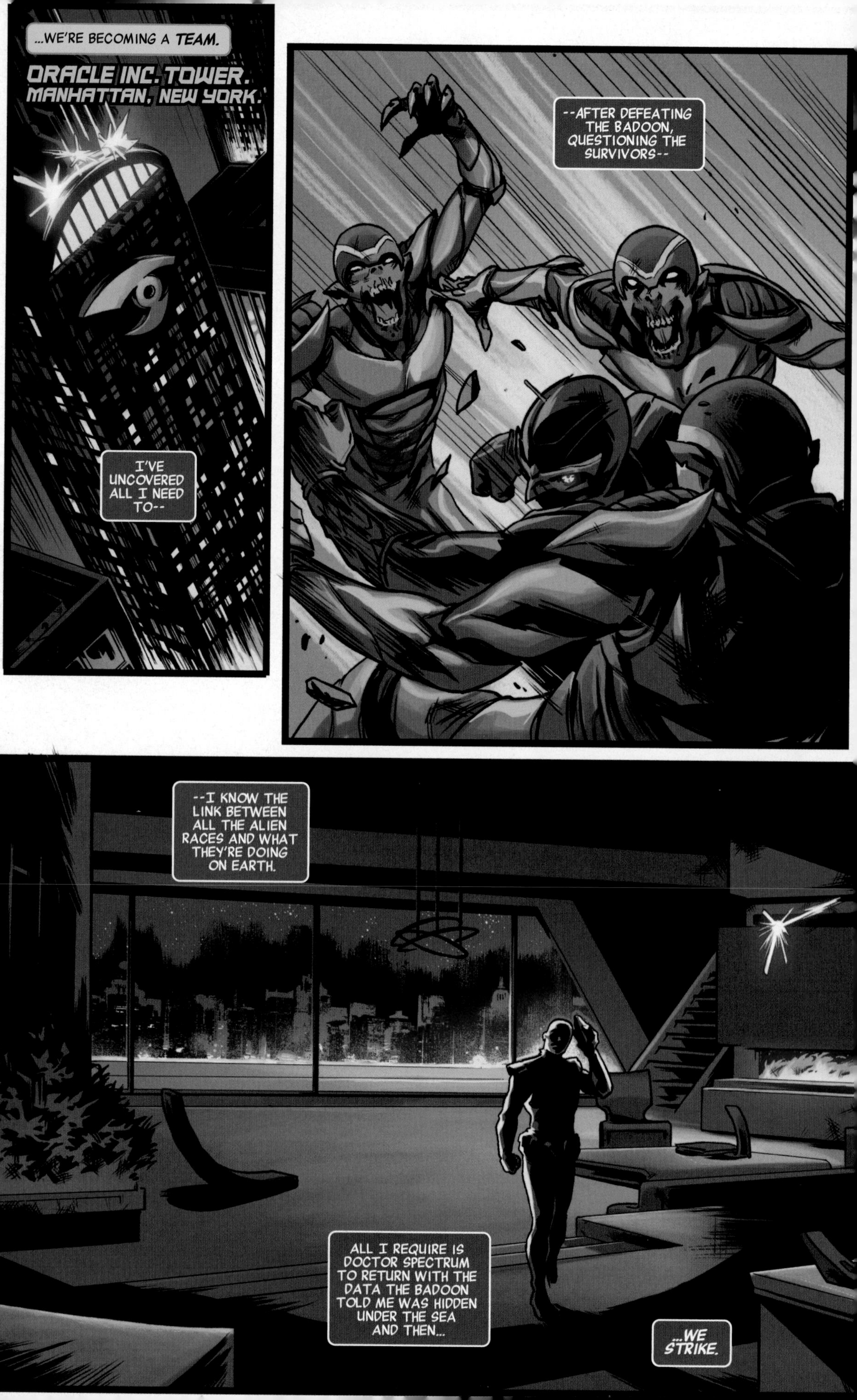
...WE'RE BECOMING A TEAM.
ORACLE INC. TOWER. MANHATTAN, NEW YORK.
I'VE UNCOVERED ALL I NEED TO--
--AFTER DEFEATING THE BADOON, QUESTIONING THE SURVIVORS--
--I KNOW THE LINK BETWEEN ALL THE ALIEN RACES AND WHAT THEY'RE DOING ON EARTH.
ALL I REQUIRE IS DOCTOR SPECTRUM TO RETURN WITH THE DATA THE BADOON TOLD ME WAS HIDDEN UNDER THE SEA AND THEN...
...WE STRIKE.

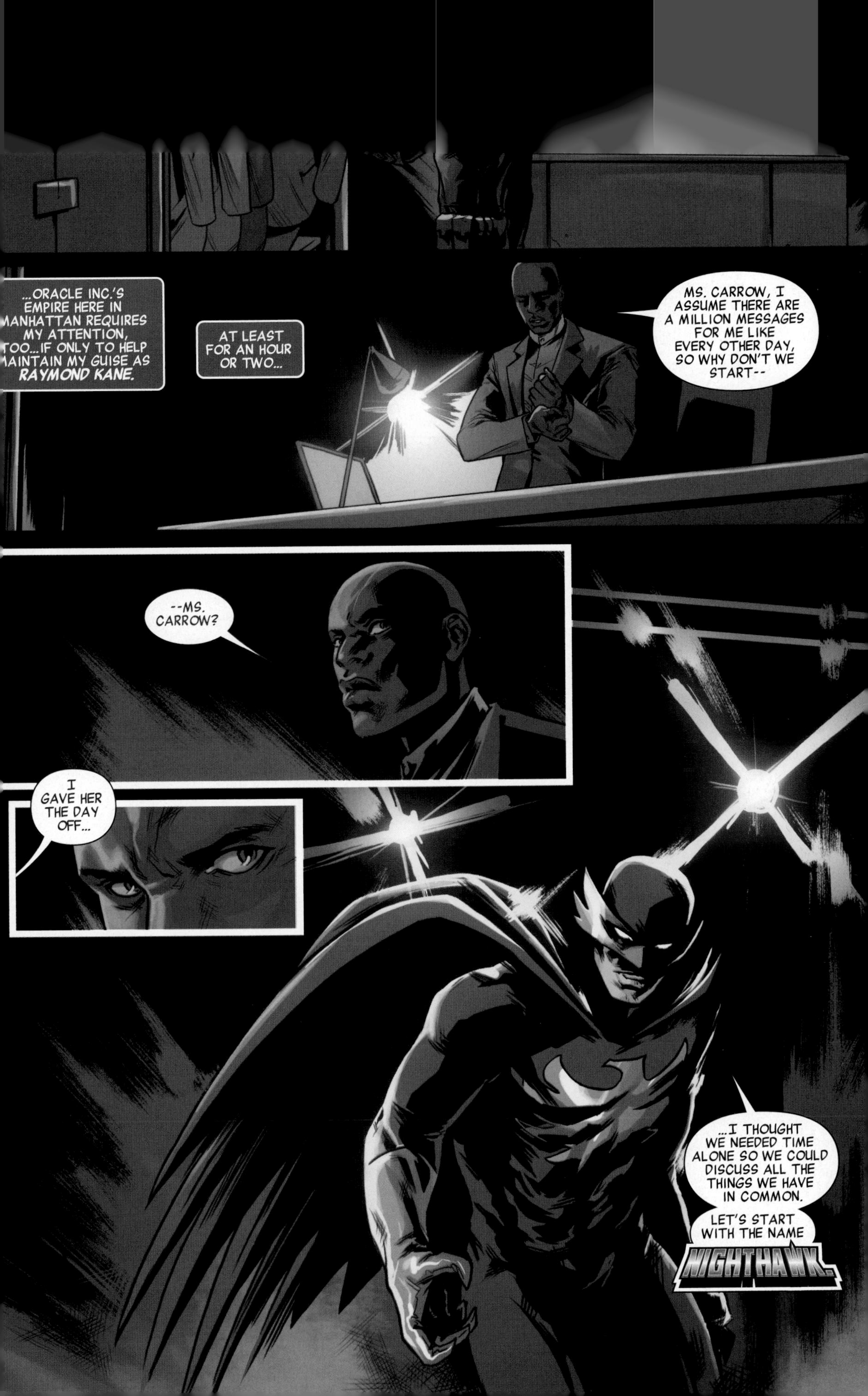
...ORACLE INC.'S EMPIRE HERE IN MANHATTAN REQUIRES MY ATTENTION, TOO...IF ONLY TO HELP MAINTAIN MY GUISE AS RAYMOND KANE.
AT LEAST FOR AN HOUR OR TWO...
MS. CARROW, I ASSUME THERE ARE A MILLION MESSAGES FOR ME LIKE EVERY OTHER DAY, SO WHY DON'T WE START--
--MS. CARROW?
I GAVE HER THE DAY OFF...
...I THOUGHT WE NEEDED TIME ALONE SO WE COULD DISCUSS ALL THE THINGS WE HAVE IN COMMON.
LET'S START WITH THE NAME
NIGHTHAWK.

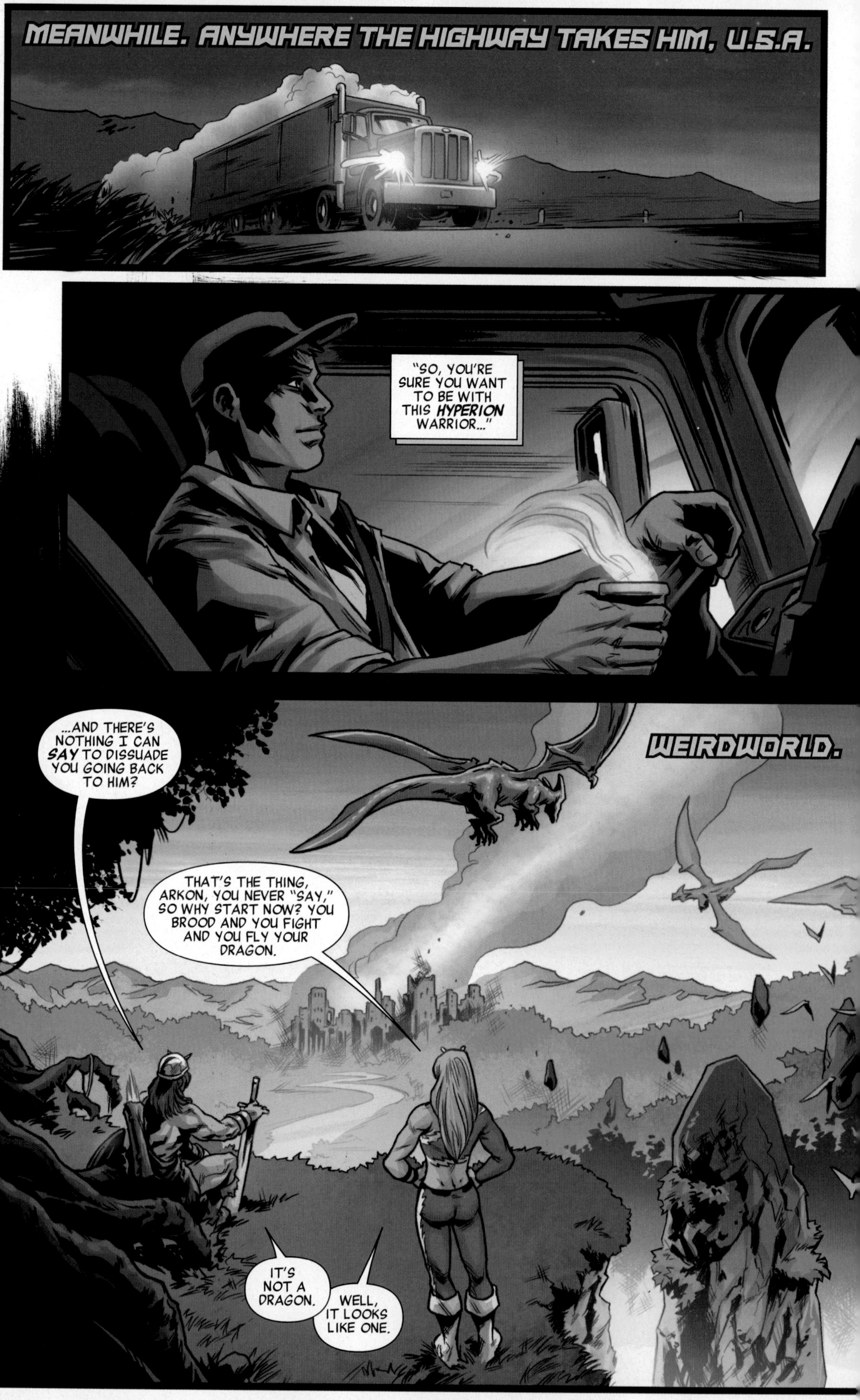
MEANWHILE. ANYWHERE THE HIGHWAY TAKES HIM, U.S.A.
"SO, YOU'RE SURE YOU WANT TO BE WITH THIS HYPERION WARRIOR..."
...AND THERE'S NOTHING I CAN SAY TO DISSUADE YOU GOING BACK TO HIM?
WEIRDWORLD.
THAT'S THE THING, ARKON, YOU NEVER "SAY," SO WHY START NOW? YOU BROOD AND YOU FIGHT AND YOU FLY YOUR DRAGON.
IT'S NOT A DRAGON.
WELL, IT LOOKS LIKE ONE.

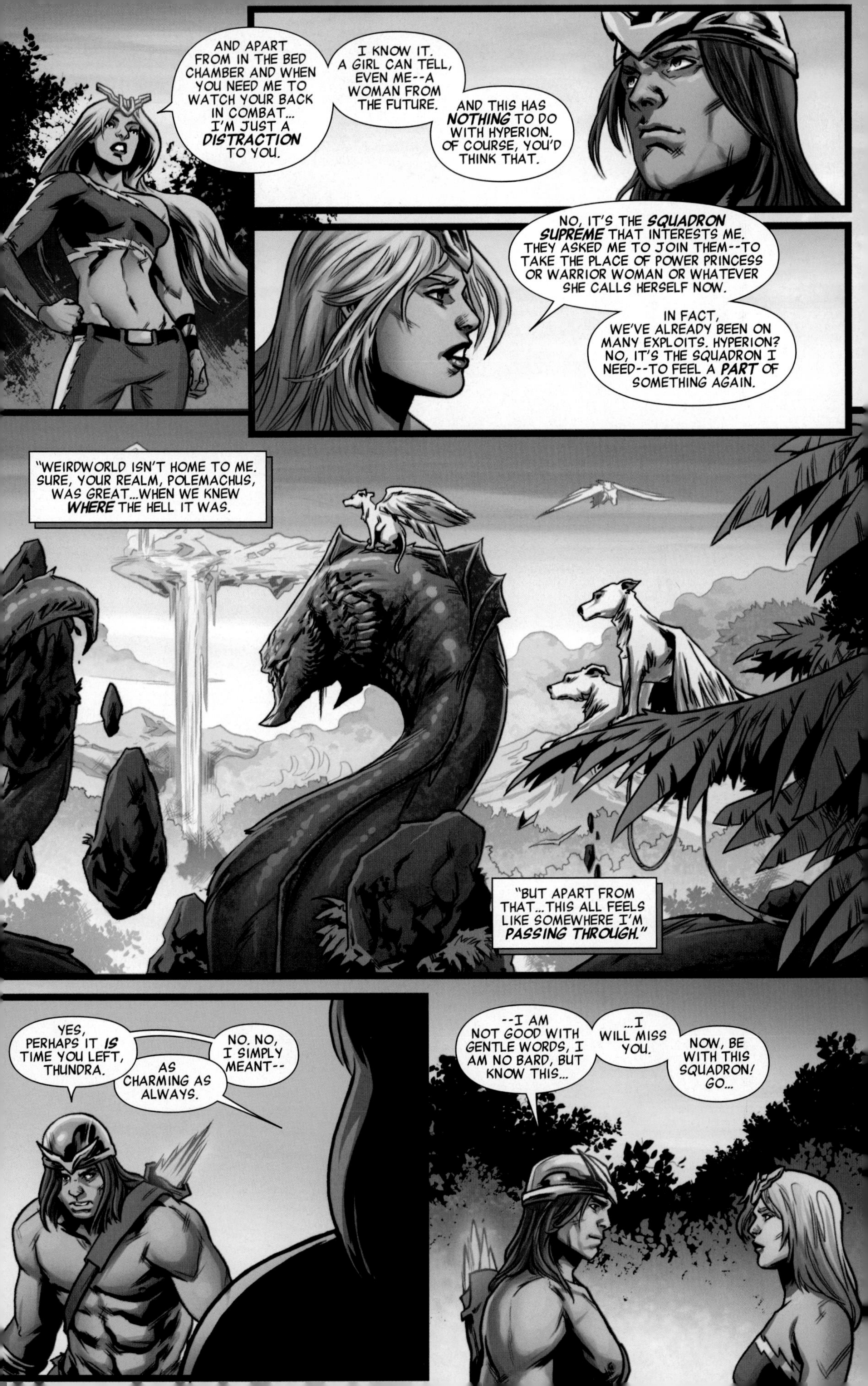
AND APART FROM IN THE BED CHAMBER AND WHEN YOU NEED ME TO WATCH YOUR BACK IN COMBAT... I'M JUST A DISTRACTION TO YOU.
I KNOW IT. A GIRL CAN TELL, EVEN ME--A WOMAN FROM THE FUTURE.
AND THIS HAS NOTHING TO DO WITH HYPERION. OF COURSE, YOU'D THINK THAT.
NO, IT'S THE SQUADRON SUPREME THAT INTERESTS ME. THEY ASKED ME TO JOIN THEM--TO TAKE THE PLACE OF POWER PRINCESS OR WARRIOR WOMAN OR WHATEVER SHE CALLS HERSELF NOW.
IN FACT, WE'VE ALREADY BEEN ON MANY EXPLOITS. HYPERION? NO, IT'S THE SQUADRON I NEED--TO FEEL A PART OF SOMETHING AGAIN.
"WEIRDWORLD ISN'T HOME TO ME. SURE, YOUR REALM, POLEMACHUS, WAS GREAT...WHEN WE KNEW WHERE THE HELL IT WAS.
"BUT APART FROM THAT...THIS ALL FEELS LIKE SOMEWHERE I'M PASSING THROUGH."
YES, PERHAPS IT IS TIME YOU LEFT, THUNDRA.
AS CHARMING AS ALWAYS.
NO. NO, I SIMPLY MEANT--
--I AM NOT GOOD WITH GENTLE WORDS, I AM NO BARD, BUT KNOW THIS...
...I WILL MISS YOU.
NOW, BE WITH THIS SQUADRON! GO...

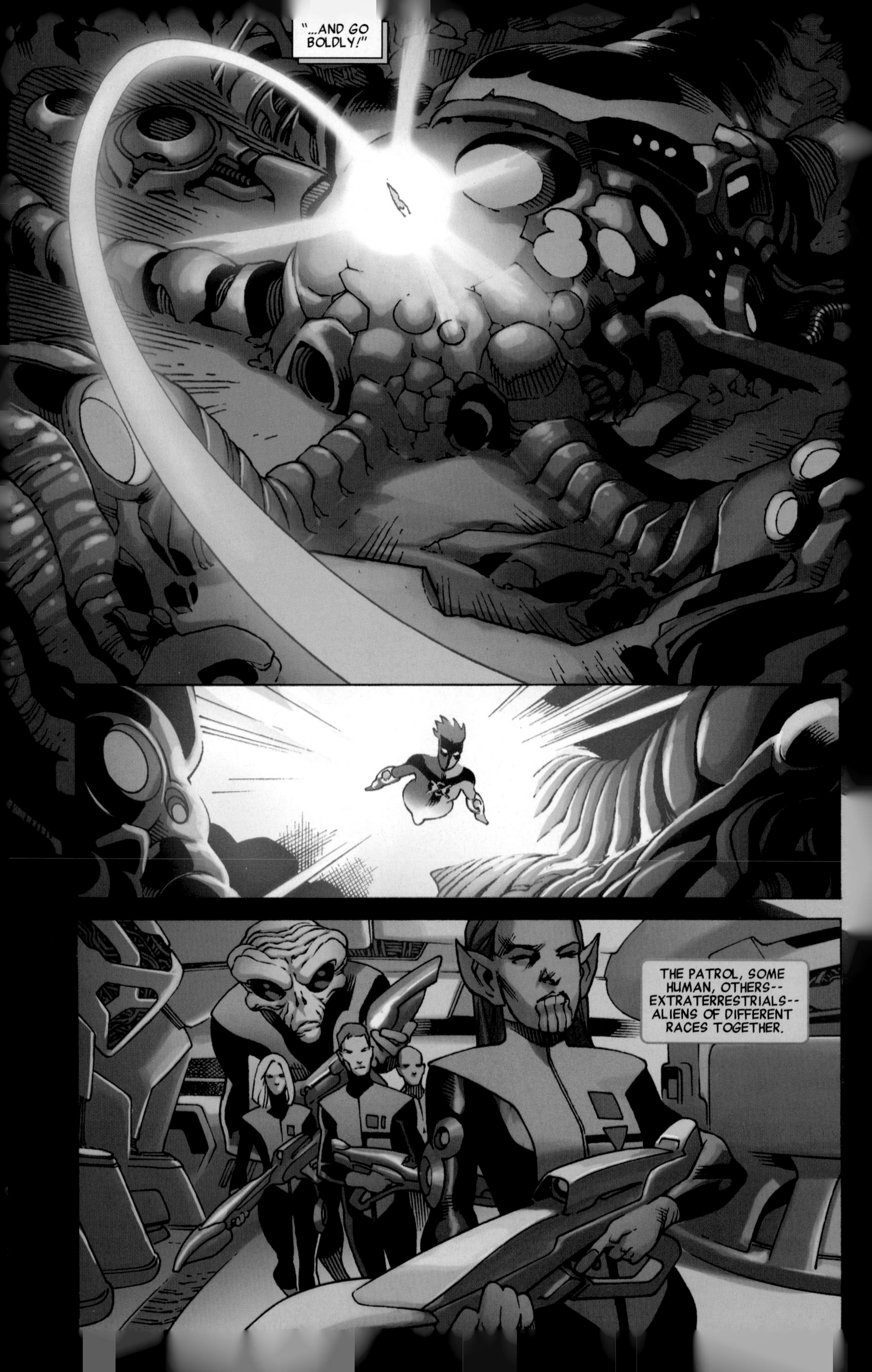
"...AND GO BOLDLY!"
THE PATROL, SOME HUMAN, OTHERS--EXTRATERRESTRIALS--ALIENS OF DIFFERENT RACES TOGETHER.

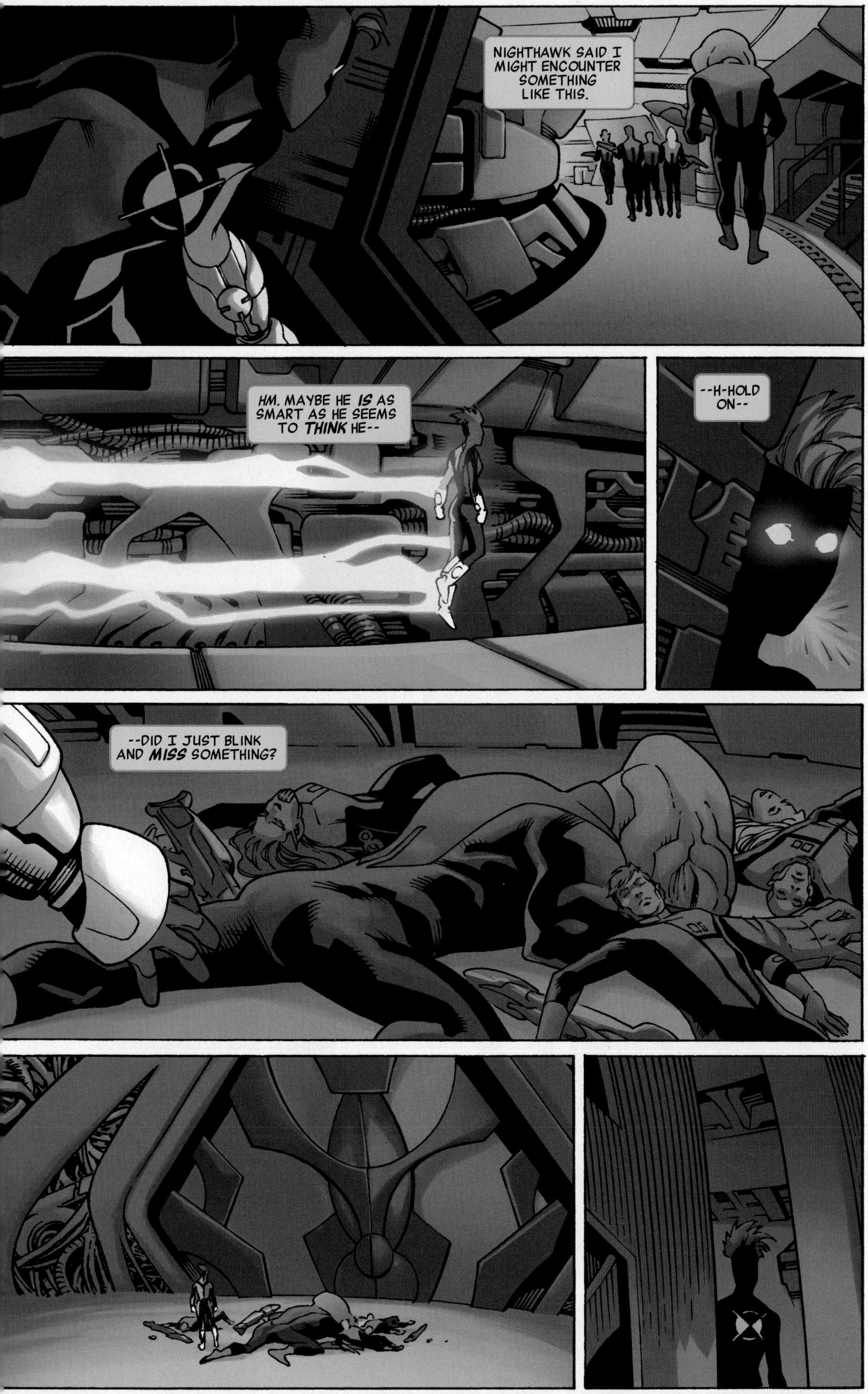
NIGHTHAWK SAID I MIGHT ENCOUNTER SOMETHING LIKE THIS.
HM. MAYBE HE IS AS SMART AS HE SEEMS TO THINK HE--
--H-HOLD ON--
--DID I JUST BLINK AND MISS SOMETHING?

ALL RIGHT
I'LL COME OUT
AND ASK IT...

NO, BUT
IT'LL DO.

ALL RIGHT...
MY NAME IS
THOMAS RAYMOND--
TOM. I USED TO BE
KNOWN AS TORO, THOUGH,
BACK WHEN I WAS THE
ORIGINAL HUMAN TORCH'S
SIDEKICK. HAD FLAME
POWERS, TOO, WHEN
I THOUGHT I WAS
A HUMAN.

HAPPY?

NOW MY ABILITIES
HAVE EVOLVED--THEY
MORE ELEMENTAL
IN NATURE--AND I
RECENTLY DISCOVER
I'M ACTUALLY AN
INHUMAN.

I WAS
SENT HERE BY
QUEEN MEDUS
ON A MISSION
INFILTRATE TH
ORGANIZATION
LEARN ABOUT
IT...

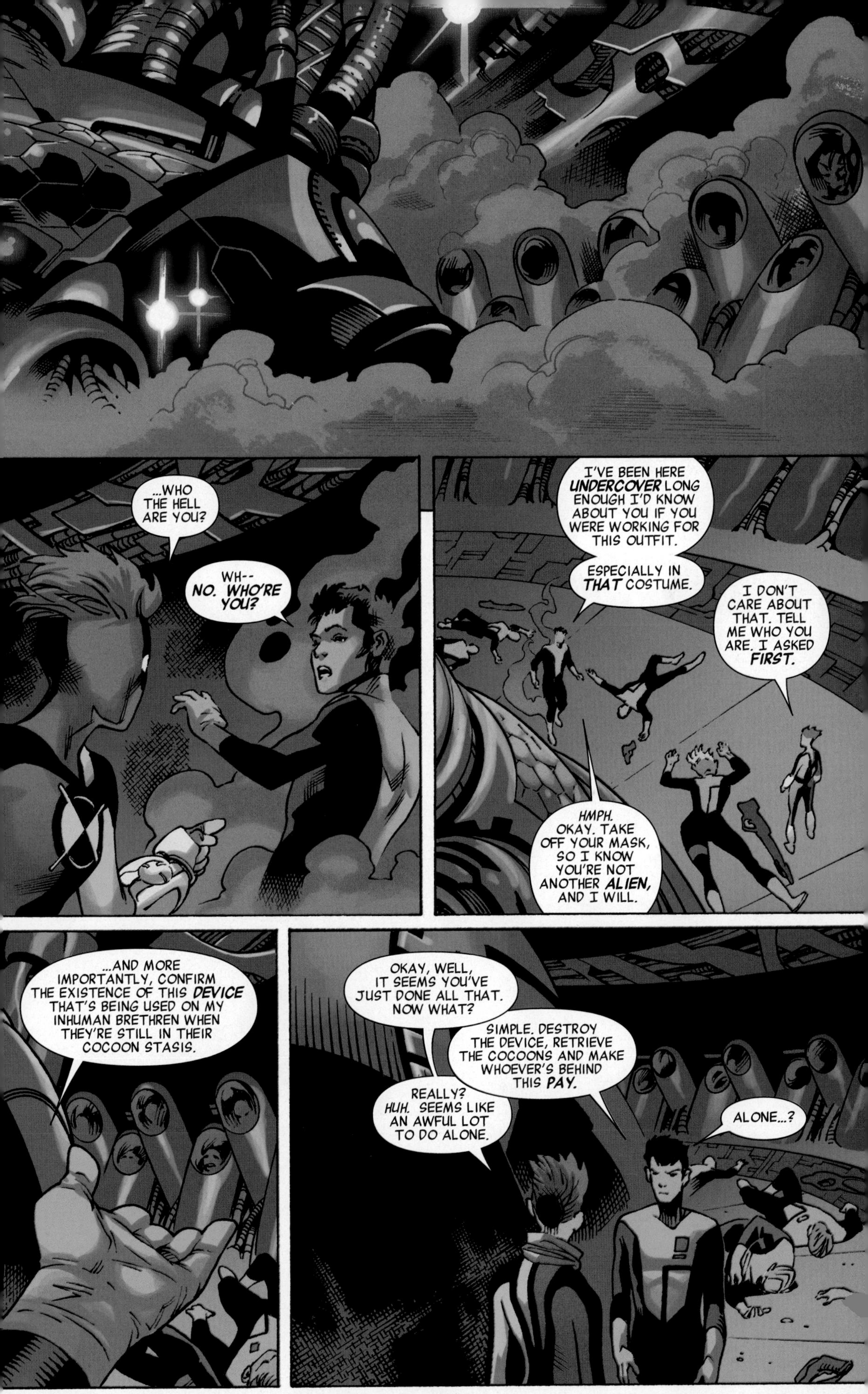
...WHO THE HELL ARE YOU?
WH-- NO. WHO'RE YOU?
I'VE BEEN HERE UNDERCOVER LONG ENOUGH I'D KNOW ABOUT YOU IF YOU WERE WORKING FOR THIS OUTFIT.
ESPECIALLY IN THAT COSTUME.
I DON'T CARE ABOUT THAT. TELL ME WHO YOU ARE. I ASKED FIRST.
HMPH. OKAY. TAKE OFF YOUR MASK, SO I KNOW YOU'RE NOT ANOTHER ALIEN, AND I WILL.
...AND MORE IMPORTANTLY, CONFIRM THE EXISTENCE OF THIS DEVICE THAT'S BEING USED ON MY INHUMAN BRETHREN WHEN THEY'RE STILL IN THEIR COCOON STASIS.
OKAY, WELL, IT SEEMS YOU'VE JUST DONE ALL THAT. NOW WHAT?
SIMPLE. DESTROY THE DEVICE, RETRIEVE THE COCOONS AND MAKE WHOEVER'S BEHIND THIS PAY.
REALLY? HUH. SEEMS LIKE AN AWFUL LOT TO DO ALONE.
ALONE...?

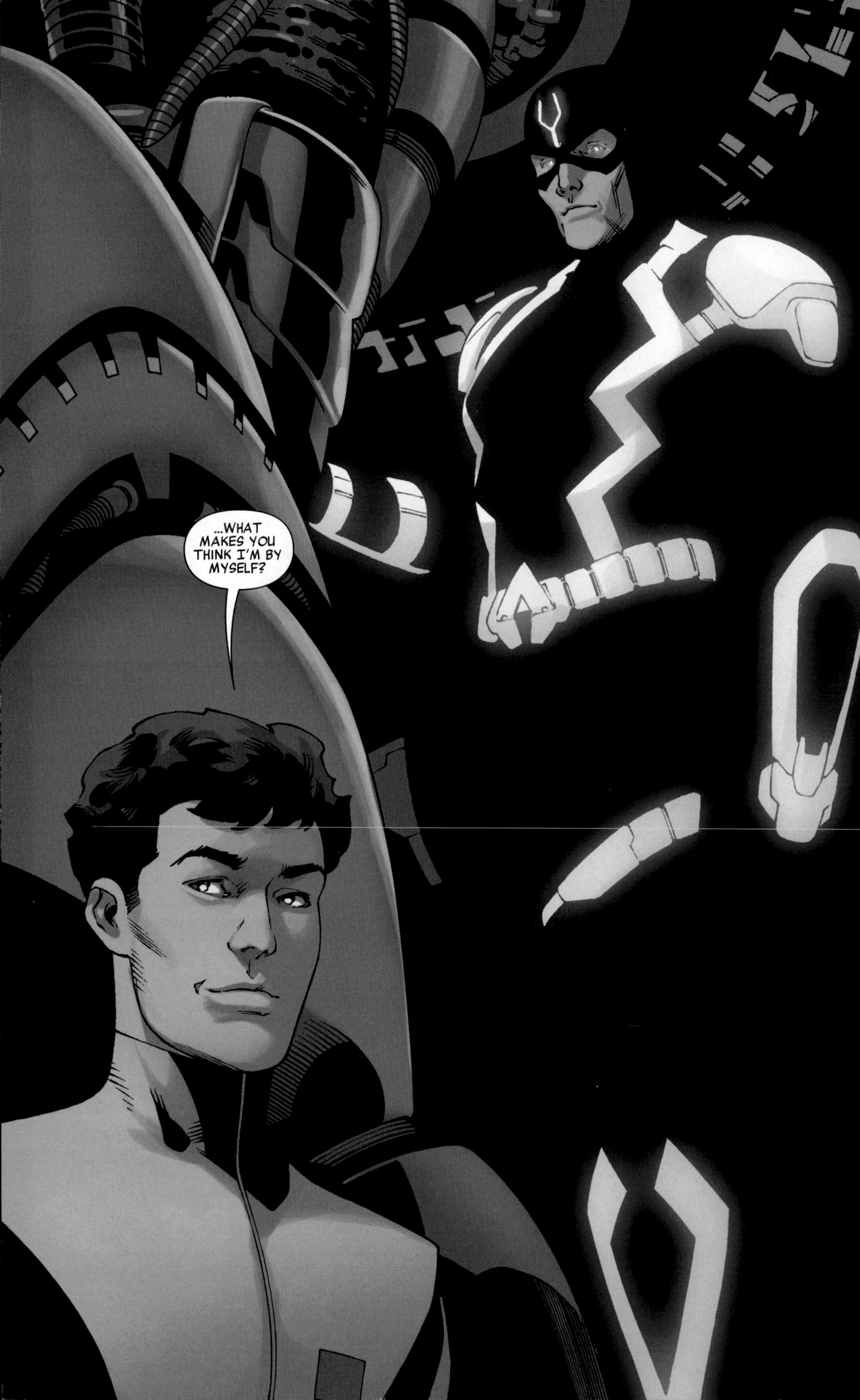
...WHAT MAKES YOU THINK I'M BY MYSELF?

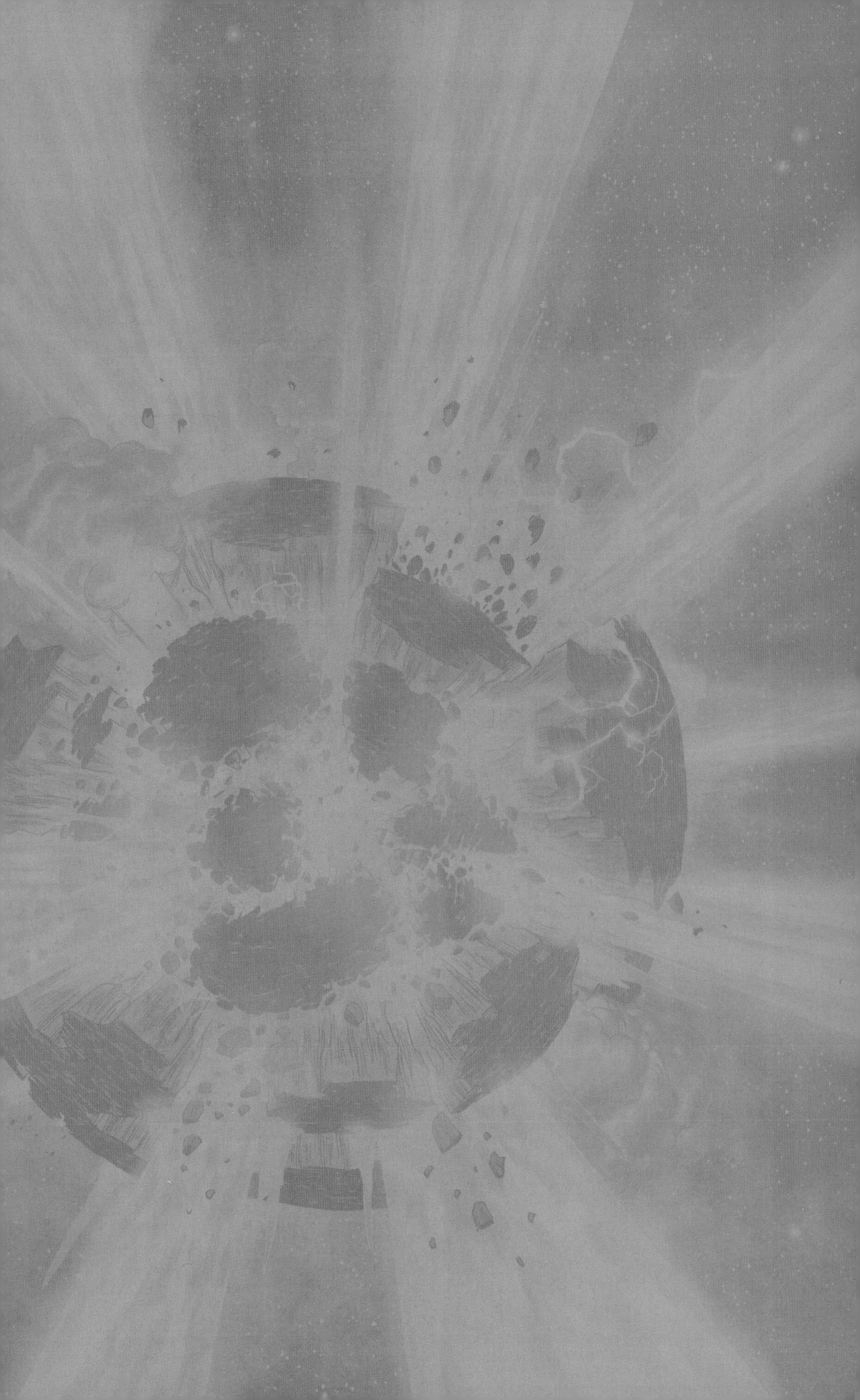

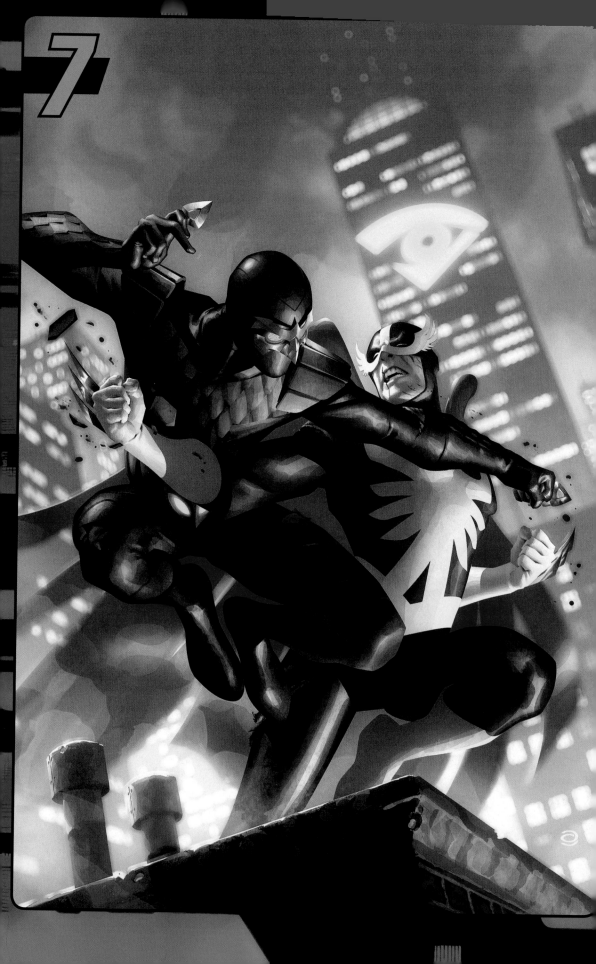

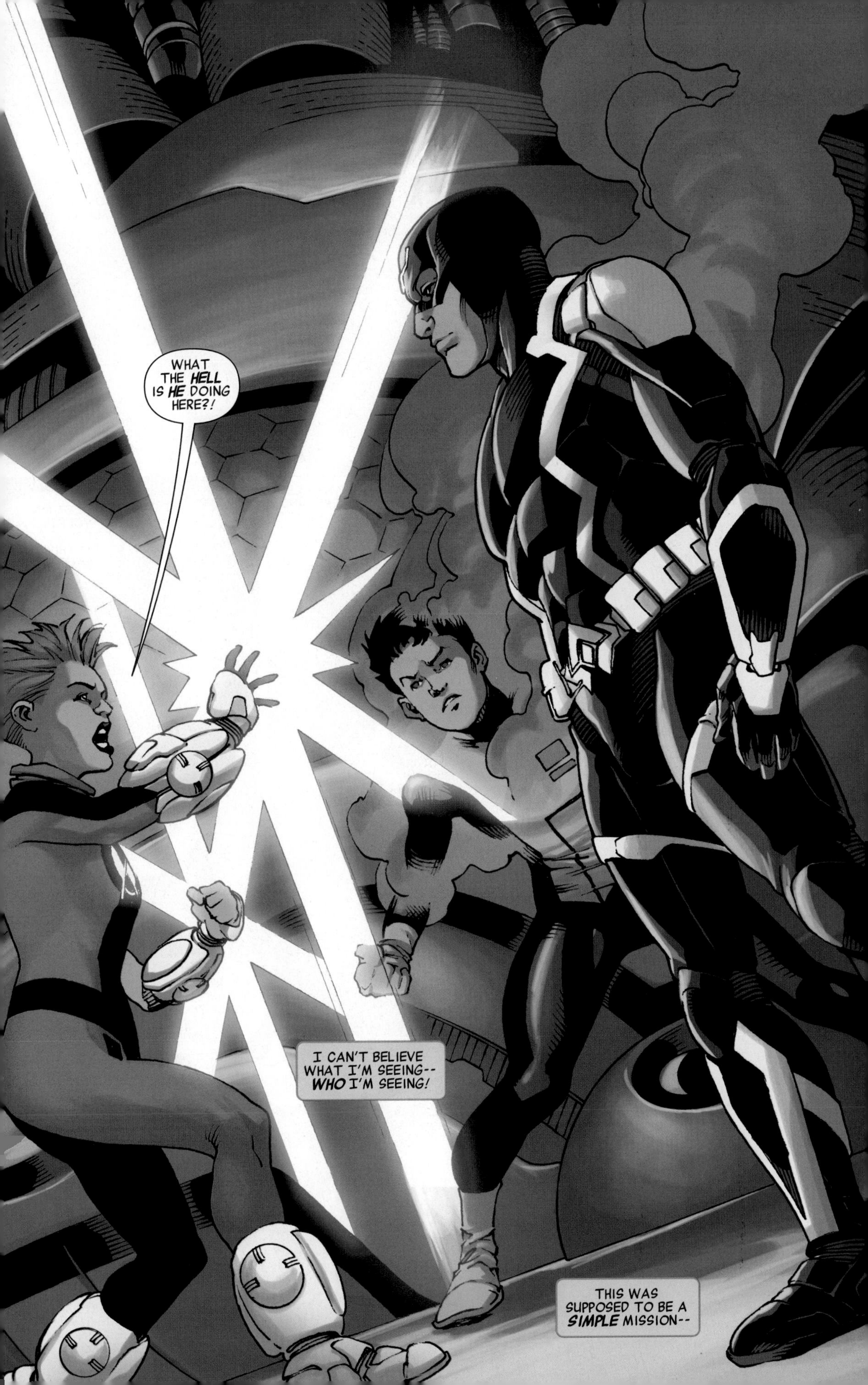
WHAT THE HELL IS HE DOING HERE?!
I CAN'T BELIEVE WHAT I'M SEEING-- WHO I'M SEEING!
THIS WAS SUPPOSED TO BE A SIMPLE MISSION--

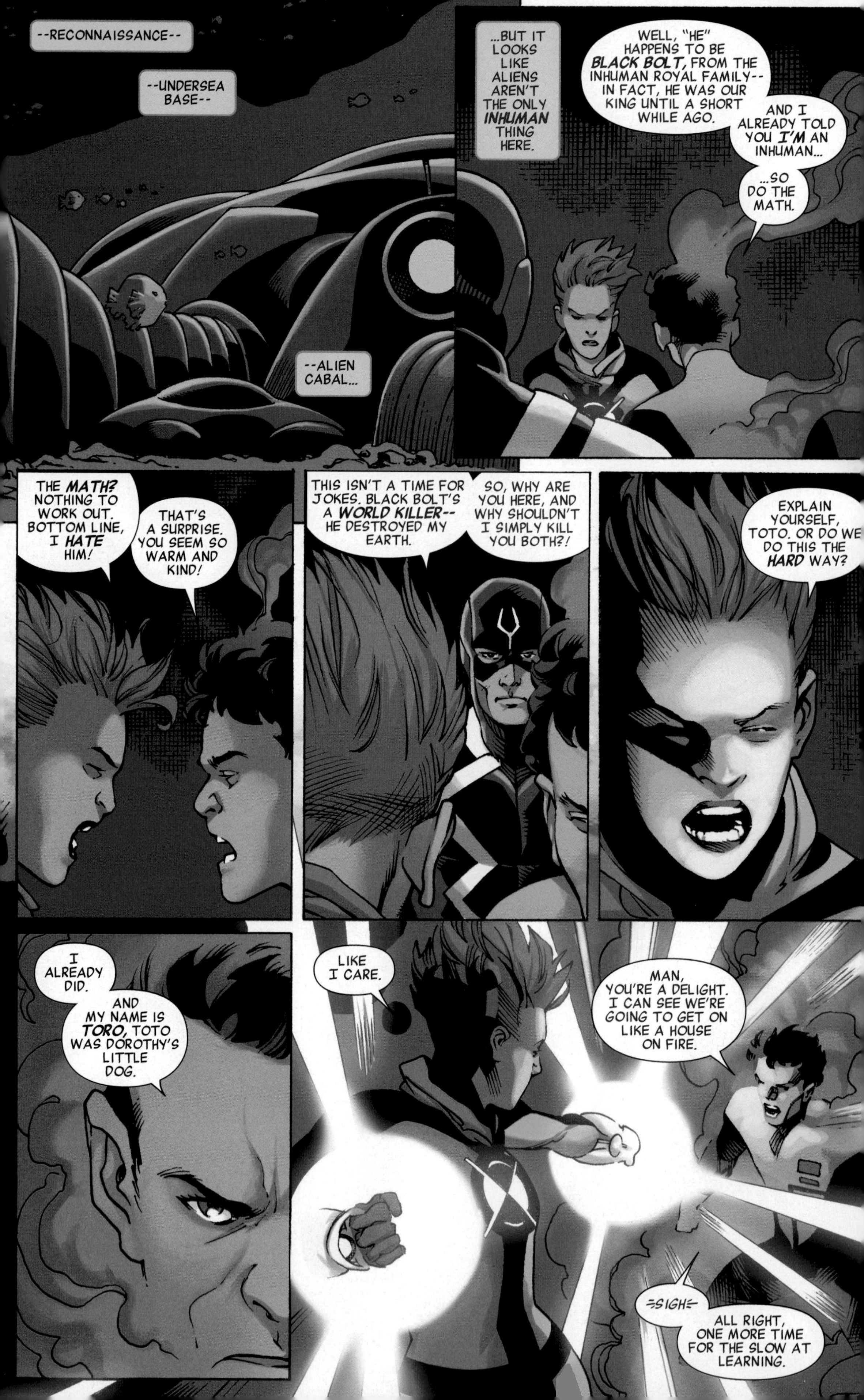
--RECONNAISSANCE--
--UNDERSEA BASE--
--ALIEN CABAL...
...BUT IT LOOKS LIKE ALIENS AREN'T THE ONLY INHUMAN THING HERE.
WELL, "HE" HAPPENS TO BE BLACK BOLT, FROM THE INHUMAN ROYAL FAMILY-- IN FACT, HE WAS OUR KING UNTIL A SHORT WHILE AGO.
AND I ALREADY TOLD YOU I'M AN INHUMAN...
...SO DO THE MATH.
THE MATH? NOTHING TO WORK OUT. BOTTOM LINE, I HATE HIM!
THAT'S A SURPRISE. YOU SEEM SO WARM AND KIND!
THIS ISN'T A TIME FOR JOKES. BLACK BOLT'S A WORLD KILLER-- HE DESTROYED MY EARTH.
SO, WHY ARE YOU HERE, AND WHY SHOULDN'T I SIMPLY KILL YOU BOTH?!
EXPLAIN YOURSELF, TOTO. OR DO WE DO THIS THE HARD WAY?
I ALREADY DID.
AND MY NAME IS TORO. TOTO WAS DOROTHY'S LITTLE DOG.
LIKE I CARE.
MAN, YOU'RE A DELIGHT. I CAN SEE WE'RE GOING TO GET ON LIKE A HOUSE ON FIRE.
=SIGH=
ALL RIGHT, ONE MORE TIME FOR THE SLOW AT LEARNING.

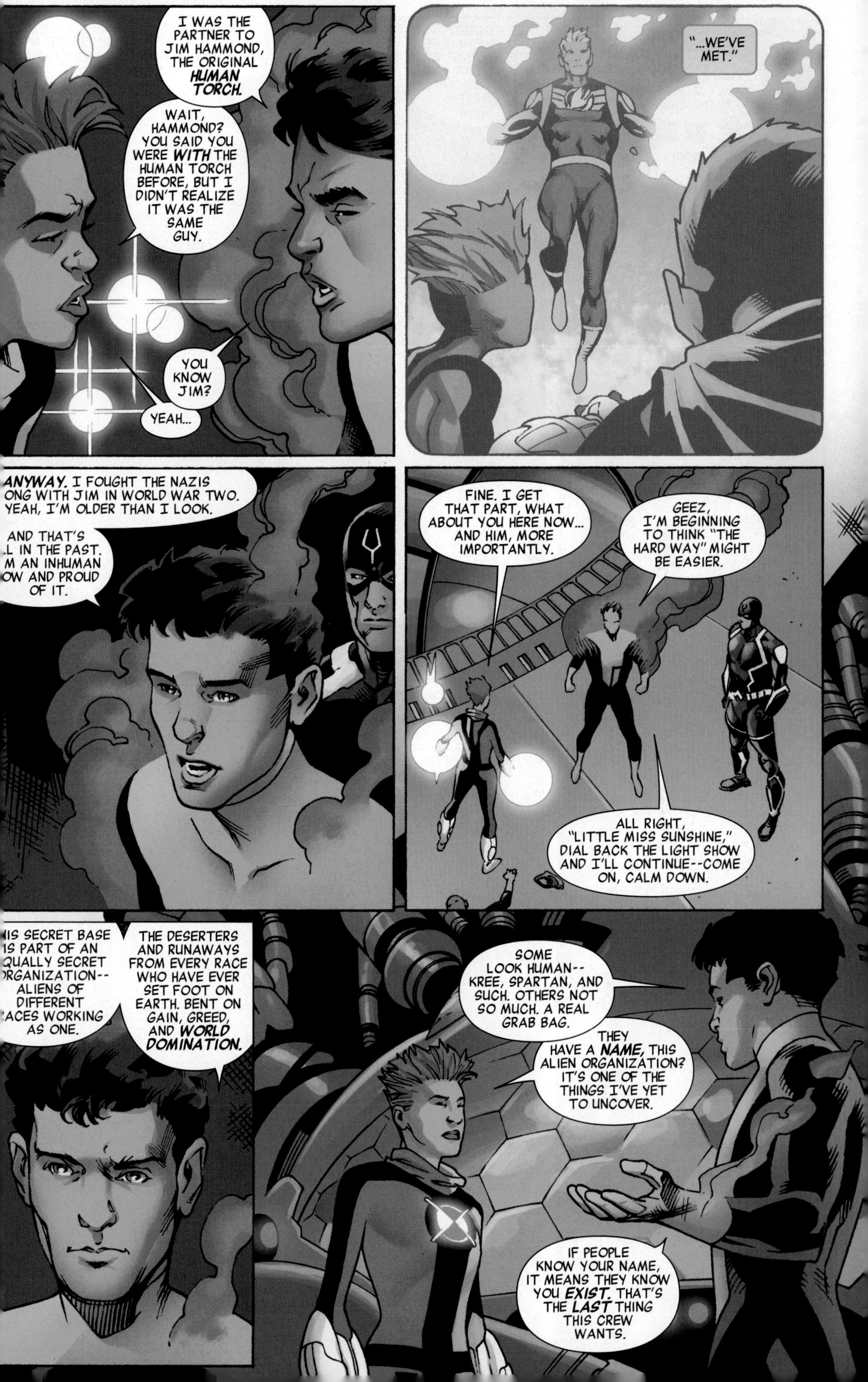
I WAS THE PARTNER TO JIM HAMMOND, THE ORIGINAL HUMAN TORCH.
WAIT, HAMMOND? YOU SAID YOU WERE WITH THE HUMAN TORCH BEFORE, BUT I DIDN'T REALIZE IT WAS THE SAME GUY.
YOU KNOW JIM?
YEAH...
"...WE'VE MET."
ANYWAY. I FOUGHT THE NAZIS ONG WITH JIM IN WORLD WAR TWO. YEAH, I'M OLDER THAN I LOOK.
AND THAT'S L IN THE PAST. M AN INHUMAN OW AND PROUD OF IT.
FINE. I GET THAT PART, WHAT ABOUT YOU HERE NOW... AND HIM, MORE IMPORTANTLY.
GEEZ, I'M BEGINNING TO THINK "THE HARD WAY" MIGHT BE EASIER.
ALL RIGHT, "LITTLE MISS SUNSHINE," DIAL BACK THE LIGHT SHOW AND I'LL CONTINUE--COME ON, CALM DOWN.
IS SECRET BASE IS PART OF AN QUALLY SECRET ORGANIZATION-- ALIENS OF DIFFERENT ACES WORKING AS ONE.
THE DESERTERS AND RUNAWAYS FROM EVERY RACE WHO HAVE EVER SET FOOT ON EARTH. BENT ON GAIN, GREED, AND WORLD DOMINATION.
SOME LOOK HUMAN-- KREE, SPARTAN, AND SUCH. OTHERS NOT SO MUCH. A REAL GRAB BAG.
THEY HAVE A NAME, THIS ALIEN ORGANIZATION? IT'S ONE OF THE THINGS I'VE YET TO UNCOVER.
IF PEOPLE KNOW YOUR NAME, IT MEANS THEY KNOW YOU EXIST. THAT'S THE LAST THING THIS CREW WANTS.

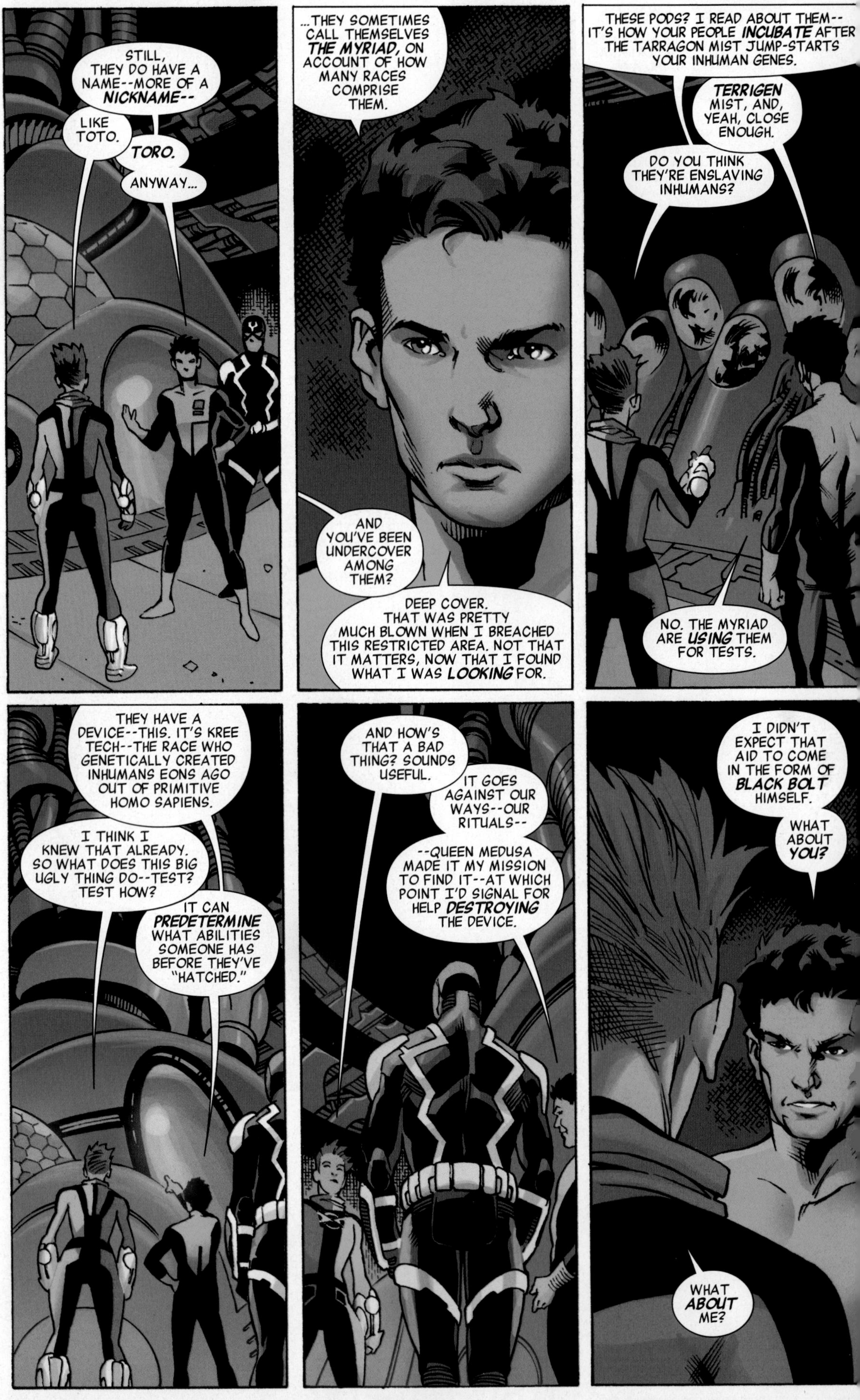
STILL, THEY DO HAVE A NAME--MORE OF A NICKNAME--
LIKE TOTO.
TORO.
ANYWAY...
...THEY SOMETIMES CALL THEMSELVES THE MYRIAD, ON ACCOUNT OF HOW MANY RACES COMPRISE THEM.
AND YOU'VE BEEN UNDERCOVER AMONG THEM?
DEEP COVER. THAT WAS PRETTY MUCH BLOWN WHEN I BREACHED THIS RESTRICTED AREA. NOT THAT IT MATTERS, NOW THAT I FOUND WHAT I WAS LOOKING FOR.
THESE PODS? I READ ABOUT THEM--IT'S HOW YOUR PEOPLE INCUBATE AFTER THE TARRAGON MIST JUMP-STARTS YOUR INHUMAN GENES.
TERRIGEN MIST, AND, YEAH, CLOSE ENOUGH.
DO YOU THINK THEY'RE ENSLAVING INHUMANS?
NO. THE MYRIAD ARE USING THEM FOR TESTS.
THEY HAVE A DEVICE--THIS. IT'S KREE TECH--THE RACE WHO GENETICALLY CREATED INHUMANS EONS AGO OUT OF PRIMITIVE HOMO SAPIENS.
I THINK I KNEW THAT ALREADY. SO WHAT DOES THIS BIG UGLY THING DO--TEST? TEST HOW?
IT CAN PREDETERMINE WHAT ABILITIES SOMEONE HAS BEFORE THEY'VE "HATCHED."
AND HOW'S THAT A BAD THING? SOUNDS USEFUL.
IT GOES AGAINST OUR WAYS--OUR RITUALS--
--QUEEN MEDUSA MADE IT MY MISSION TO FIND IT--AT WHICH POINT I'D SIGNAL FOR HELP DESTROYING THE DEVICE.
I DIDN'T EXPECT THAT AID TO COME IN THE FORM OF BLACK BOLT HIMSELF.
WHAT ABOUT YOU?
WHAT ABOUT ME?

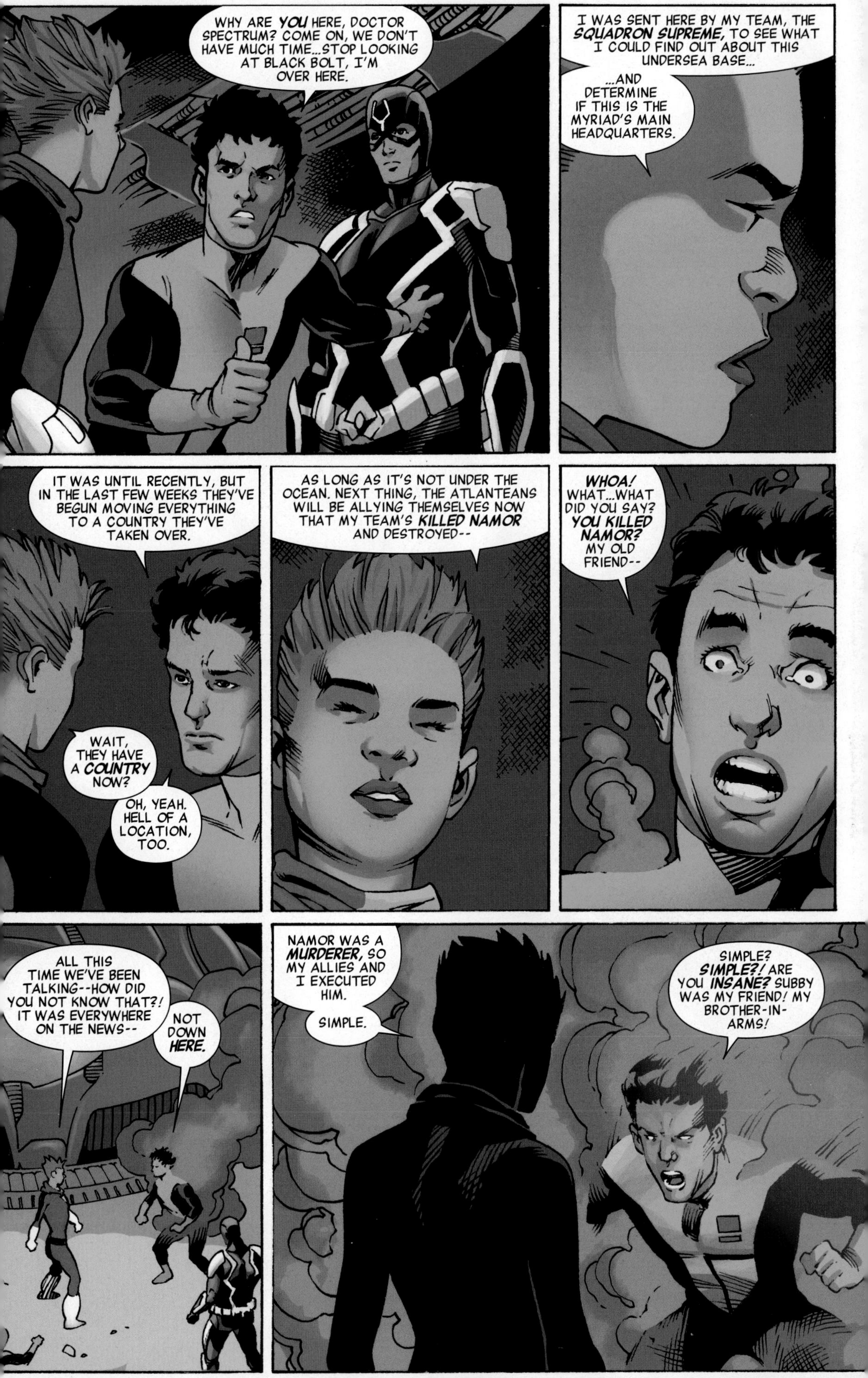

WHY ARE YOU HERE, DOCTOR SPECTRUM? COME ON, WE DON'T HAVE MUCH TIME...STOP LOOKING AT BLACK BOLT, I'M OVER HERE.
I WAS SENT HERE BY MY TEAM, THE SQUADRON SUPREME, TO SEE WHAT I COULD FIND OUT ABOUT THIS UNDERSEA BASE...
...AND DETERMINE IF THIS IS THE MYRIAD'S MAIN HEADQUARTERS.
IT WAS UNTIL RECENTLY, BUT IN THE LAST FEW WEEKS THEY'VE BEGUN MOVING EVERYTHING TO A COUNTRY THEY'VE TAKEN OVER.
WAIT, THEY HAVE A COUNTRY NOW?
OH, YEAH. HELL OF A LOCATION, TOO.
AS LONG AS IT'S NOT UNDER THE OCEAN. NEXT THING, THE ATLANTEANS WILL BE ALLYING THEMSELVES NOW THAT MY TEAM'S KILLED NAMOR AND DESTROYED--
WHOA! WHAT...WHAT DID YOU SAY? YOU KILLED NAMOR? MY OLD FRIEND--
ALL THIS TIME WE'VE BEEN TALKING--HOW DID YOU NOT KNOW THAT?! IT WAS EVERYWHERE ON THE NEWS--
NOT DOWN HERE.
NAMOR WAS A MURDERER, SO MY ALLIES AND I EXECUTED HIM.
SIMPLE.
SIMPLE? SIMPLE?! ARE YOU INSANE? SUBBY WAS MY FRIEND! MY BROTHER-IN-ARMS!

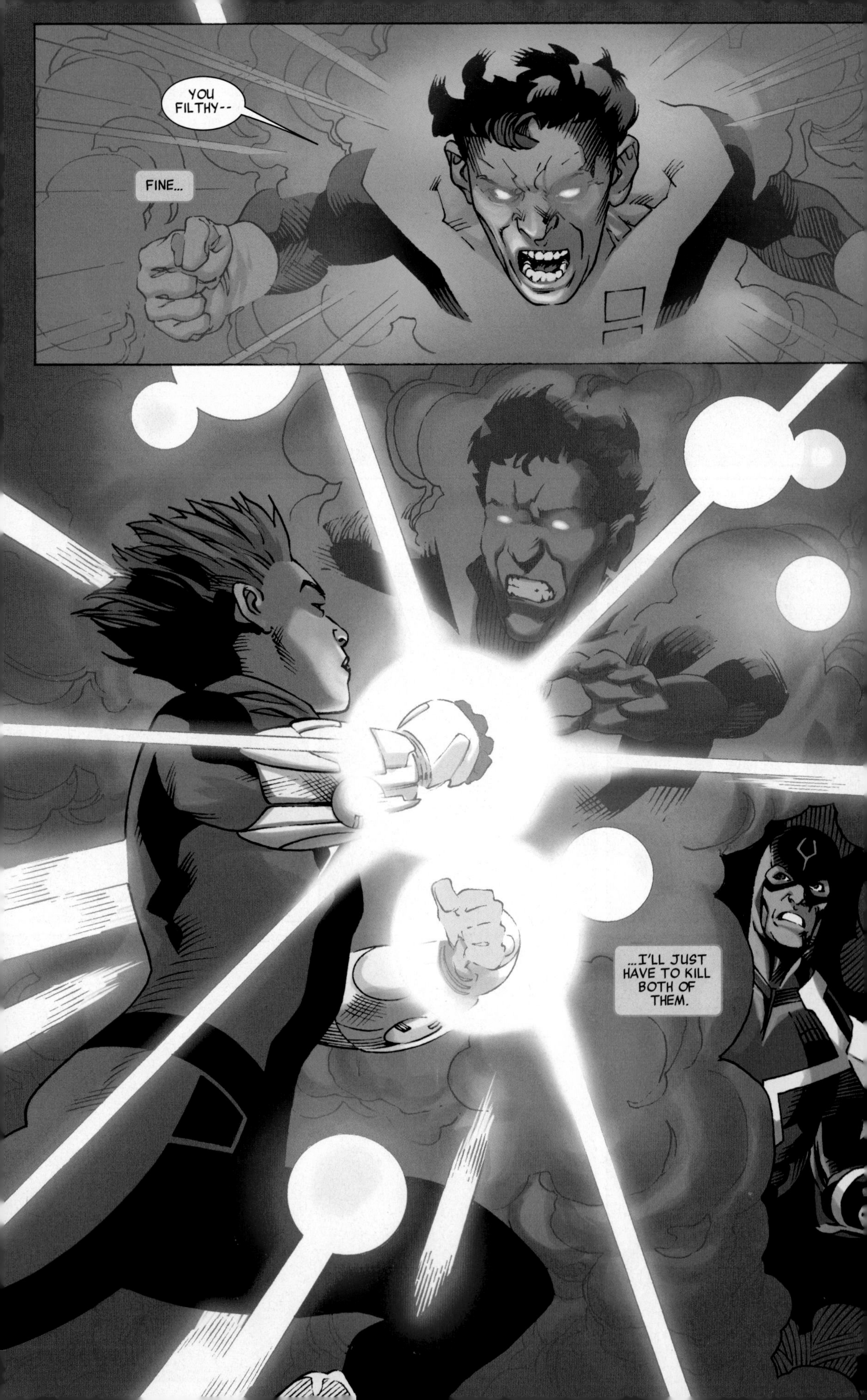
YOU FILTHY--
FINE...
...I'LL JUST HAVE TO KILL BOTH OF THEM.

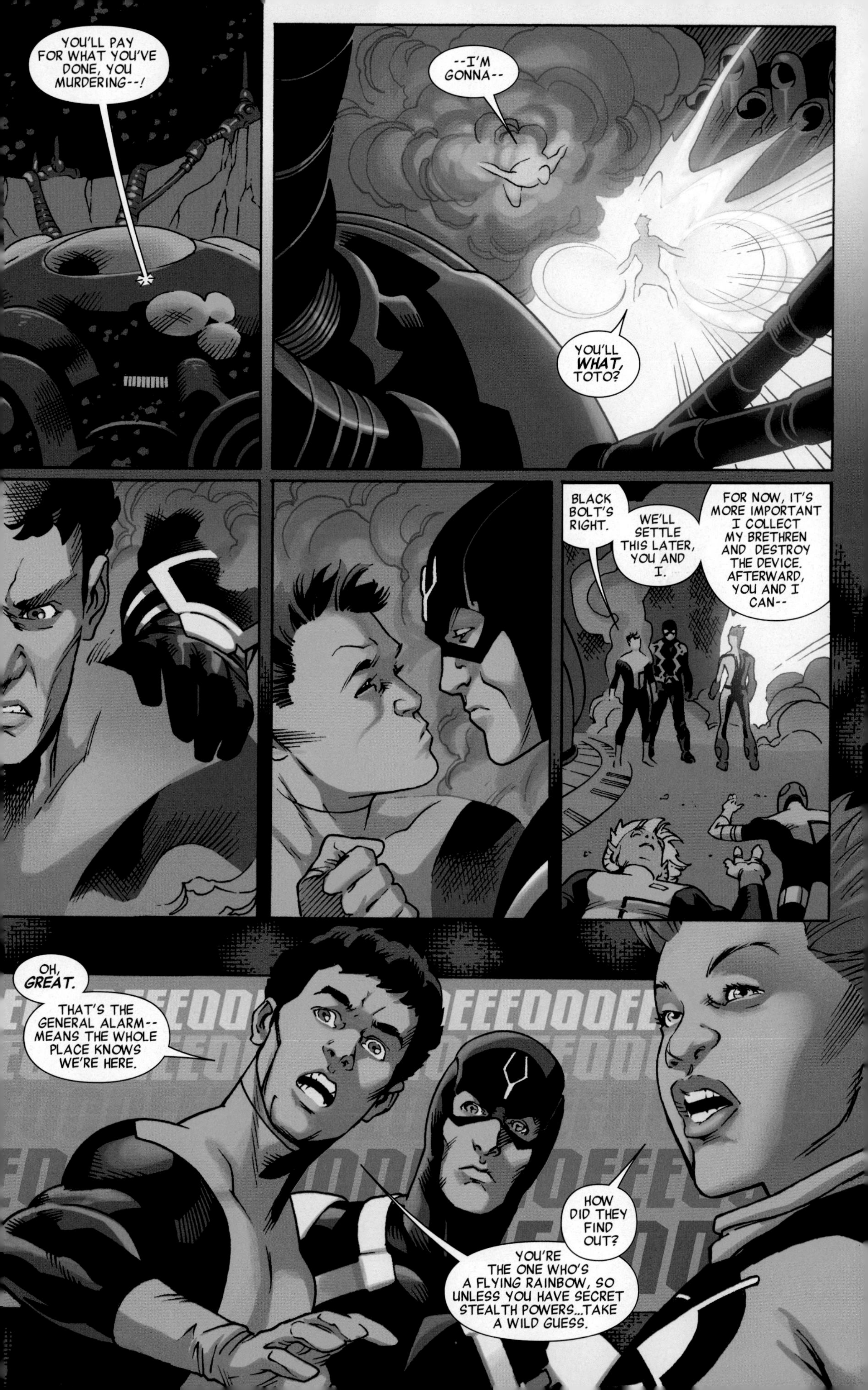

YOU'LL PAY FOR WHAT YOU'VE DONE, YOU MURDERING--!
--I'M GONNA--
YOU'LL *WHAT*, TOTO?
BLACK BOLT'S RIGHT.
WE'LL SETTLE THIS LATER, YOU AND I.
FOR NOW, IT'S MORE IMPORTANT I COLLECT MY BRETHREN AND DESTROY THE DEVICE. AFTERWARD, YOU AND I CAN--
OH, *GREAT.*
THAT'S THE GENERAL ALARM--MEANS THE WHOLE PLACE KNOWS WE'RE HERE.
HOW DID THEY FIND OUT?
YOU'RE THE ONE WHO'S A FLYING RAINBOW, SO UNLESS YOU HAVE SECRET STEALTH POWERS...TAKE A WILD GUESS.

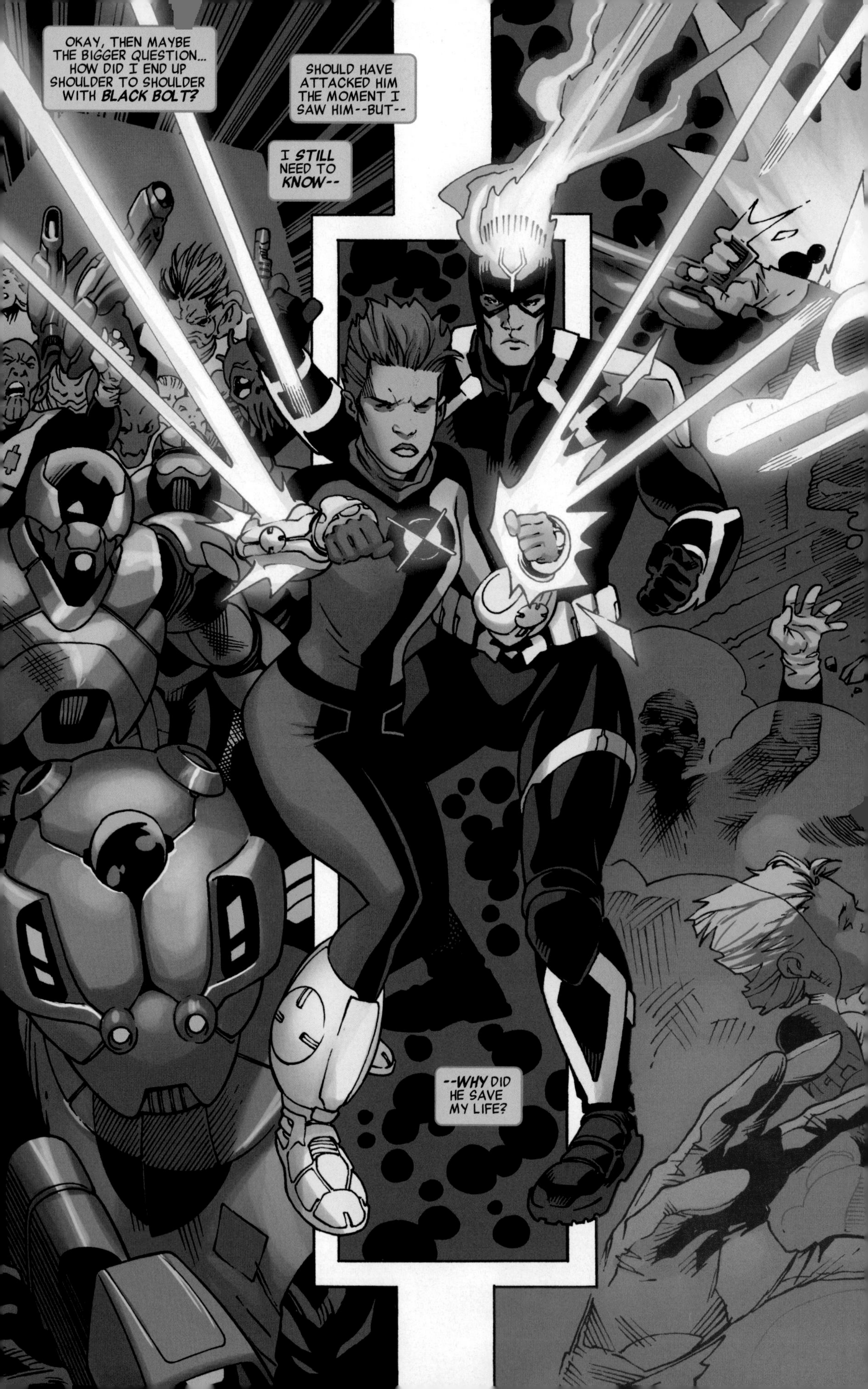
OKAY, THEN MAYBE THE BIGGER QUESTION... HOW DID I END UP SHOULDER TO SHOULDER WITH **BLACK BOLT?**
SHOULD HAVE ATTACKED HIM THE MOMENT I SAW HIM--BUT--
I **STILL** NEED TO **KNOW--**
--**WHY** DID HE SAVE MY LIFE?

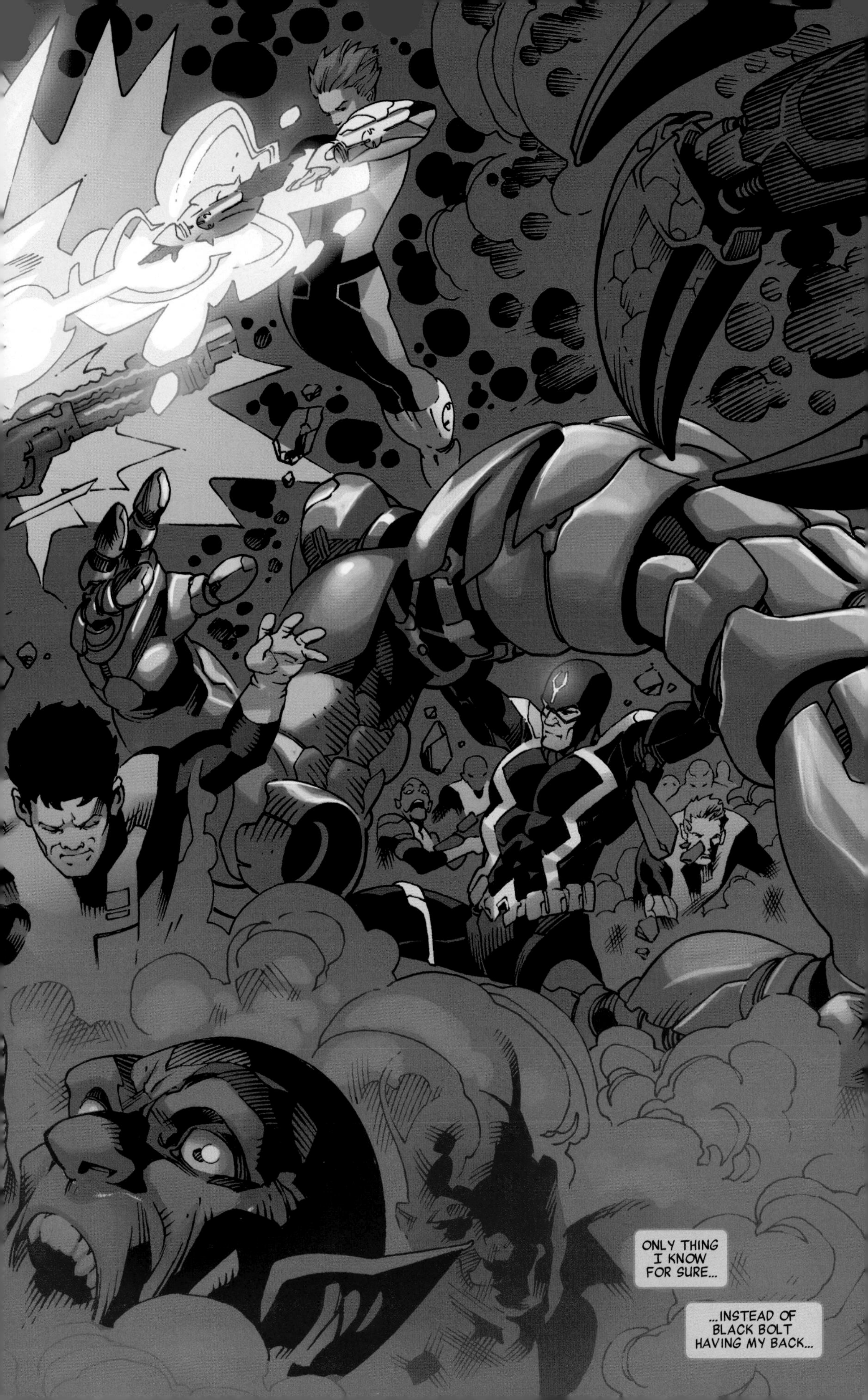
ONLY THING I KNOW FOR SURE...
...INSTEAD OF BLACK BOLT HAVING MY BACK...

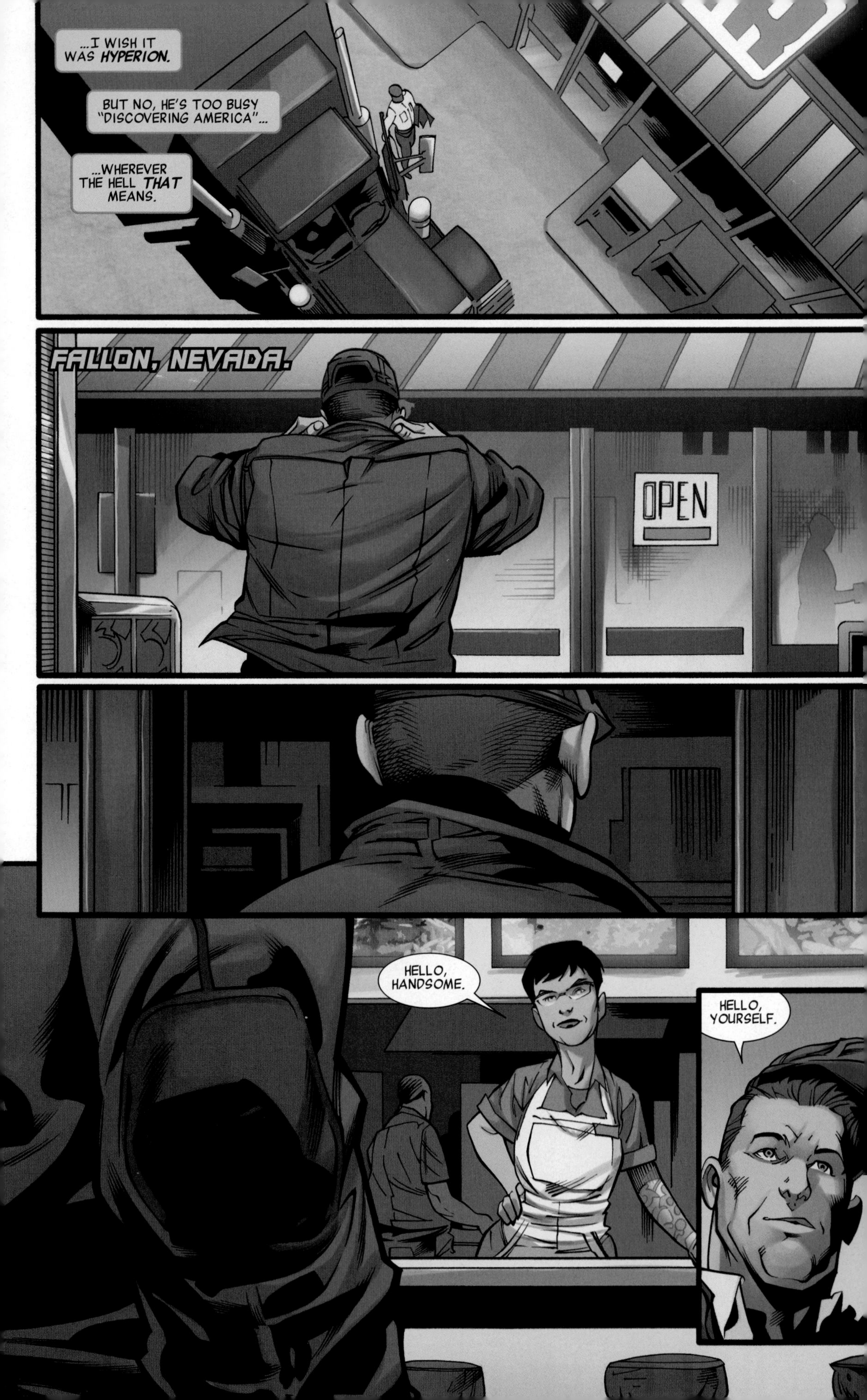
...I WISH IT WAS HYPERION.
BUT NO, HE'S TOO BUSY "DISCOVERING AMERICA"...
...WHEREVER THE HELL THAT MEANS.
FALLON, NEVADA.
OPEN
HELLO, HANDSOME.
HELLO, YOURSELF.

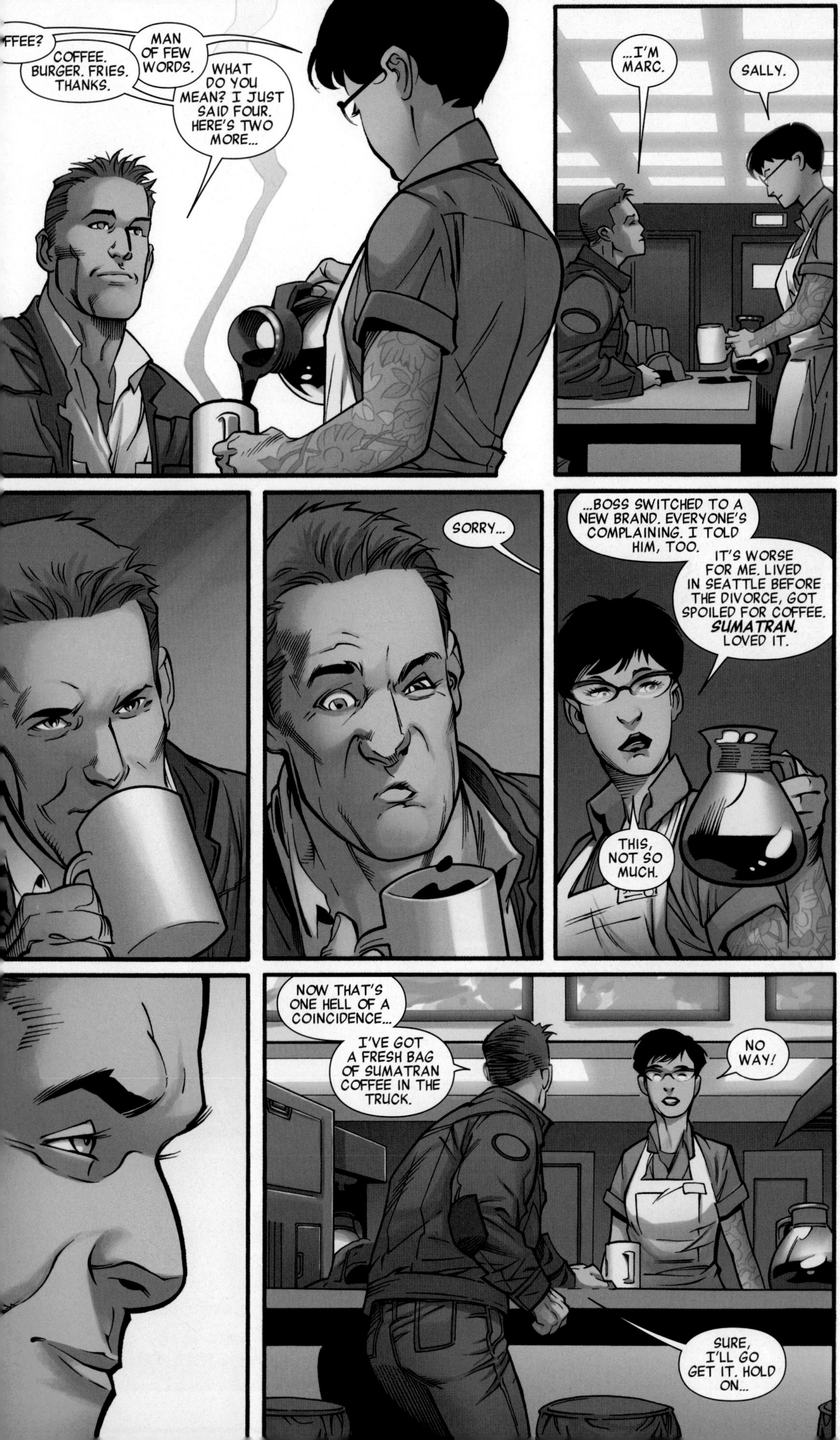
FFEE?
COFFEE. BURGER. FRIES. THANKS.
MAN OF FEW WORDS.
WHAT DO YOU MEAN? I JUST SAID FOUR. HERE'S TWO MORE...
...I'M MARC.
SALLY.
SORRY...
...BOSS SWITCHED TO A NEW BRAND. EVERYONE'S COMPLAINING. I TOLD HIM, TOO.
IT'S WORSE FOR ME. LIVED IN SEATTLE BEFORE THE DIVORCE, GOT SPOILED FOR COFFEE. SUMATRAN. LOVED IT.
THIS, NOT SO MUCH.
NOW THAT'S ONE HELL OF A COINCIDENCE...
I'VE GOT A FRESH BAG OF SUMATRAN COFFEE IN THE TRUCK.
NO WAY!
SURE, I'LL GO GET IT. HOLD ON...

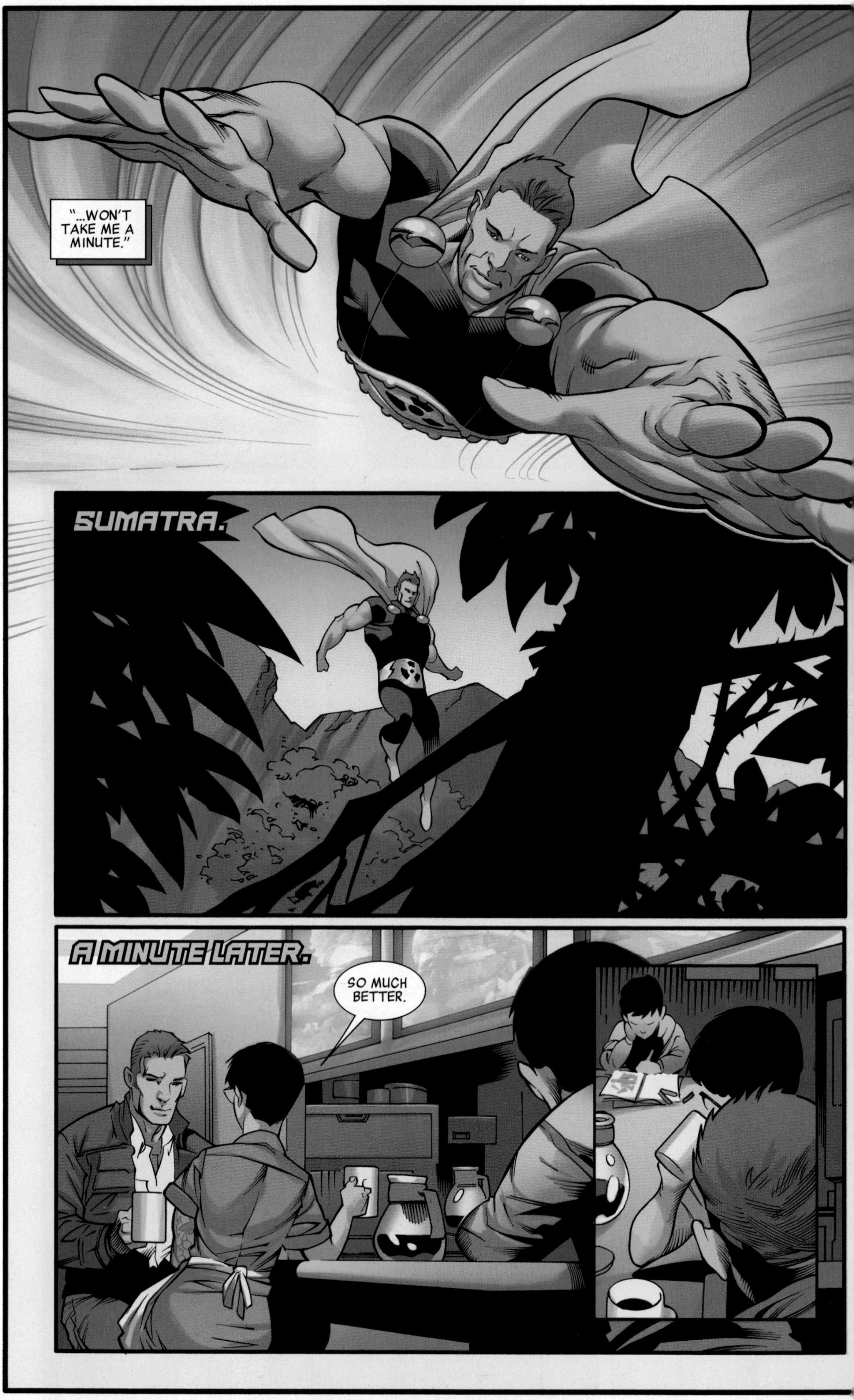
"...WON'T TAKE ME A MINUTE."
SUMATRA.
A MINUTE LATER.
SO MUCH BETTER.

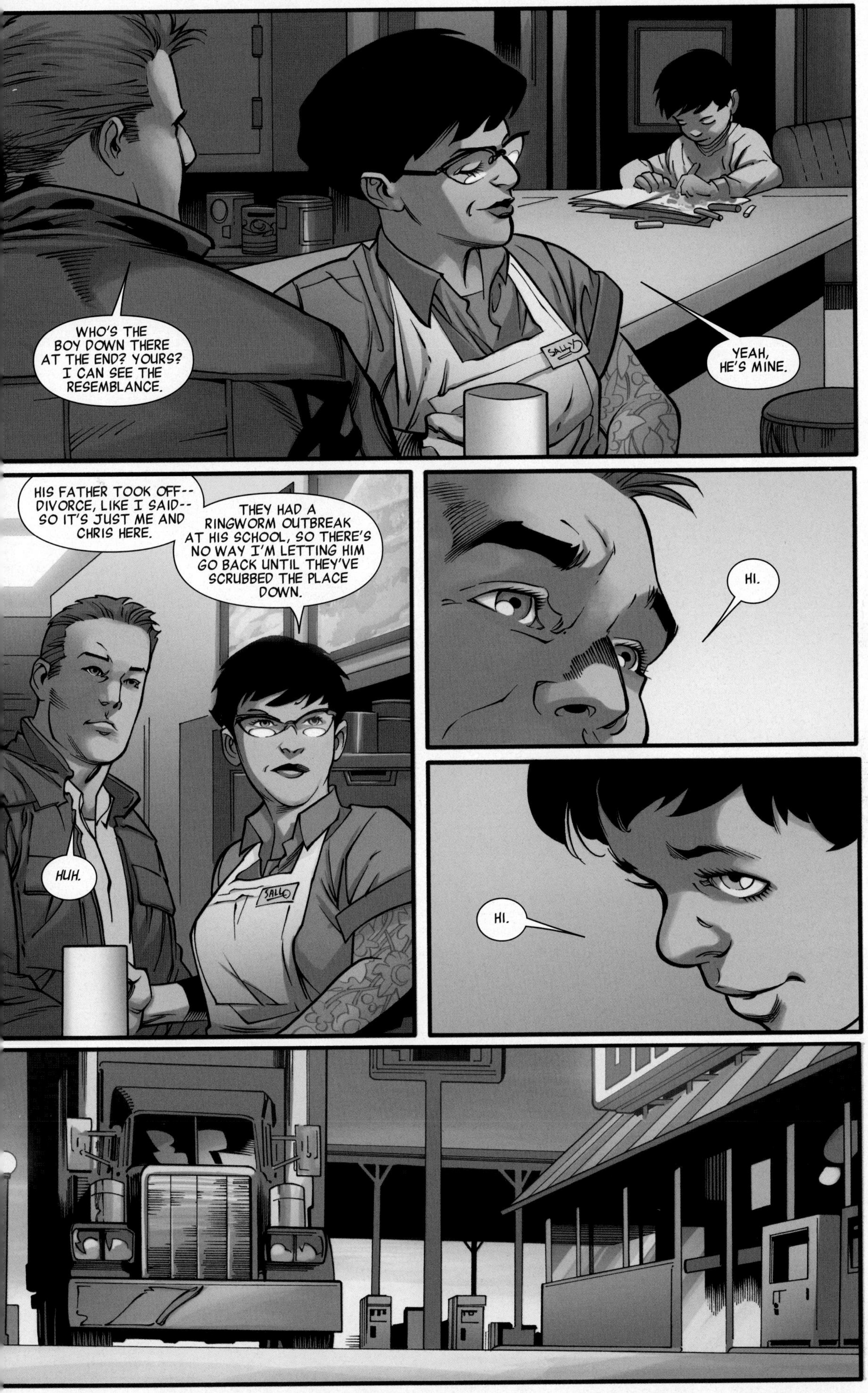
WHO'S THE BOY DOWN THERE AT THE END? YOURS? I CAN SEE THE RESEMBLANCE.
YEAH, HE'S MINE.
HIS FATHER TOOK OFF-- DIVORCE, LIKE I SAID-- SO IT'S JUST ME AND CHRIS HERE.
THEY HAD A RINGWORM OUTBREAK AT HIS SCHOOL, SO THERE'S NO WAY I'M LETTING HIM GO BACK UNTIL THEY'VE SCRUBBED THE PLACE DOWN.
HUH.
HI.
HI.

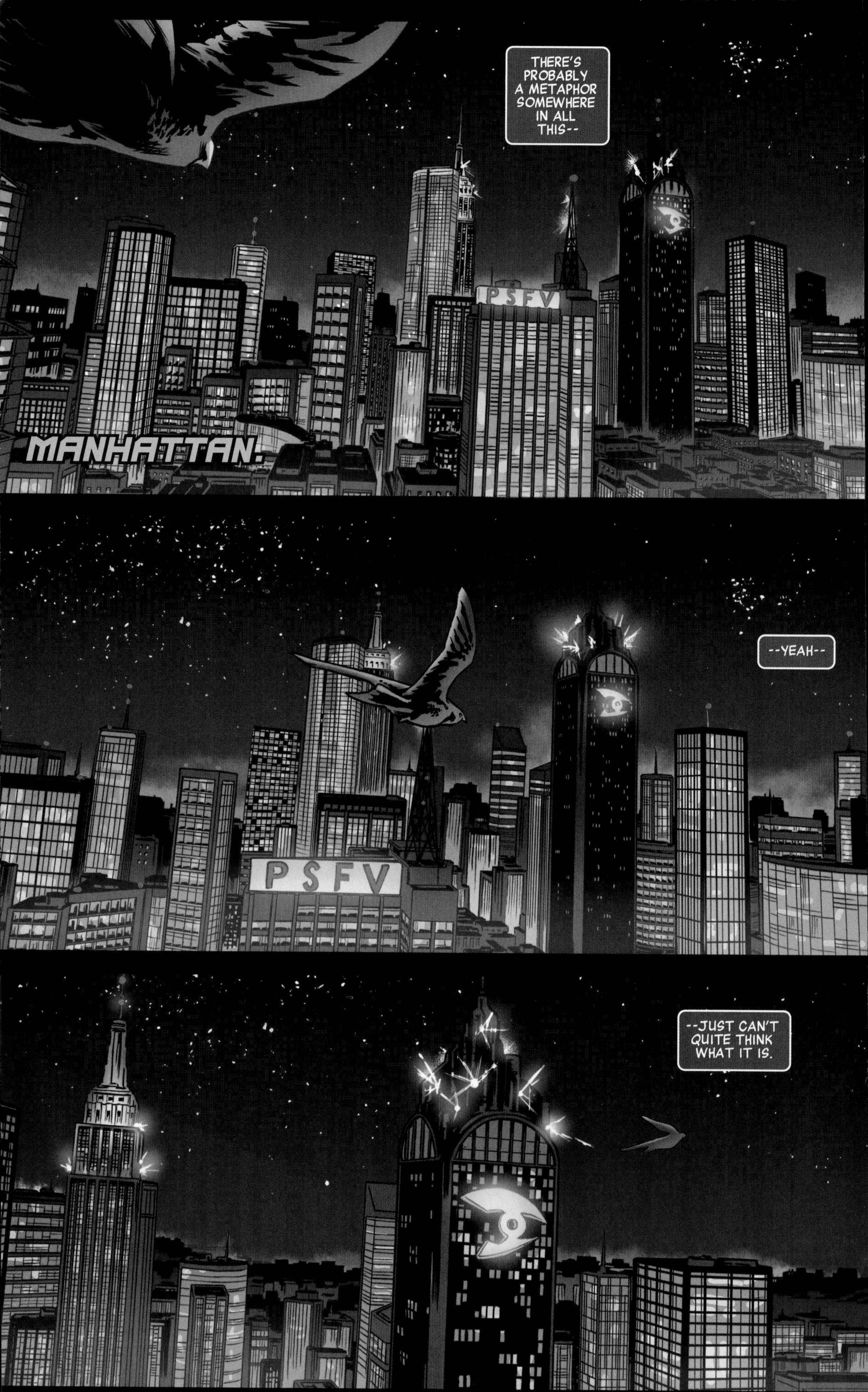
THERE'S PROBABLY A METAPHOR SOMEWHERE IN ALL THIS--
MANHATTAN.
PSFV
--YEAH--
PSFV
--JUST CAN'T QUITE THINK WHAT IT IS.

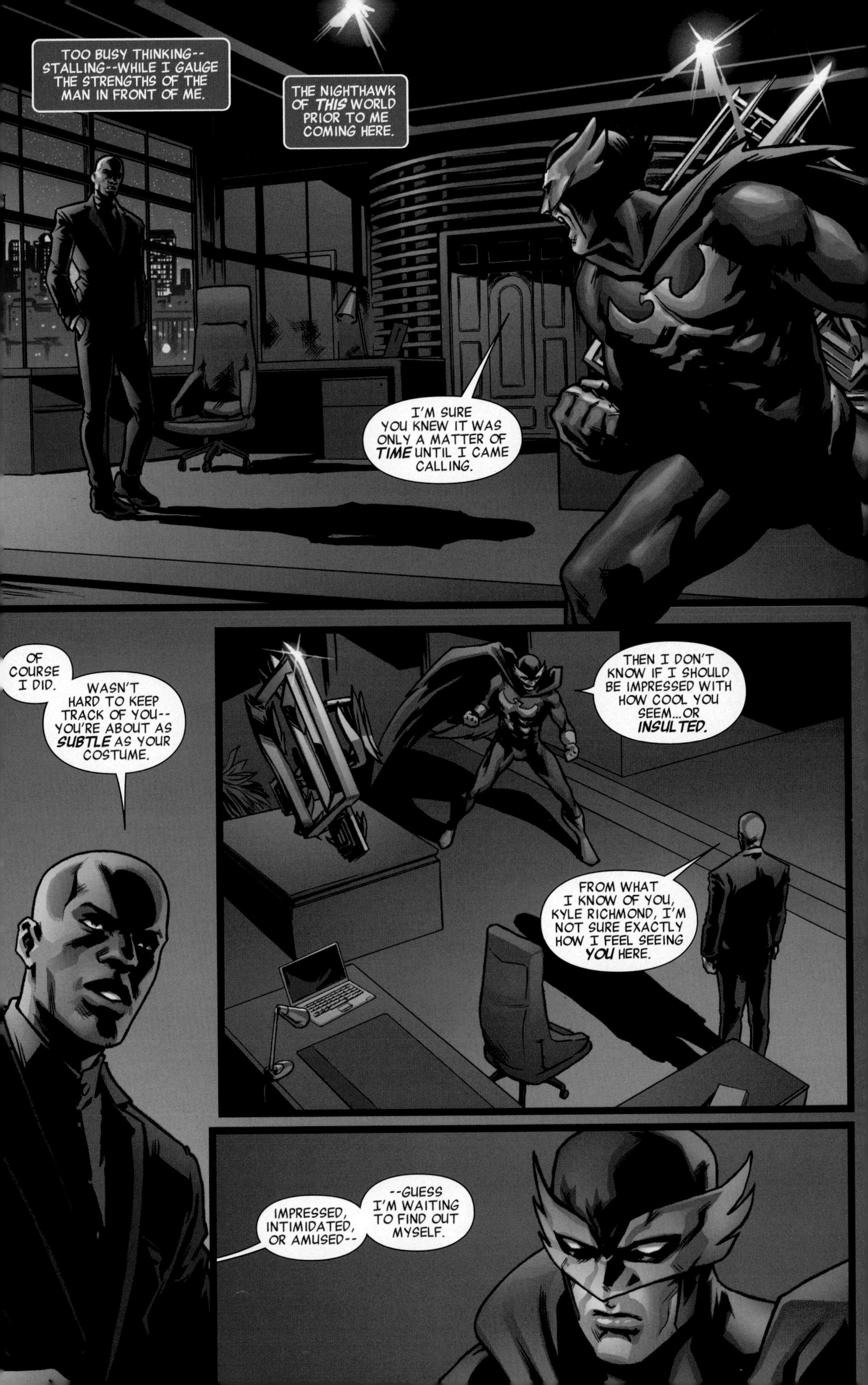
TOO BUSY THINKING--STALLING--WHILE I GAUGE THE STRENGTHS OF THE MAN IN FRONT OF ME.
THE NIGHTHAWK OF THIS WORLD PRIOR TO ME COMING HERE.
I'M SURE YOU KNEW IT WAS ONLY A MATTER OF TIME UNTIL I CAME CALLING.
OF COURSE I DID.
WASN'T HARD TO KEEP TRACK OF YOU--YOU'RE ABOUT AS SUBTLE AS YOUR COSTUME.
THEN I DON'T KNOW IF I SHOULD BE IMPRESSED WITH HOW COOL YOU SEEM...OR INSULTED.
FROM WHAT I KNOW OF YOU, KYLE RICHMOND, I'M NOT SURE EXACTLY HOW I FEEL SEEING YOU HERE.
IMPRESSED, INTIMIDATED, OR AMUSED--
--GUESS I'M WAITING TO FIND OUT MYSELF.

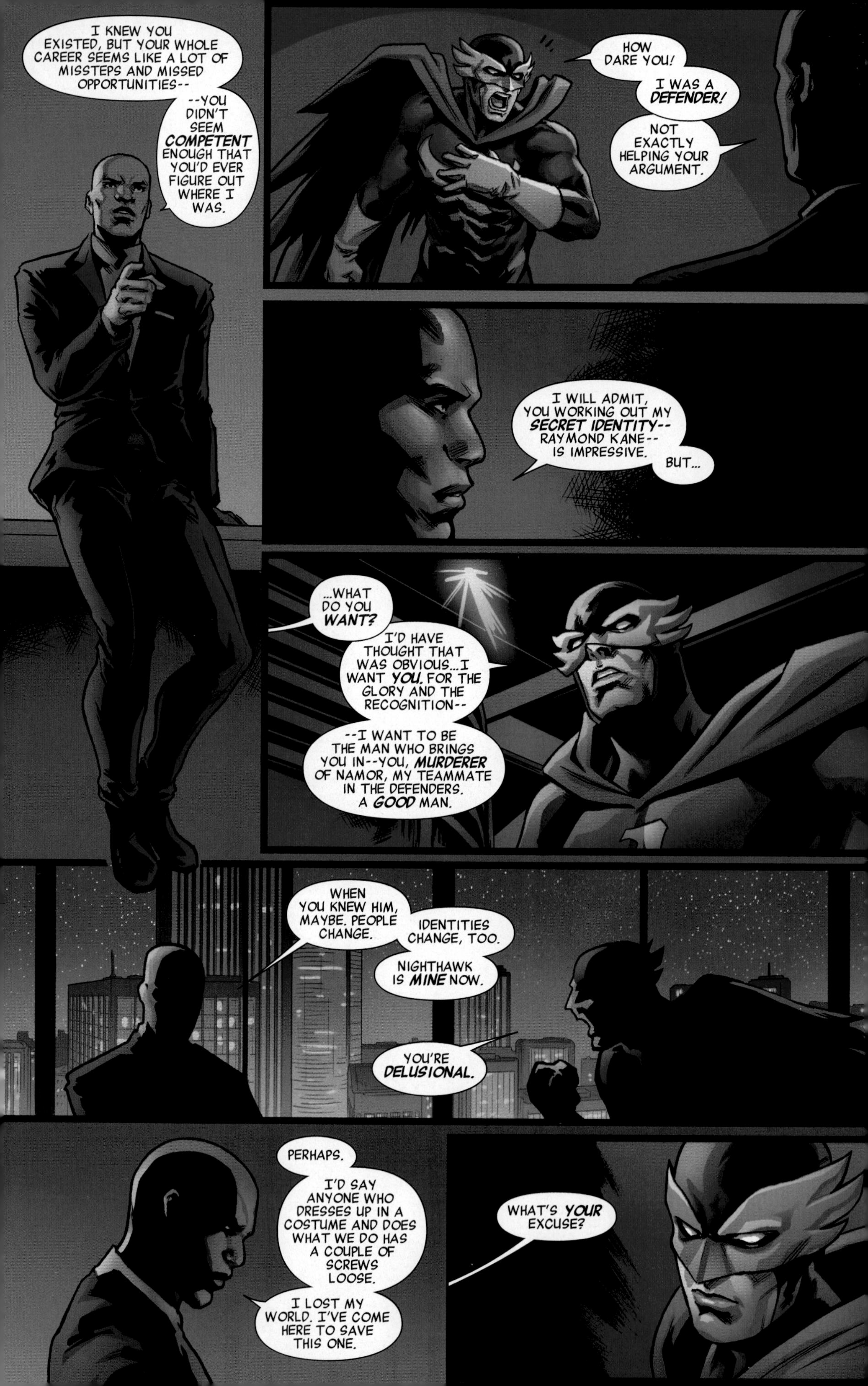
I KNEW YOU EXISTED, BUT YOUR WHOLE CAREER SEEMS LIKE A LOT OF MISSTEPS AND MISSED OPPORTUNITIES--
--YOU DIDN'T SEEM COMPETENT ENOUGH THAT YOU'D EVER FIGURE OUT WHERE I WAS.
HOW DARE YOU!
I WAS A DEFENDER!
NOT EXACTLY HELPING YOUR ARGUMENT.
I WILL ADMIT, YOU WORKING OUT MY SECRET IDENTITY-- RAYMOND KANE-- IS IMPRESSIVE.
BUT...
...WHAT DO YOU WANT?
I'D HAVE THOUGHT THAT WAS OBVIOUS...I WANT YOU. FOR THE GLORY AND THE RECOGNITION--
--I WANT TO BE THE MAN WHO BRINGS YOU IN--YOU, MURDERER OF NAMOR, MY TEAMMATE IN THE DEFENDERS. A GOOD MAN.
WHEN YOU KNEW HIM, MAYBE. PEOPLE CHANGE.
IDENTITIES CHANGE, TOO.
NIGHTHAWK IS MINE NOW.
YOU'RE DELUSIONAL.
PERHAPS.
I'D SAY ANYONE WHO DRESSES UP IN A COSTUME AND DOES WHAT WE DO HAS A COUPLE OF SCREWS LOOSE.
WHAT'S YOUR EXCUSE?
I LOST MY WORLD. I'VE COME HERE TO SAVE THIS ONE.

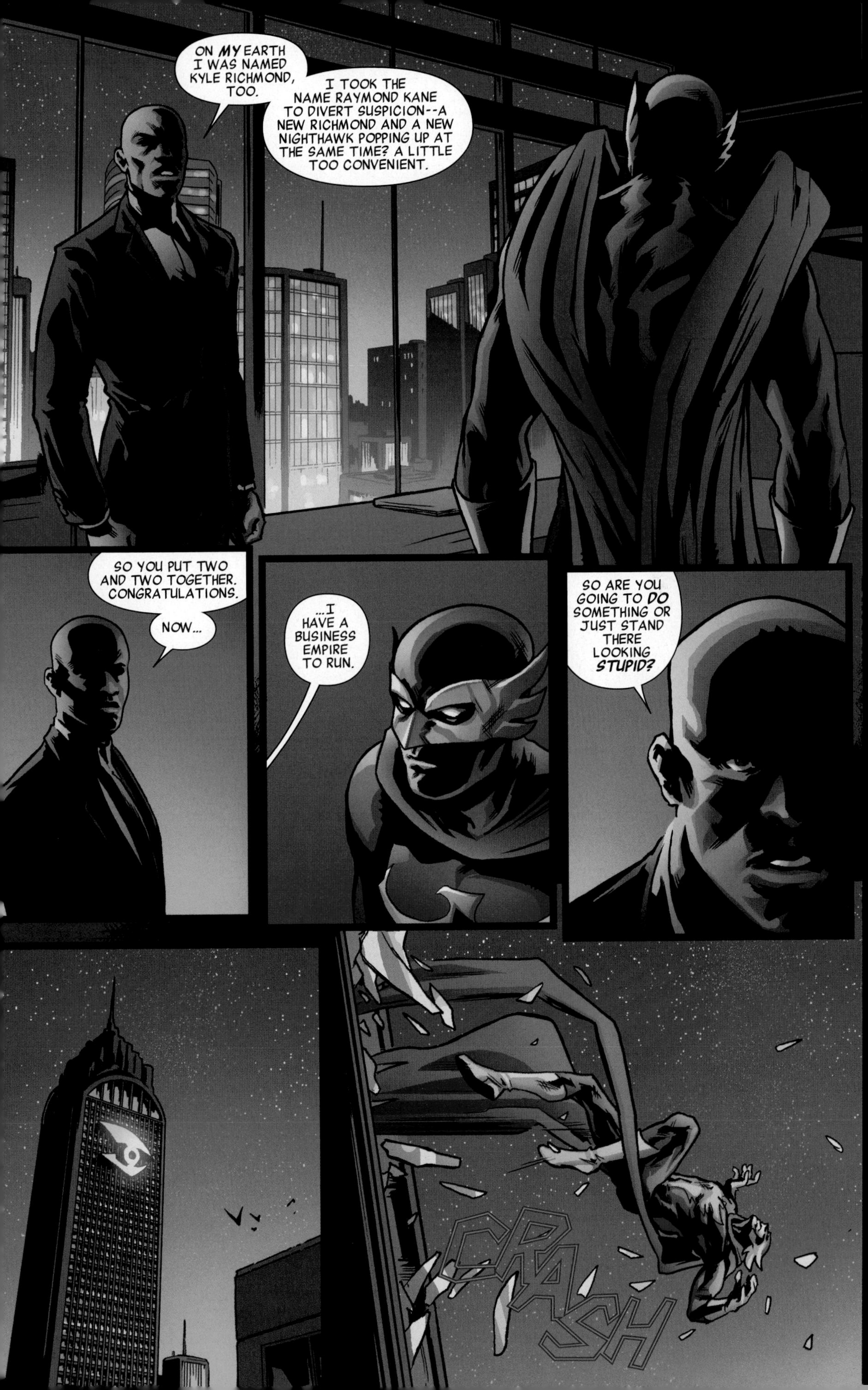
ON MY EARTH I WAS NAMED KYLE RICHMOND, TOO.
I TOOK THE NAME RAYMOND KANE TO DIVERT SUSPICION--A NEW RICHMOND AND A NEW NIGHTHAWK POPPING UP AT THE SAME TIME? A LITTLE TOO CONVENIENT.
SO YOU PUT TWO AND TWO TOGETHER. CONGRATULATIONS.
NOW...
...I HAVE A BUSINESS EMPIRE TO RUN.
SO ARE YOU GOING TO DO SOMETHING OR JUST STAND THERE LOOKING STUPID?
CRASH

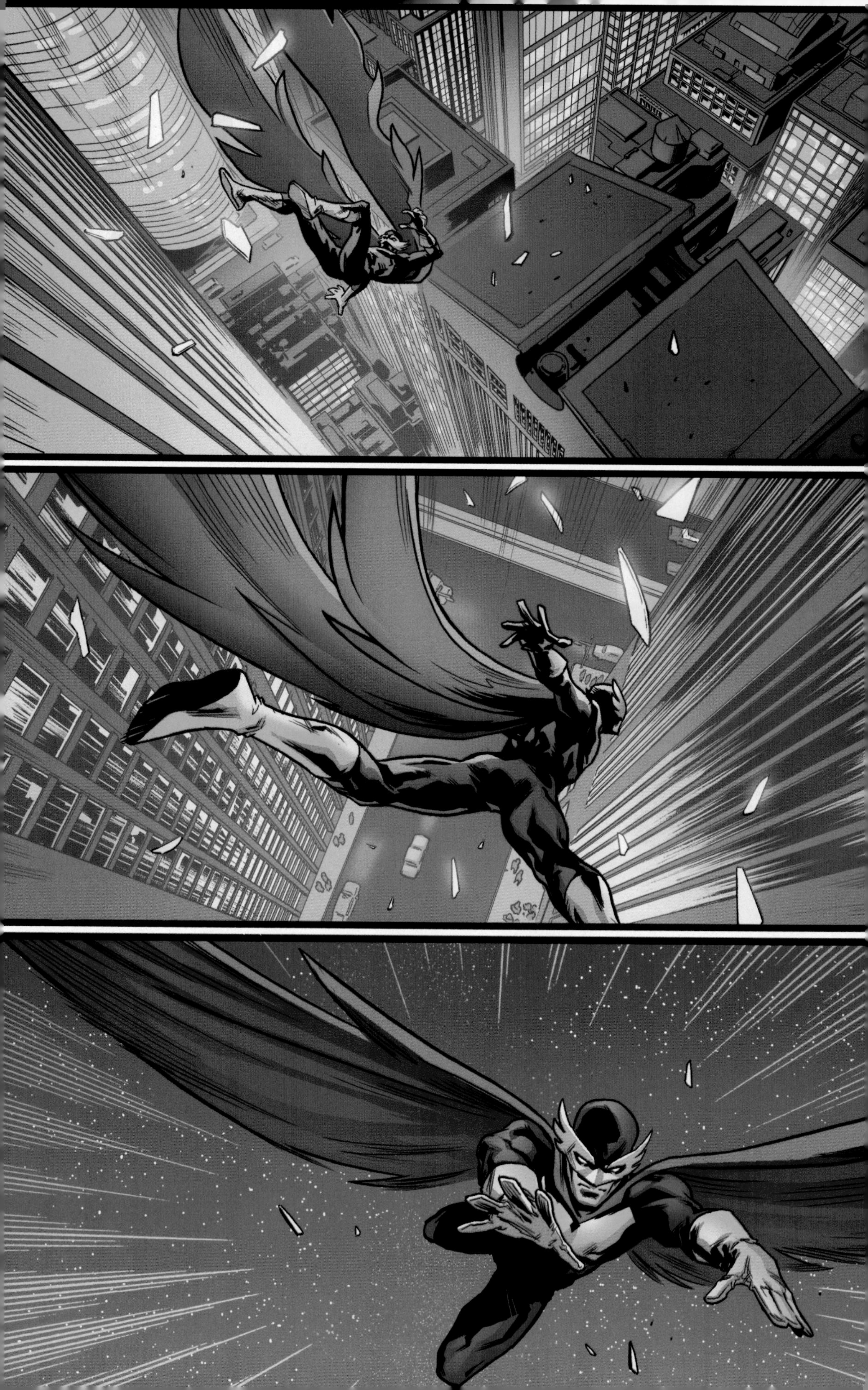

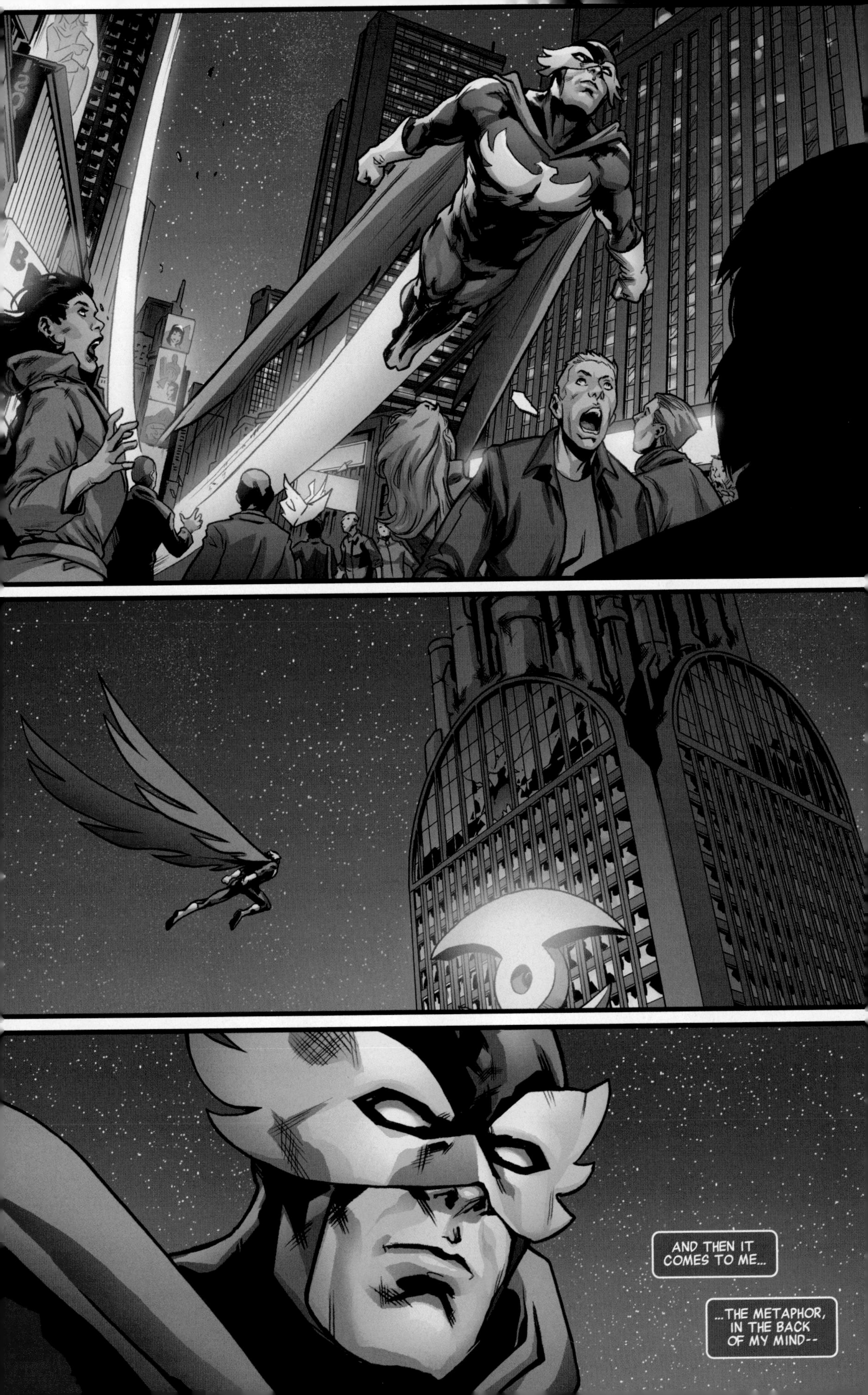
AND THEN IT COMES TO ME...
...THE METAPHOR, IN THE BACK OF MY MIND--

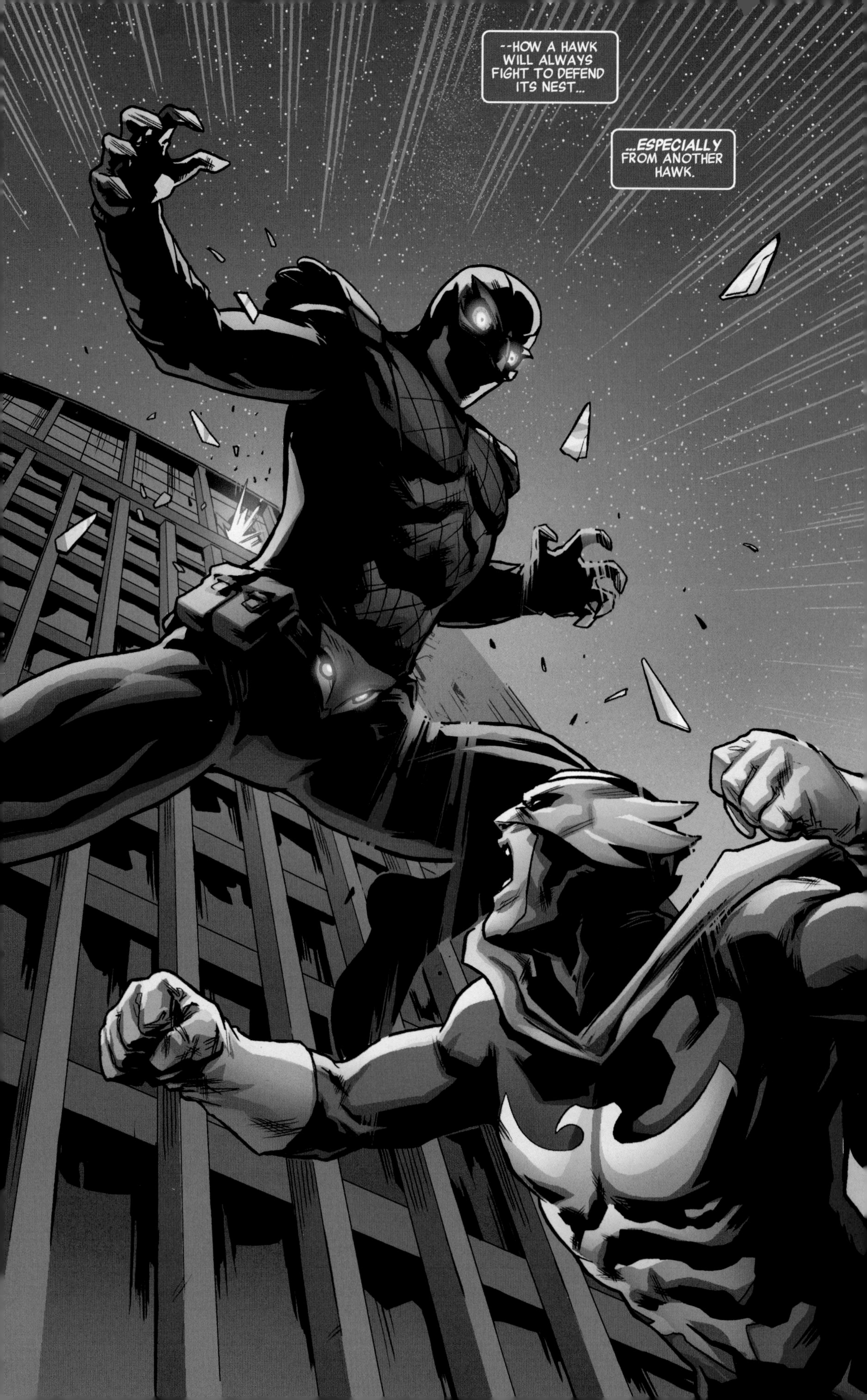
--HOW A HAWK WILL ALWAYS FIGHT TO DEFEND ITS NEST...
...ESPECIALLY FROM ANOTHER HAWK.

# 8

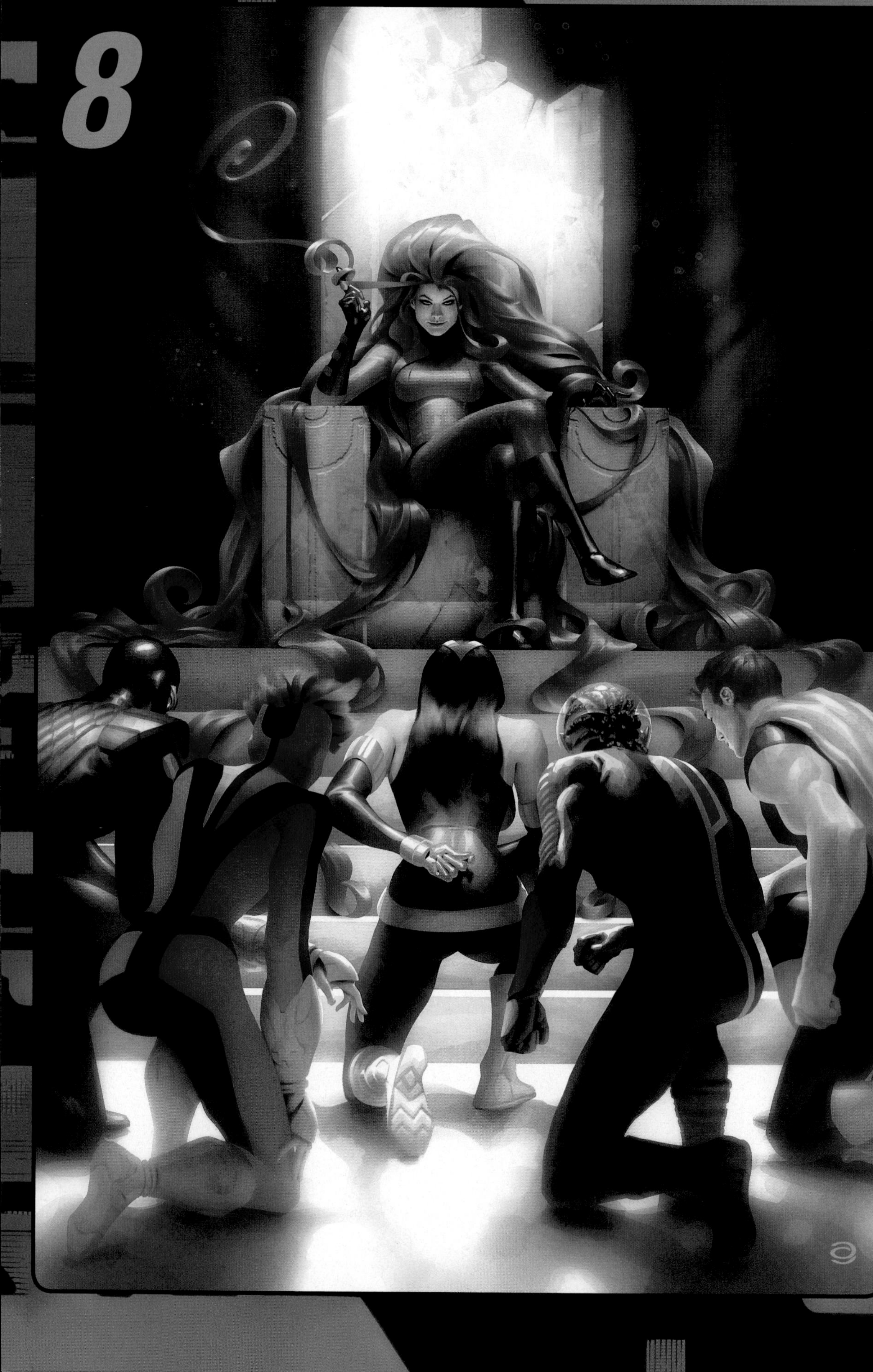

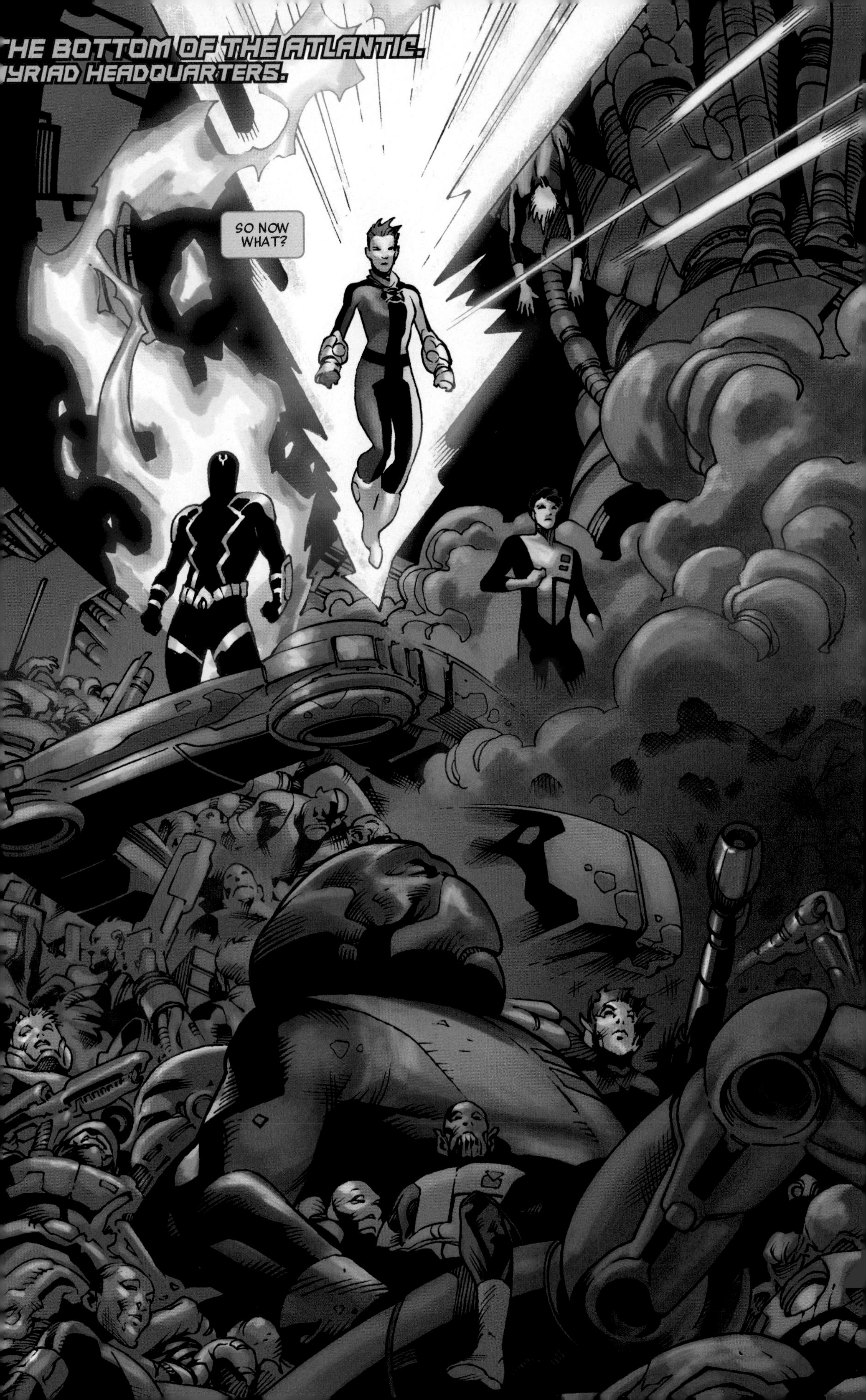

THE BOTTOM OF THE ATLANTIC.
YRIAD HEADQUARTERS.
SO NOW WHAT?

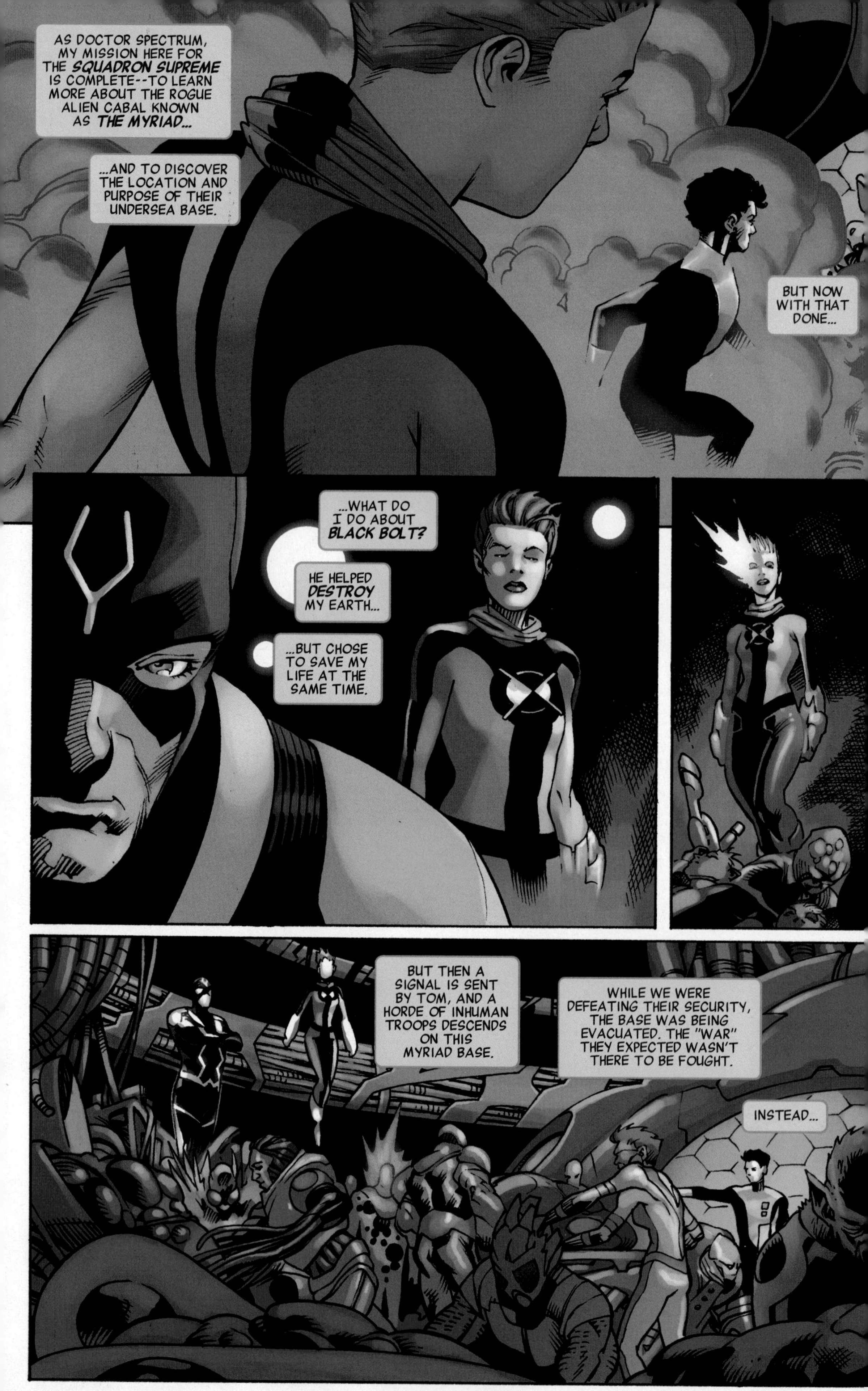
AS DOCTOR SPECTRUM, MY MISSION HERE FOR THE SQUADRON SUPREME IS COMPLETE--TO LEARN MORE ABOUT THE ROGUE ALIEN CABAL KNOWN AS THE MYRIAD...
...AND TO DISCOVER THE LOCATION AND PURPOSE OF THEIR UNDERSEA BASE.
BUT NOW WITH THAT DONE...
...WHAT DO I DO ABOUT BLACK BOLT?
HE HELPED DESTROY MY EARTH...
...BUT CHOSE TO SAVE MY LIFE AT THE SAME TIME.
BUT THEN A SIGNAL IS SENT BY TOM, AND A HORDE OF INHUMAN TROOPS DESCENDS ON THIS MYRIAD BASE.
WHILE WE WERE DEFEATING THEIR SECURITY, THE BASE WAS BEING EVACUATED. THE "WAR" THEY EXPECTED WASN'T THERE TO BE FOUGHT.
INSTEAD...

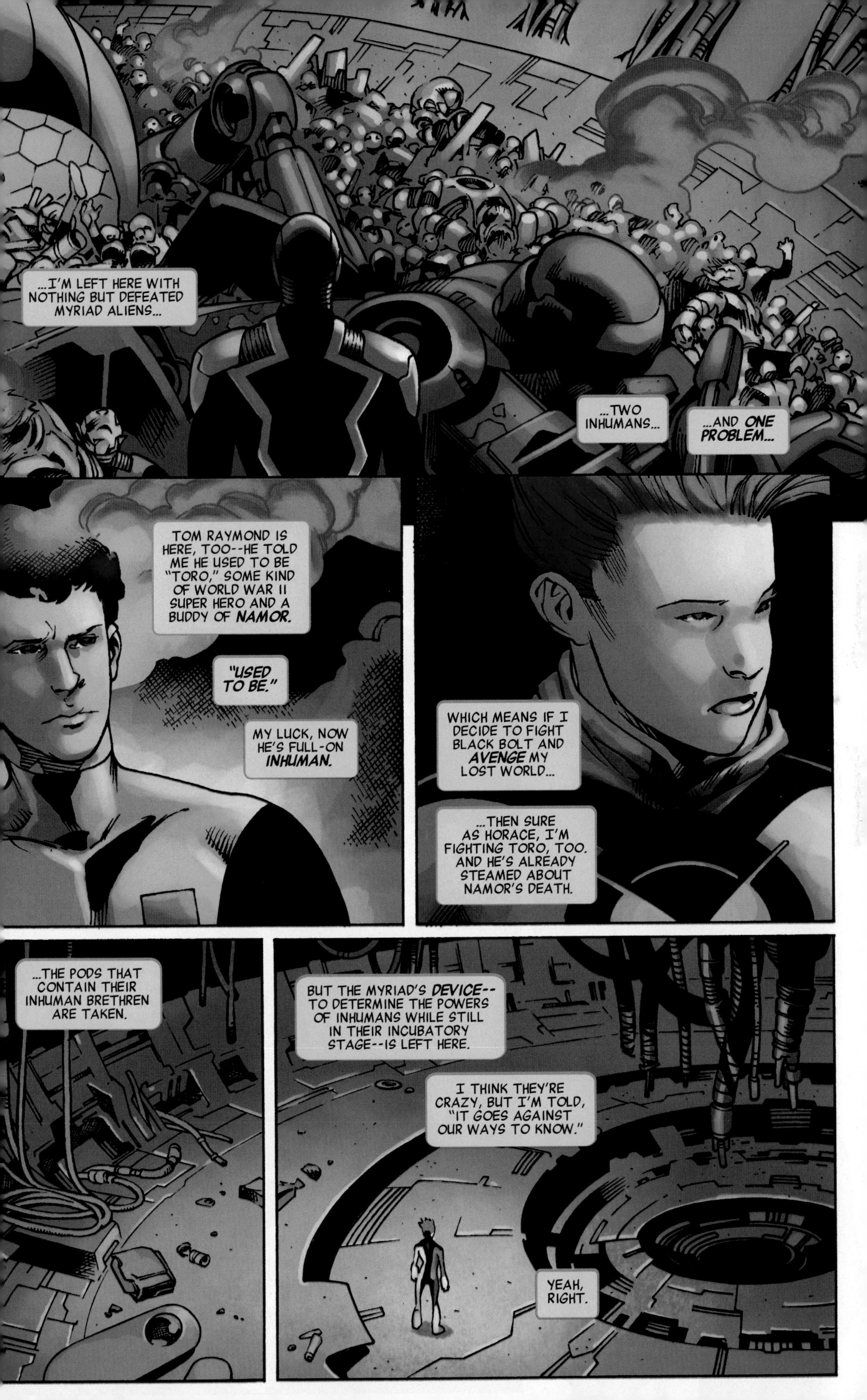
...I'M LEFT HERE WITH NOTHING BUT DEFEATED MYRIAD ALIENS...
...TWO INHUMANS...
...AND ONE PROBLEM...
TOM RAYMOND IS HERE, TOO--HE TOLD ME HE USED TO BE "TORO," SOME KIND OF WORLD WAR II SUPER HERO AND A BUDDY OF NAMOR.
"USED TO BE."
MY LUCK, NOW HE'S FULL-ON INHUMAN.
WHICH MEANS IF I DECIDE TO FIGHT BLACK BOLT AND AVENGE MY LOST WORLD...
...THEN SURE AS HORACE, I'M FIGHTING TORO, TOO. AND HE'S ALREADY STEAMED ABOUT NAMOR'S DEATH.
...THE PODS THAT CONTAIN THEIR INHUMAN BRETHREN ARE TAKEN.
BUT THE MYRIAD'S DEVICE--TO DETERMINE THE POWERS OF INHUMANS WHILE STILL IN THEIR INCUBATORY STAGE--IS LEFT HERE.
I THINK THEY'RE CRAZY, BUT I'M TOLD, "IT GOES AGAINST OUR WAYS TO KNOW."
YEAH, RIGHT.

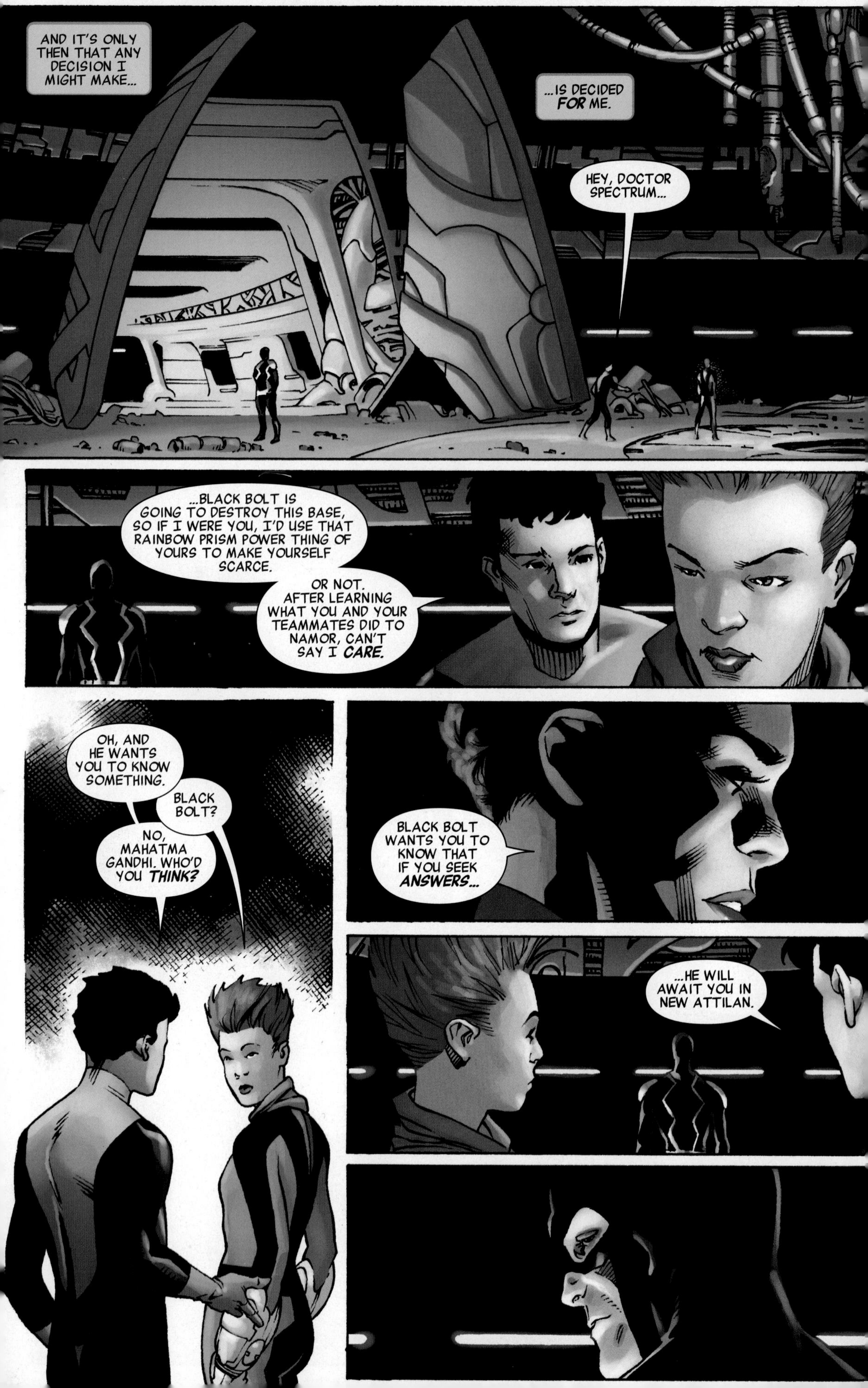
AND IT'S ONLY THEN THAT ANY DECISION I MIGHT MAKE...
...IS DECIDED FOR ME.
HEY, DOCTOR SPECTRUM...
...BLACK BOLT IS GOING TO DESTROY THIS BASE, SO IF I WERE YOU, I'D USE THAT RAINBOW PRISM POWER THING OF YOURS TO MAKE YOURSELF SCARCE.
OR NOT. AFTER LEARNING WHAT YOU AND YOUR TEAMMATES DID TO NAMOR, CAN'T SAY I CARE.
OH, AND HE WANTS YOU TO KNOW SOMETHING.
BLACK BOLT?
NO, MAHATMA GANDHI. WHO'D YOU THINK?
BLACK BOLT WANTS YOU TO KNOW THAT IF YOU SEEK ANSWERS...
...HE WILL AWAIT YOU IN NEW ATTILAN.

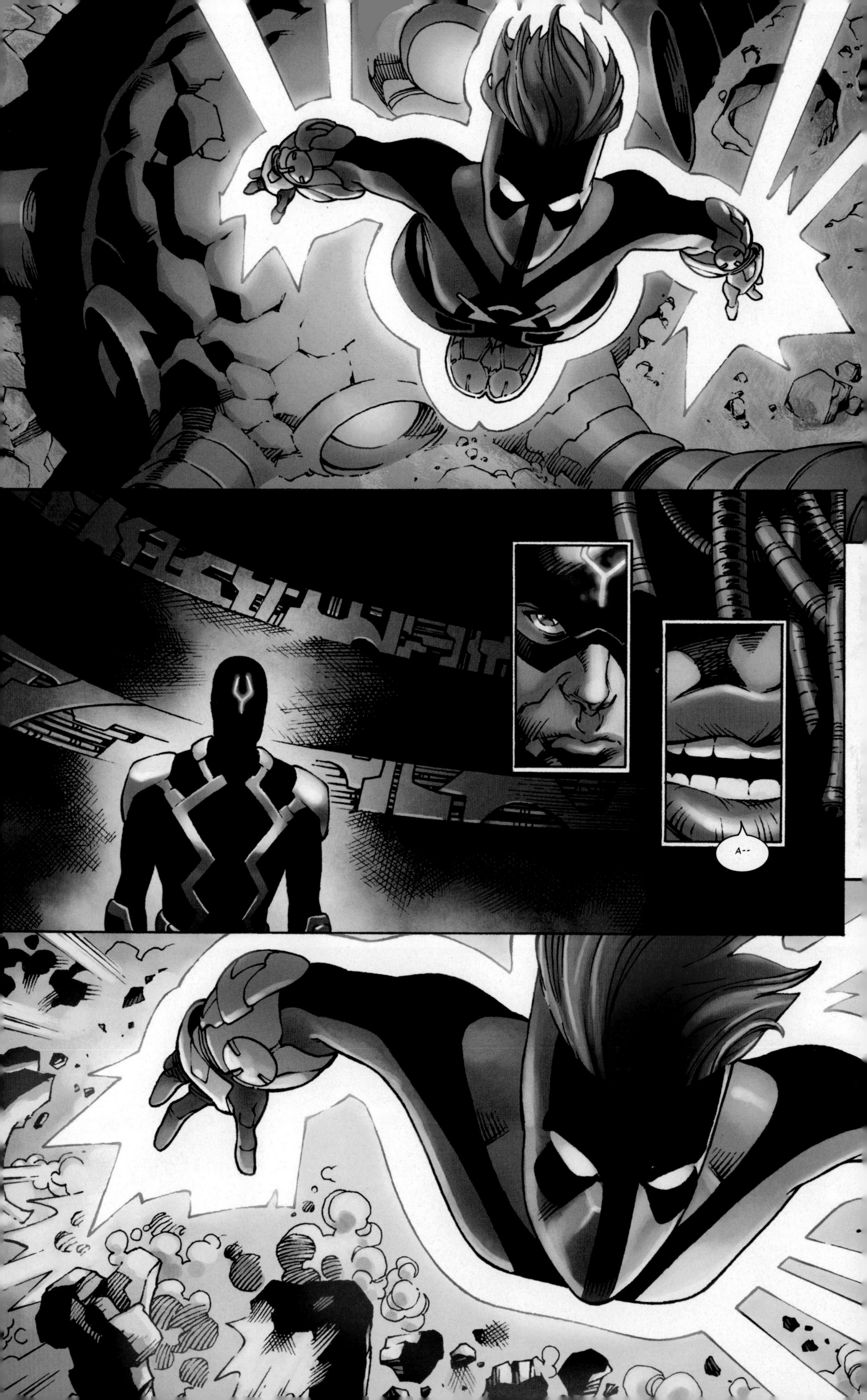
A--

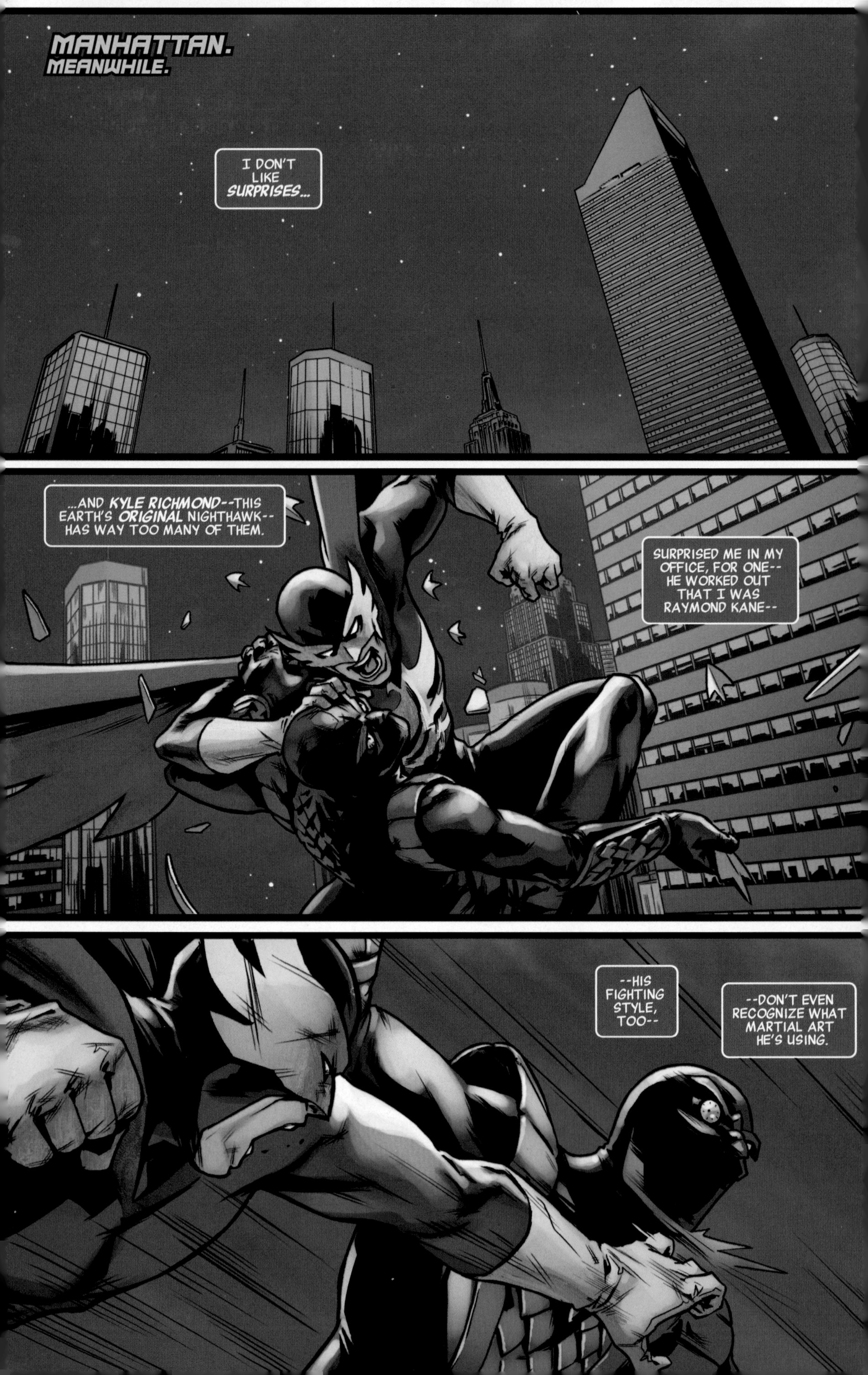
MANHATTAN.
MEANWHILE.
I DON'T LIKE SURPRISES...
...AND KYLE RICHMOND--THIS EARTH'S ORIGINAL NIGHTHAWK--HAS WAY TOO MANY OF THEM.
SURPRISED ME IN MY OFFICE, FOR ONE--HE WORKED OUT THAT I WAS RAYMOND KANE--
--HIS FIGHTING STYLE, TOO--
--DON'T EVEN RECOGNIZE WHAT MARTIAL ART HE'S USING.

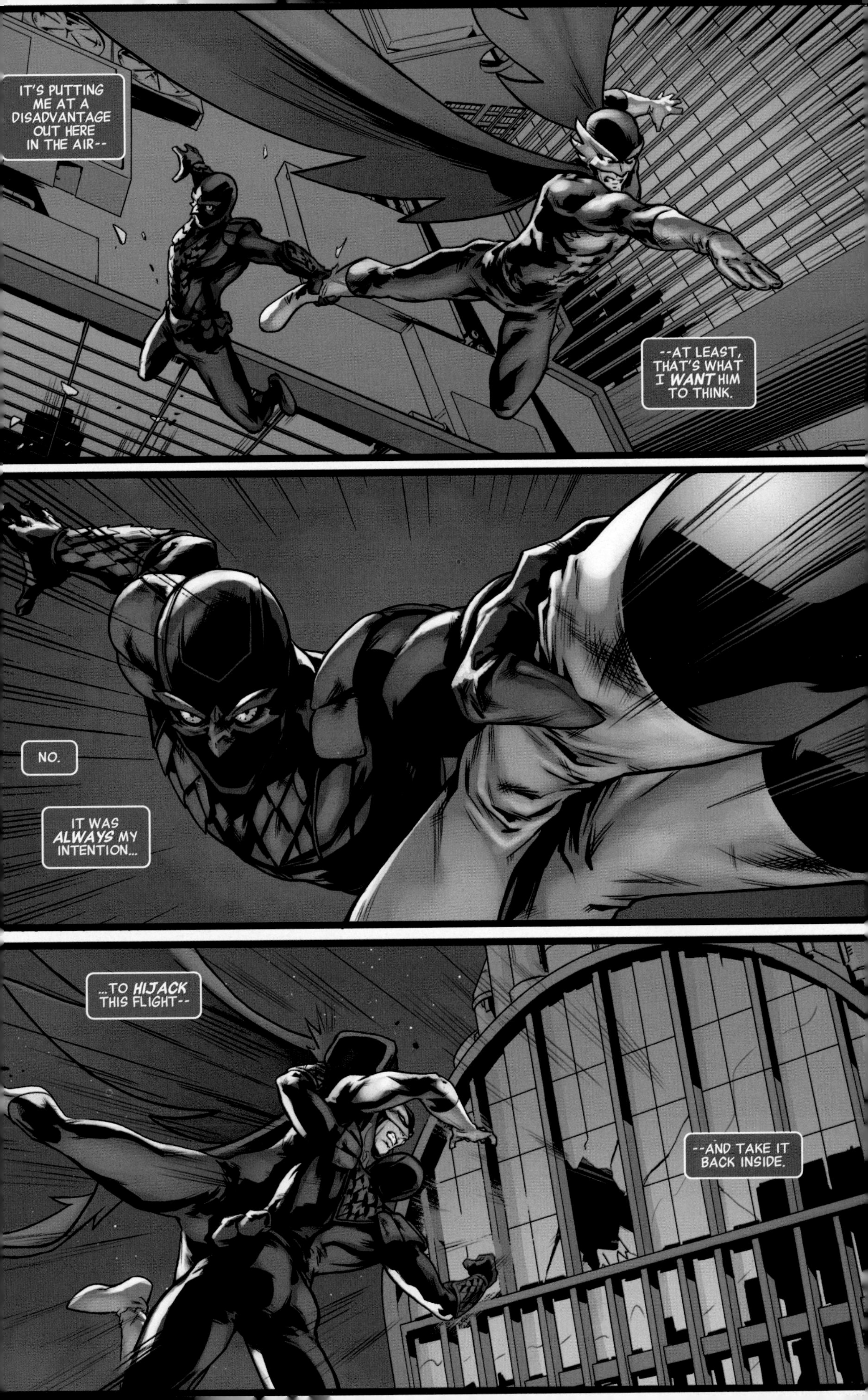
IT'S PUTTING ME AT A DISADVANTAGE OUT HERE IN THE AIR--
--AT LEAST, THAT'S WHAT I WANT HIM TO THINK.
NO.
IT WAS ALWAYS MY INTENTION...
...TO HIJACK THIS FLIGHT--
--AND TAKE IT BACK INSIDE.

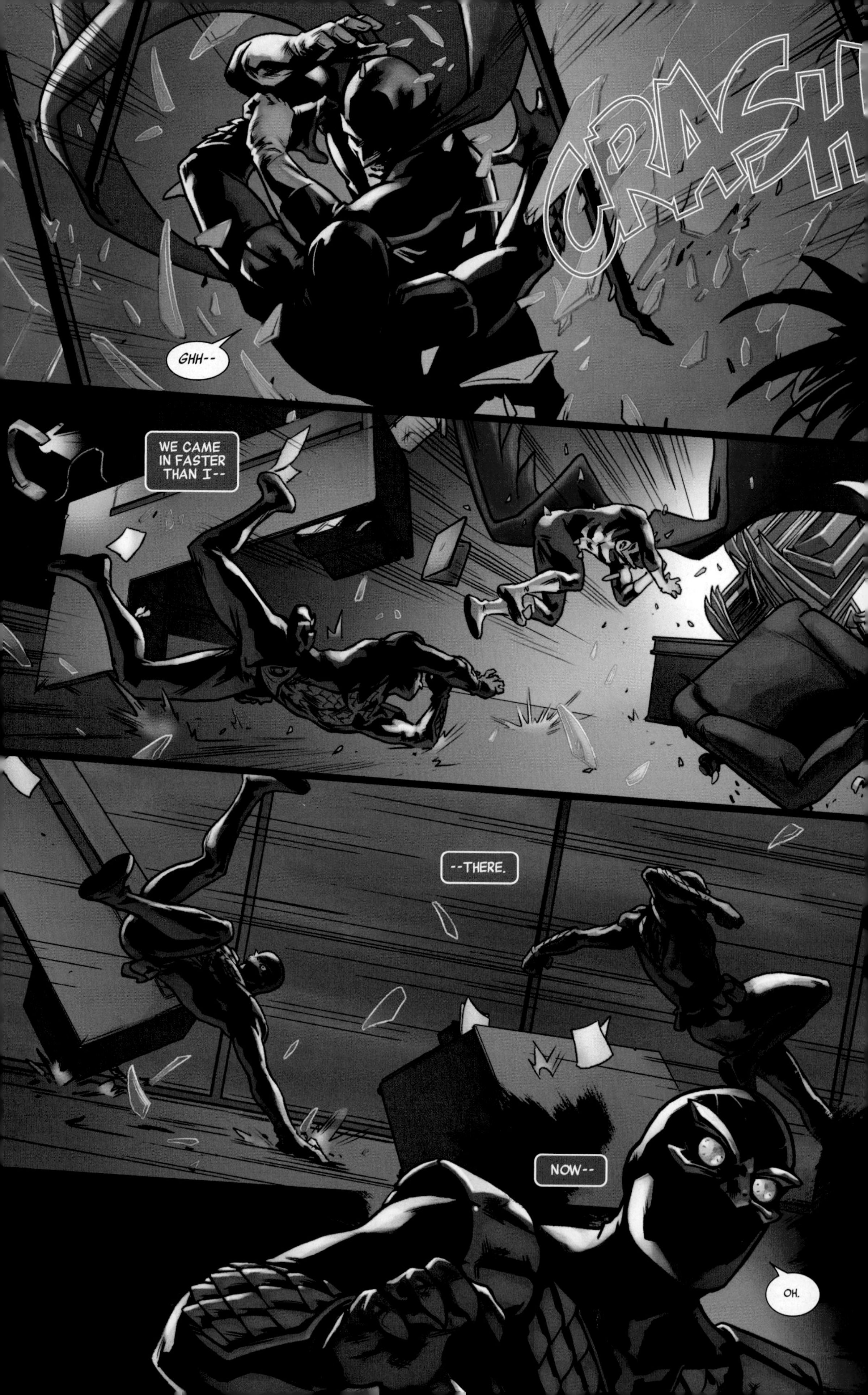
GHH--
WE CAME IN FASTER THAN I--
--THERE.
NOW--
OH.

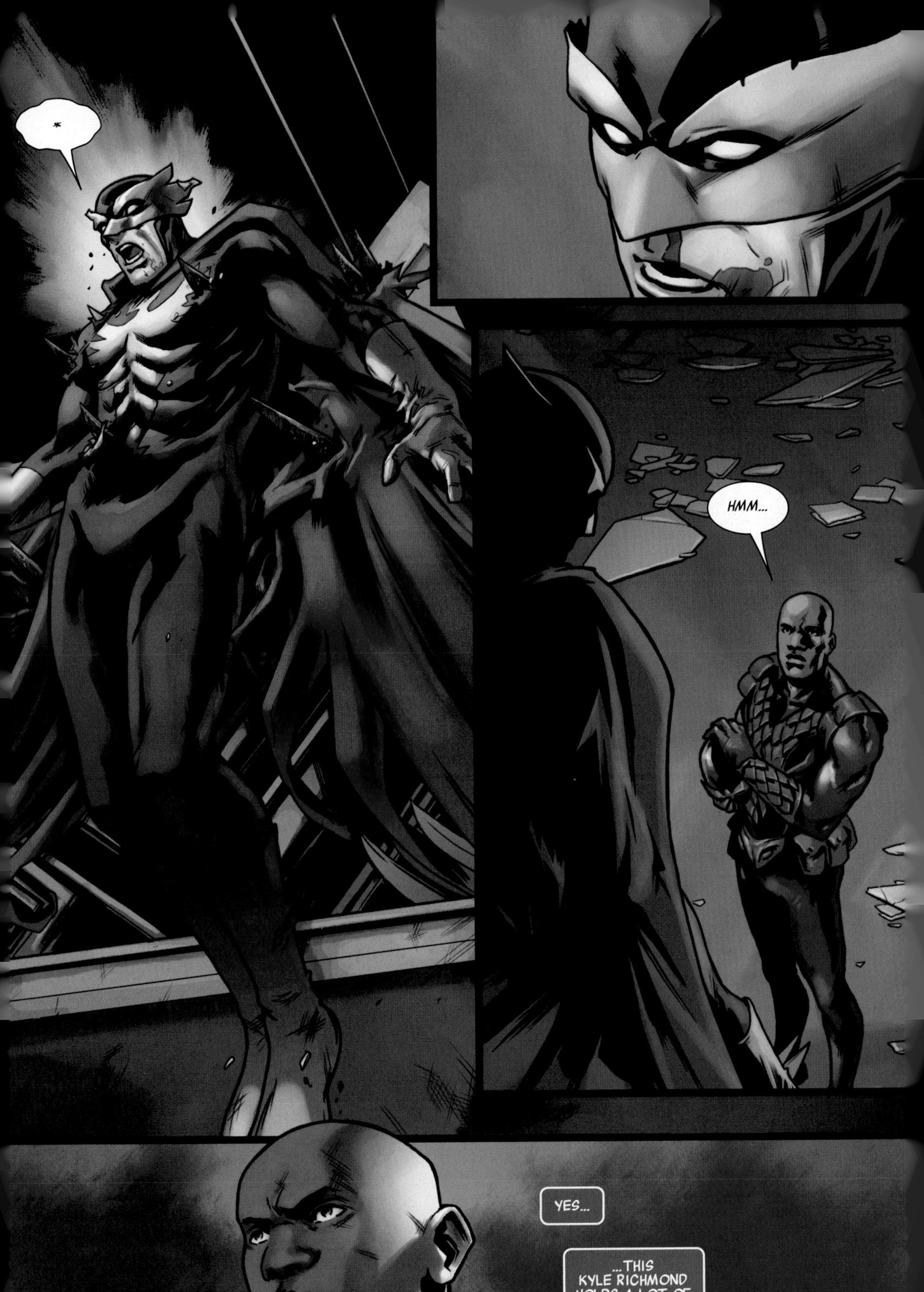
*
HMM...
YES...
...THIS KYLE RICHMOND HOLDS A LOT OF SURPRISES.

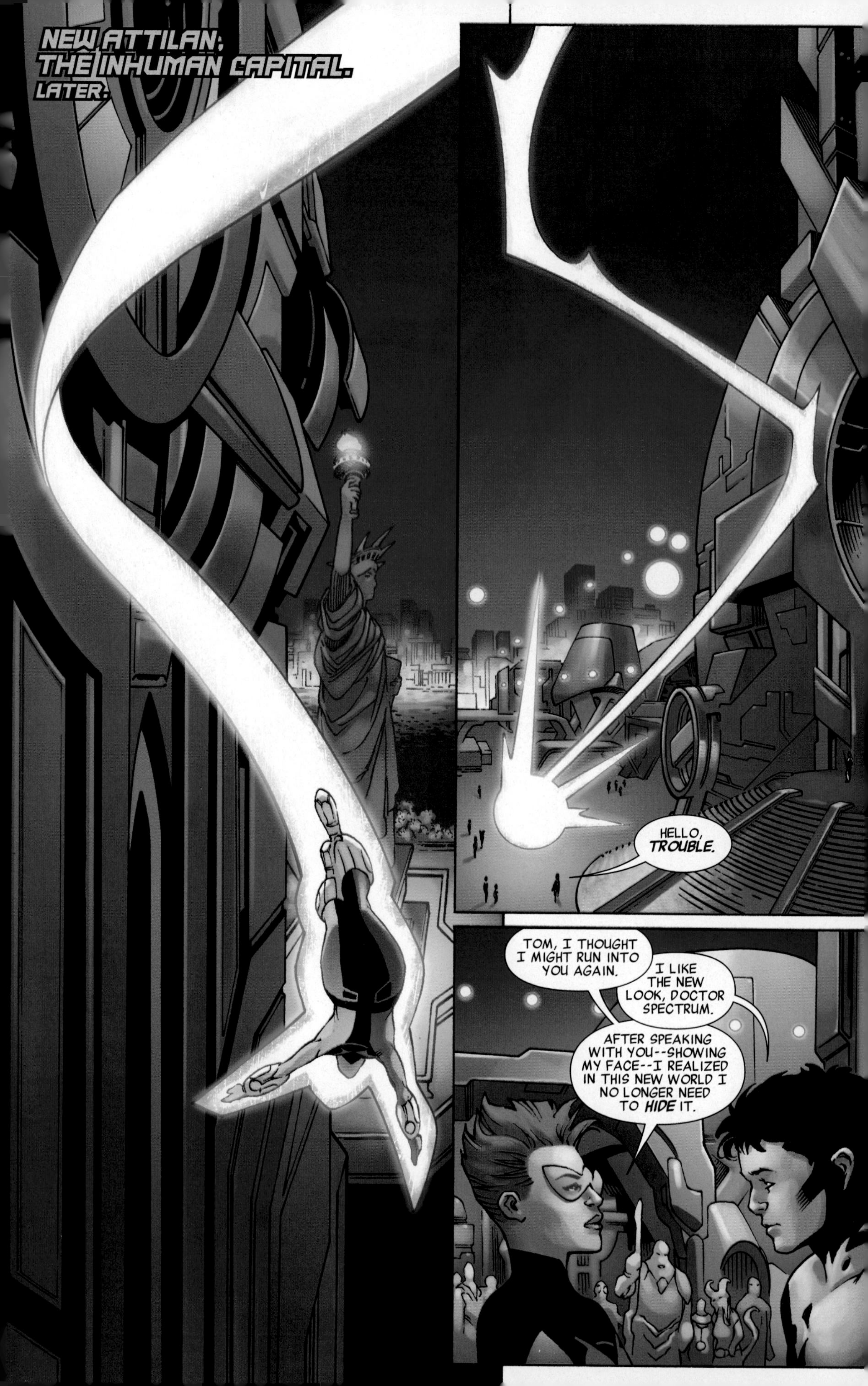
NEW ATTILAN: THE INHUMAN CAPITAL.
LATER.
HELLO, TROUBLE.
TOM, I THOUGHT I MIGHT RUN INTO YOU AGAIN.
I LIKE THE NEW LOOK, DOCTOR SPECTRUM.
AFTER SPEAKING WITH YOU--SHOWING MY FACE--I REALIZED IN THIS NEW WORLD I NO LONGER NEED TO HIDE IT.

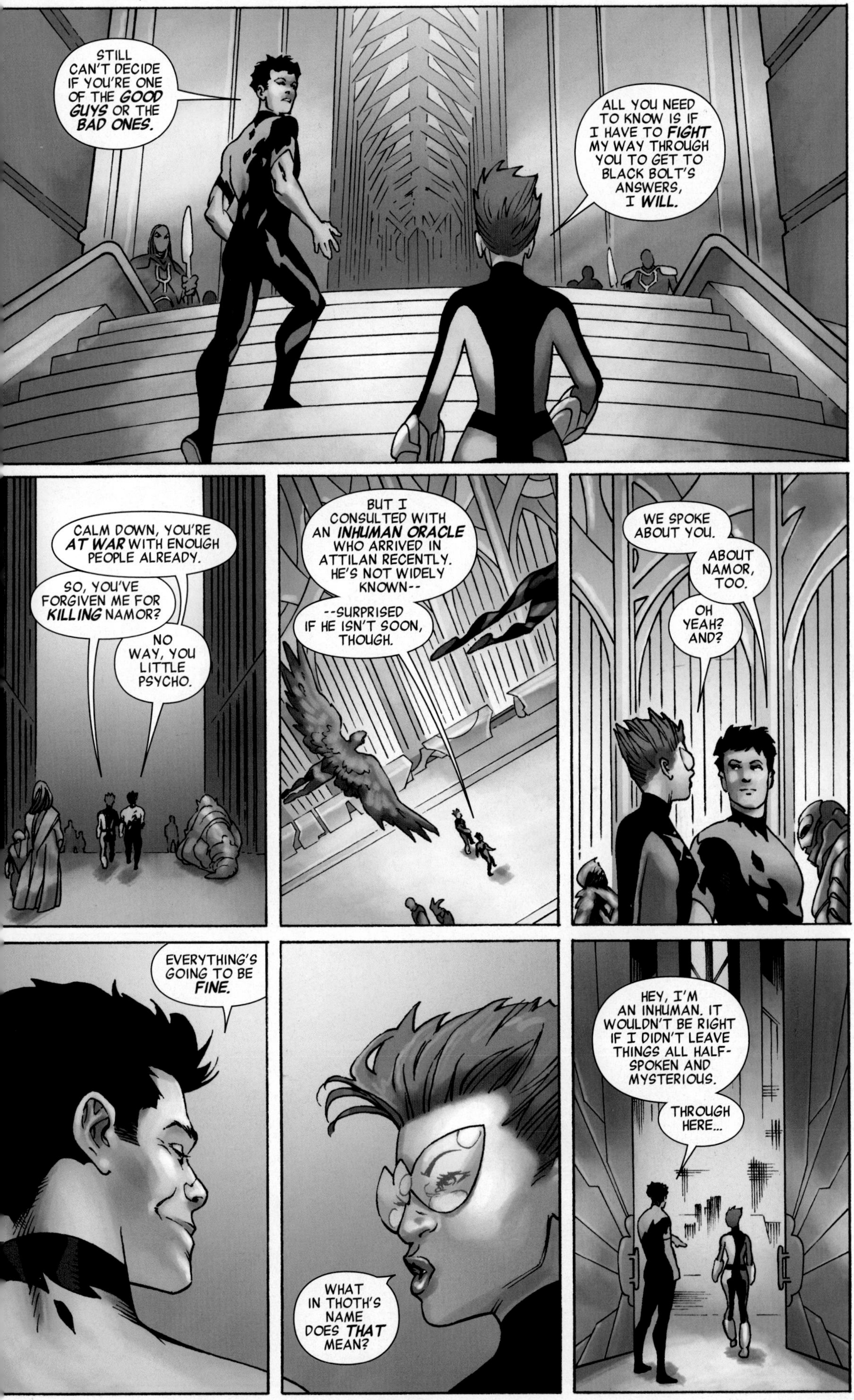
STILL CAN'T DECIDE IF YOU'RE ONE OF THE GOOD GUYS OR THE BAD ONES.
ALL YOU NEED TO KNOW IS IF I HAVE TO FIGHT MY WAY THROUGH YOU TO GET TO BLACK BOLT'S ANSWERS, I WILL.
CALM DOWN, YOU'RE AT WAR WITH ENOUGH PEOPLE ALREADY.
SO, YOU'VE FORGIVEN ME FOR KILLING NAMOR?
NO WAY, YOU LITTLE PSYCHO.
BUT I CONSULTED WITH AN INHUMAN ORACLE WHO ARRIVED IN ATTILAN RECENTLY. HE'S NOT WIDELY KNOWN--
--SURPRISED IF HE ISN'T SOON, THOUGH.
WE SPOKE ABOUT YOU.
ABOUT NAMOR, TOO.
OH YEAH? AND?
EVERYTHING'S GOING TO BE FINE.
WHAT IN THOTH'S NAME DOES THAT MEAN?
HEY, I'M AN INHUMAN. IT WOULDN'T BE RIGHT IF I DIDN'T LEAVE THINGS ALL HALF-SPOKEN AND MYSTERIOUS.
THROUGH HERE...

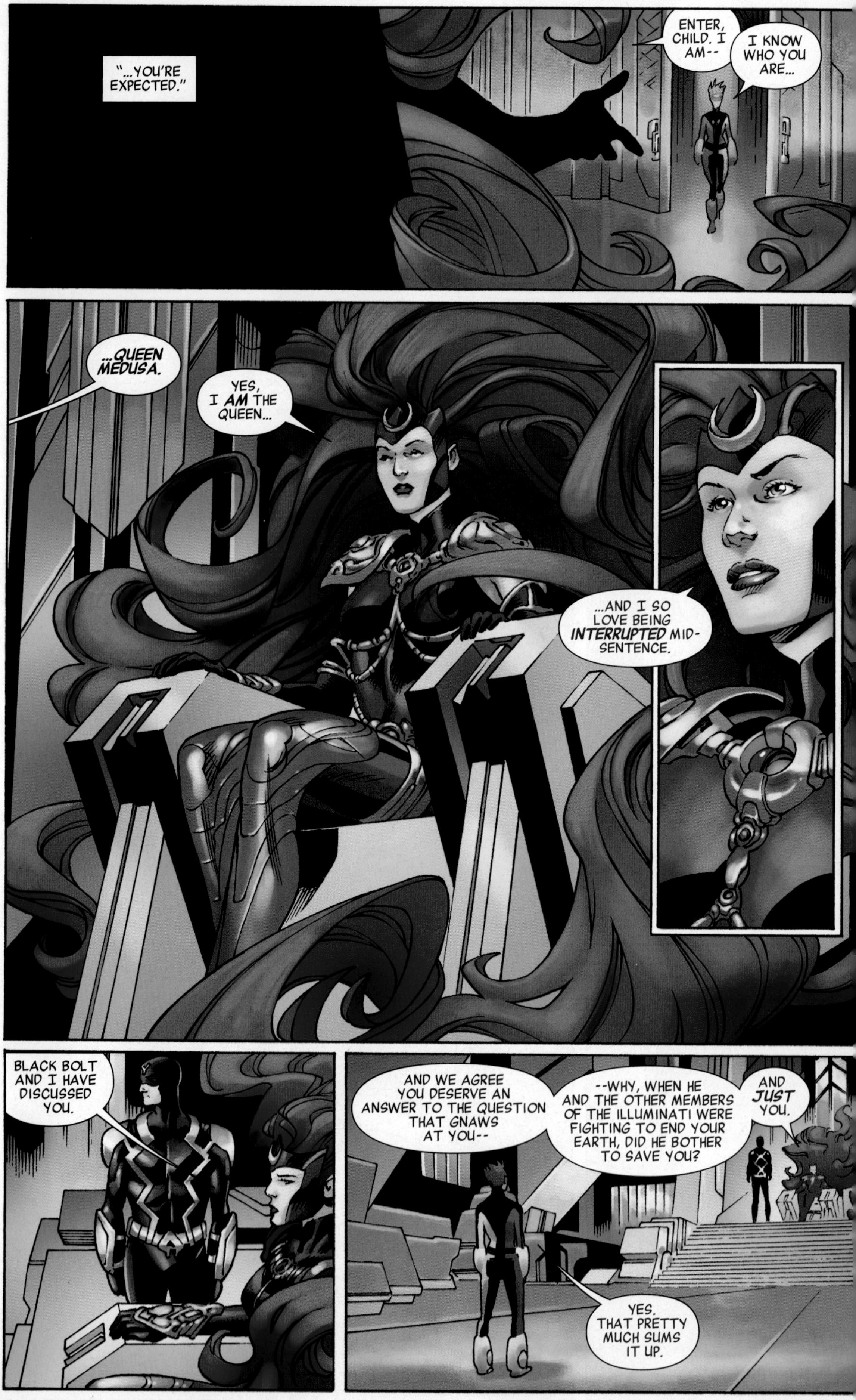
"...YOU'RE EXPECTED."
ENTER, CHILD. I AM--
I KNOW WHO YOU ARE...
...QUEEN MEDUSA.
YES, I AM THE QUEEN...
...AND I SO LOVE BEING INTERRUPTED MID-SENTENCE.
BLACK BOLT AND I HAVE DISCUSSED YOU.
AND WE AGREE YOU DESERVE AN ANSWER TO THE QUESTION THAT GNAWS AT YOU--
--WHY, WHEN HE AND THE OTHER MEMBERS OF THE ILLUMINATI WERE FIGHTING TO END YOUR EARTH, DID HE BOTHER TO SAVE YOU?
AND JUST YOU.
YES. THAT PRETTY MUCH SUMS IT UP.

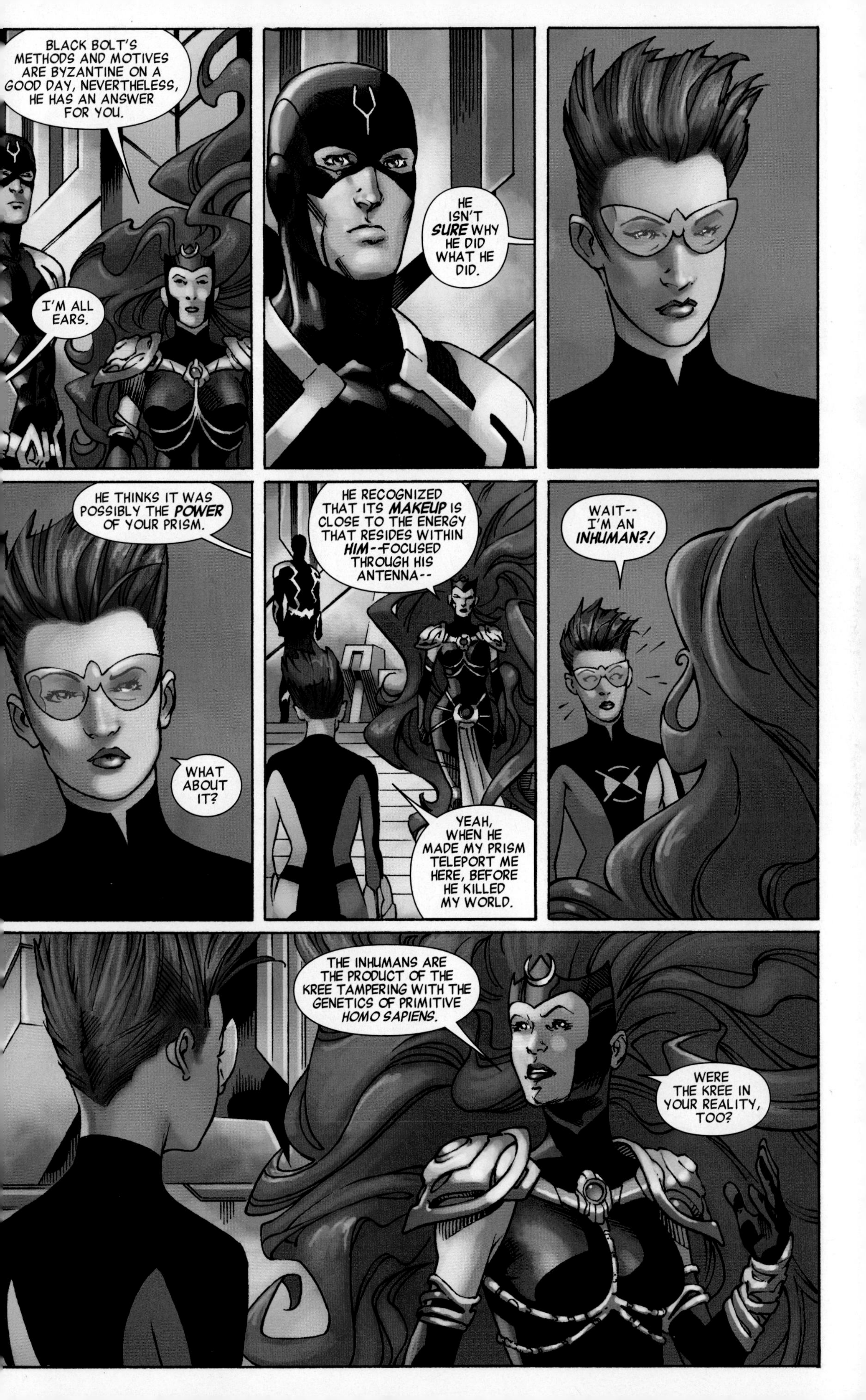
BLACK BOLT'S METHODS AND MOTIVES ARE BYZANTINE ON A GOOD DAY, NEVERTHELESS, HE HAS AN ANSWER FOR YOU.
I'M ALL EARS.
HE ISN'T SURE WHY HE DID WHAT HE DID.
HE THINKS IT WAS POSSIBLY THE POWER OF YOUR PRISM.
WHAT ABOUT IT?
HE RECOGNIZED THAT ITS MAKEUP IS CLOSE TO THE ENERGY THAT RESIDES WITHIN HIM--FOCUSED THROUGH HIS ANTENNA--
YEAH, WHEN HE MADE MY PRISM TELEPORT ME HERE, BEFORE HE KILLED MY WORLD.
WAIT-- I'M AN INHUMAN?!
THE INHUMANS ARE THE PRODUCT OF THE KREE TAMPERING WITH THE GENETICS OF PRIMITIVE HOMO SAPIENS.
WERE THE KREE IN YOUR REALITY, TOO?

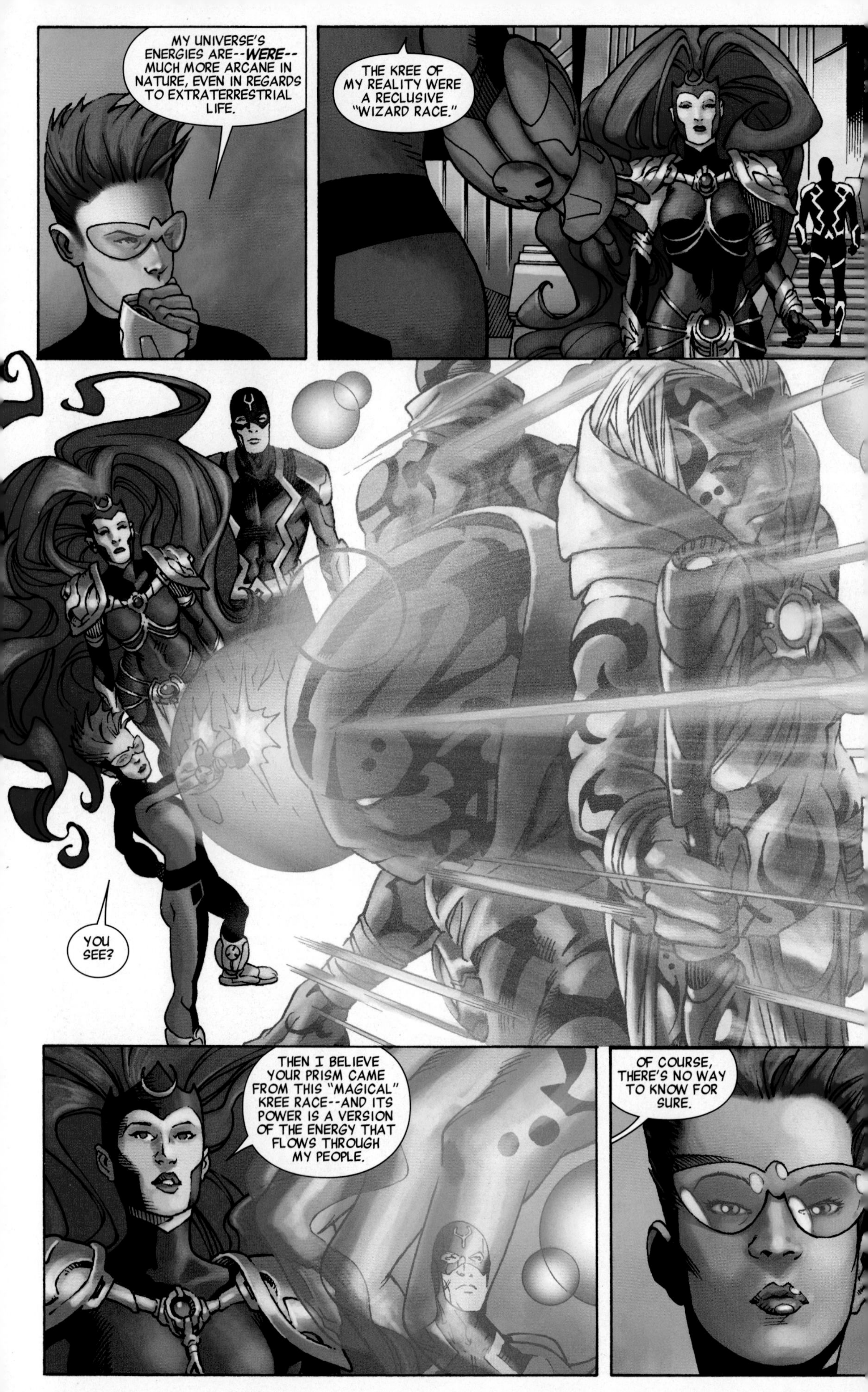
MY UNIVERSE'S ENERGIES ARE--**WERE**--MUCH MORE ARCANE IN NATURE, EVEN IN REGARDS TO EXTRATERRESTRIAL LIFE.
THE KREE OF MY REALITY WERE A RECLUSIVE "WIZARD RACE."
YOU SEE?
THEN I BELIEVE YOUR PRISM CAME FROM THIS "MAGICAL" KREE RACE--AND ITS POWER IS A VERSION OF THE ENERGY THAT FLOWS THROUGH MY PEOPLE.
OF COURSE, THERE'S NO WAY TO KNOW FOR SURE.

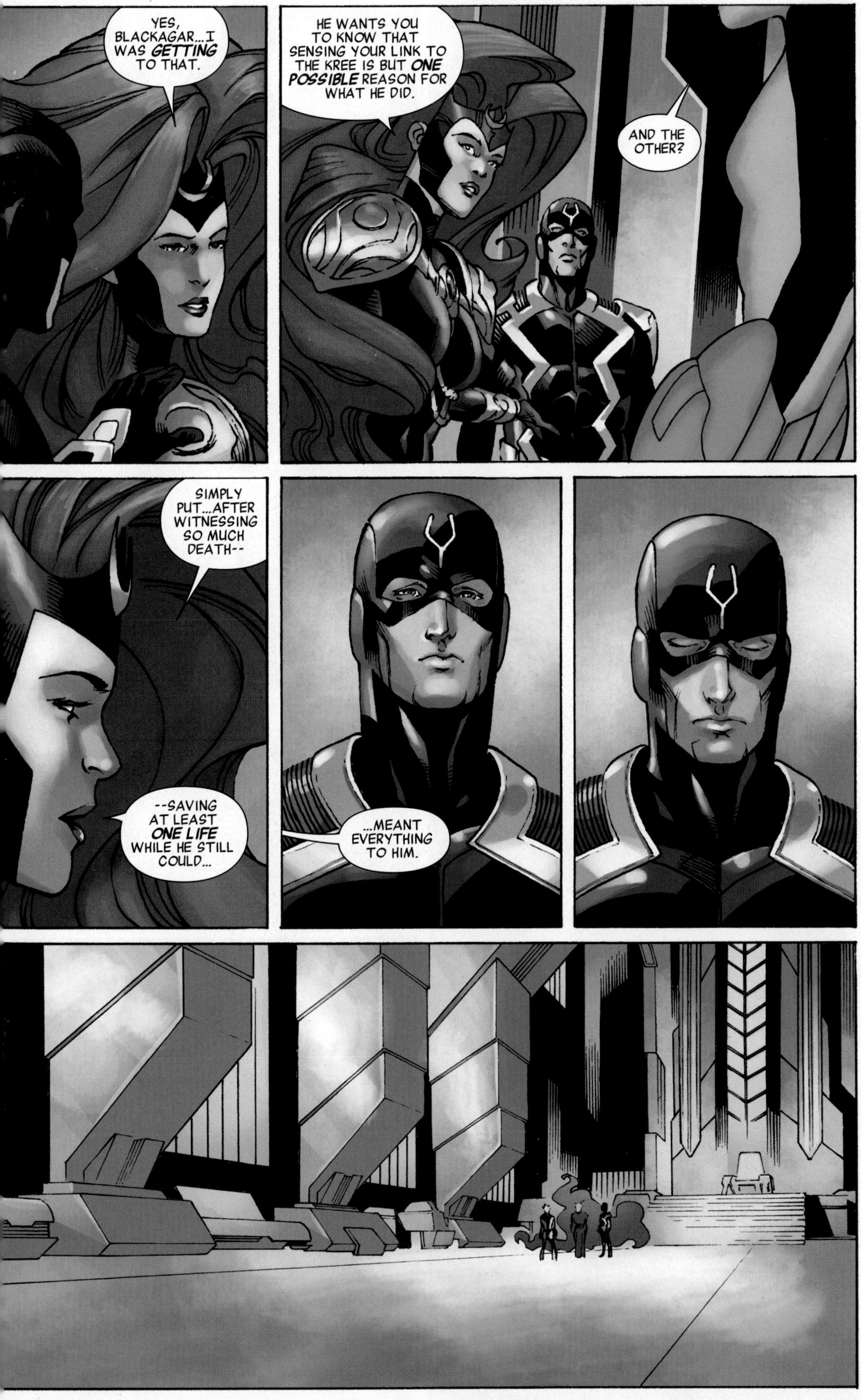
YES, BLACKAGAR...I WAS GETTING TO THAT.
HE WANTS YOU TO KNOW THAT SENSING YOUR LINK TO THE KREE IS BUT ONE POSSIBLE REASON FOR WHAT HE DID.
AND THE OTHER?
SIMPLY PUT...AFTER WITNESSING SO MUCH DEATH--
--SAVING AT LEAST ONE LIFE WHILE HE STILL COULD...
...MEANT EVERYTHING TO HIM.

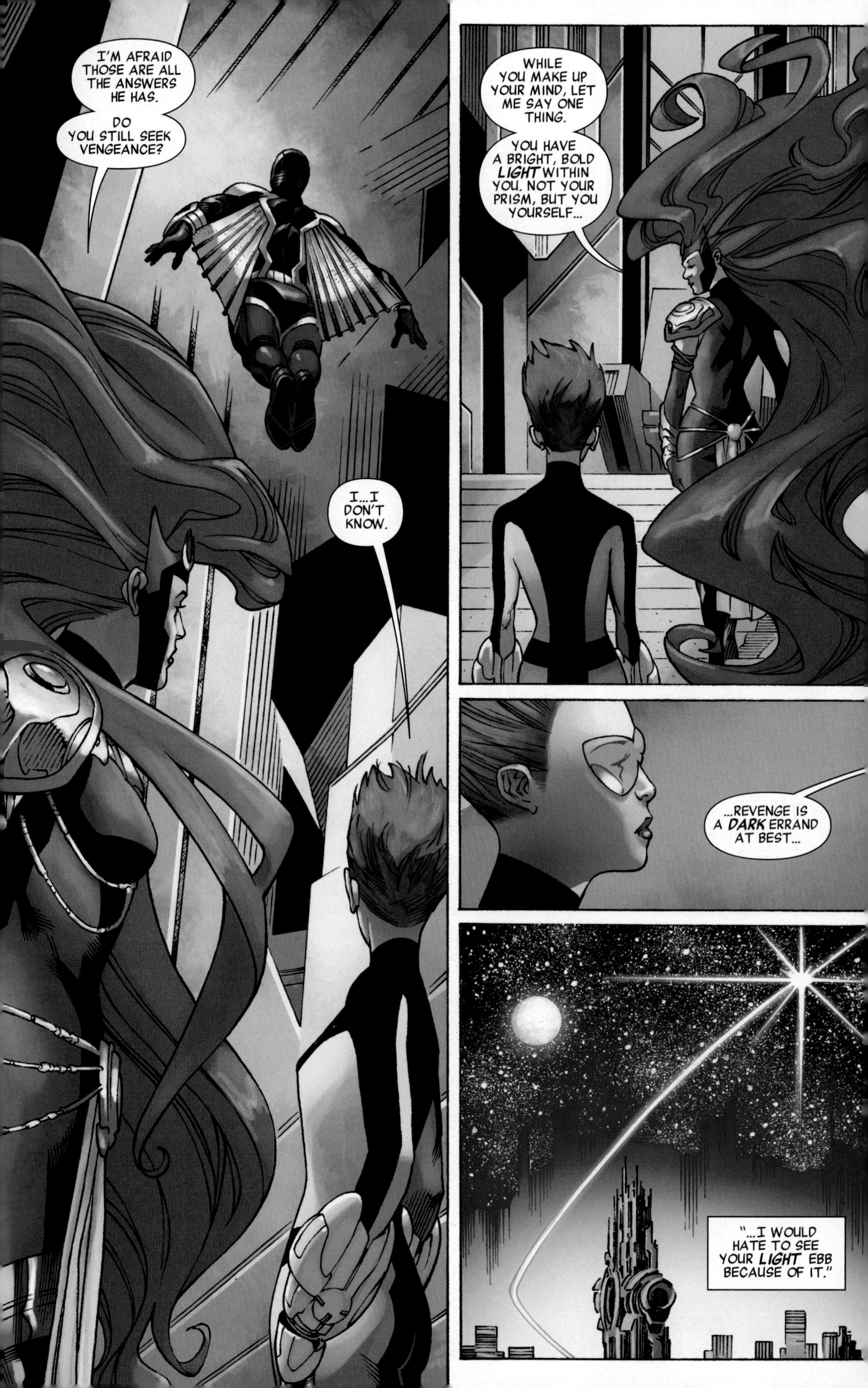
I'M AFRAID THOSE ARE ALL THE ANSWERS HE HAS.
DO YOU STILL SEEK VENGEANCE?
I...I DON'T KNOW.
WHILE YOU MAKE UP YOUR MIND, LET ME SAY ONE THING.
YOU HAVE A BRIGHT, BOLD LIGHT WITHIN YOU. NOT YOUR PRISM, BUT YOU YOURSELF...
...REVENGE IS A DARK ERRAND AT BEST...
"...I WOULD HATE TO SEE YOUR LIGHT EBB BECAUSE OF IT."

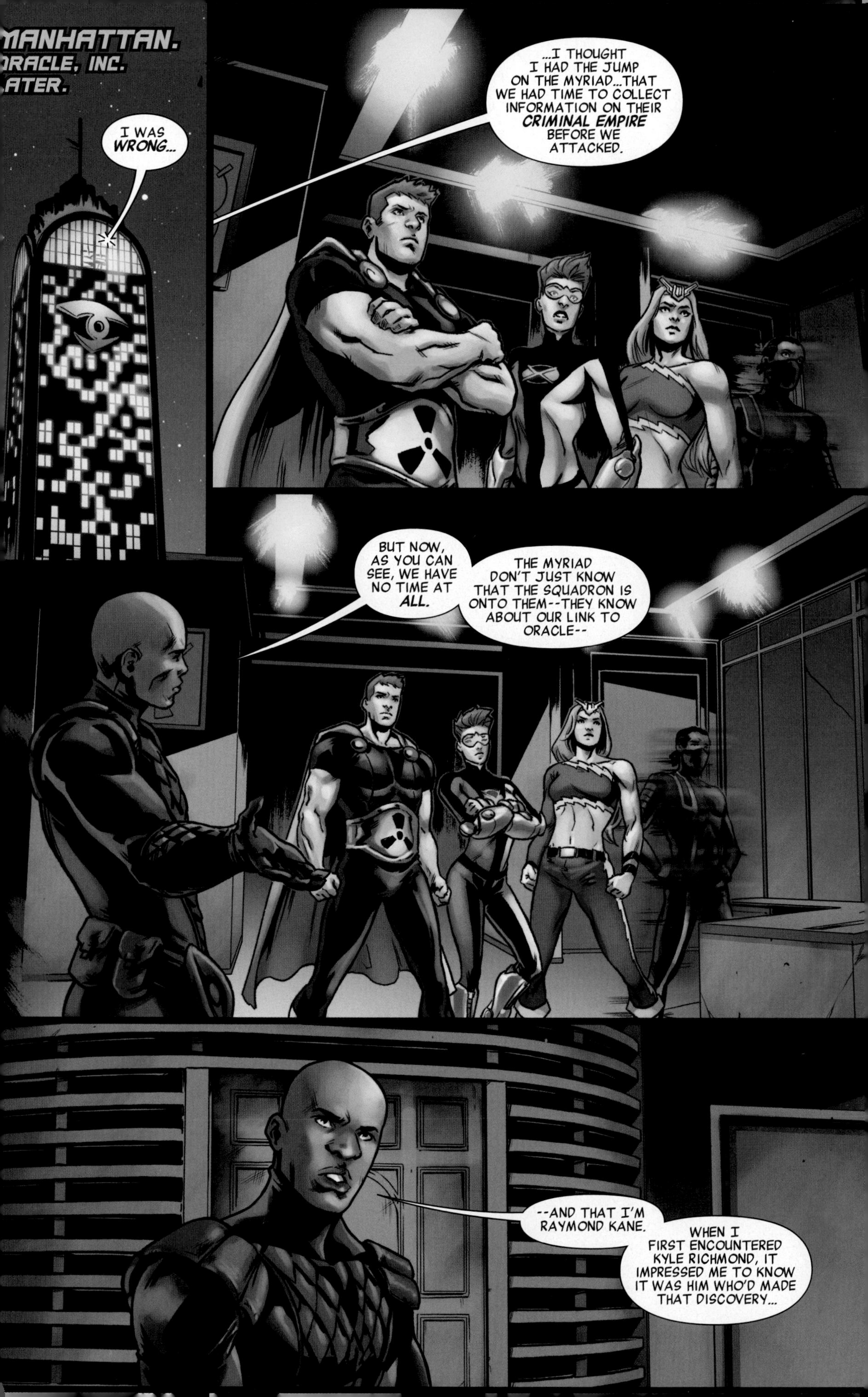
MANHATTAN.
ORACLE, INC.
LATER.
I WAS WRONG...
...I THOUGHT I HAD THE JUMP ON THE MYRIAD...THAT WE HAD TIME TO COLLECT INFORMATION ON THEIR CRIMINAL EMPIRE BEFORE WE ATTACKED.
BUT NOW, AS YOU CAN SEE, WE HAVE NO TIME AT ALL.
THE MYRIAD DON'T JUST KNOW THAT THE SQUADRON IS ONTO THEM--THEY KNOW ABOUT OUR LINK TO ORACLE--
--AND THAT I'M RAYMOND KANE.
WHEN I FIRST ENCOUNTERED KYLE RICHMOND, IT IMPRESSED ME TO KNOW IT WAS HIM WHO'D MADE THAT DISCOVERY...

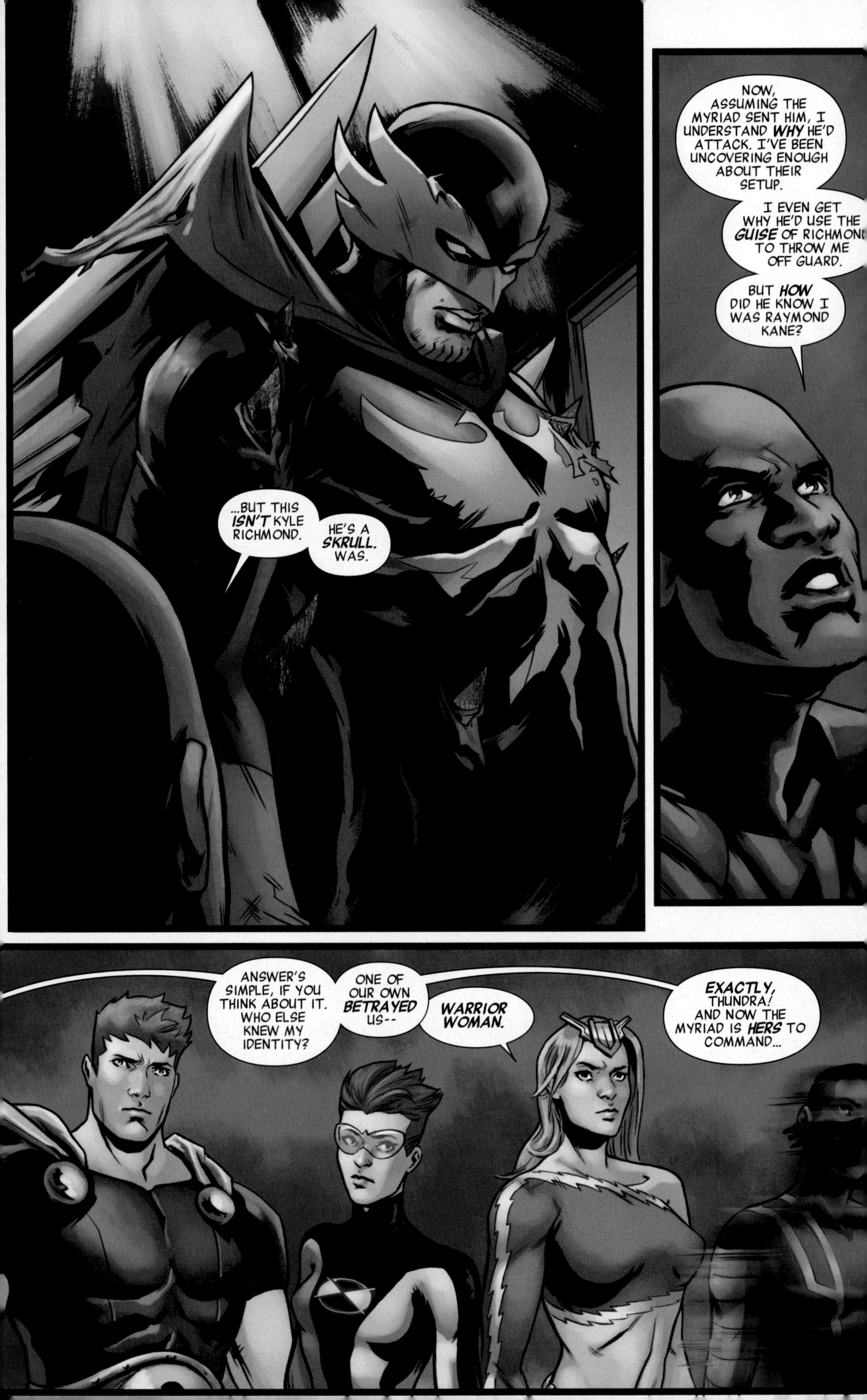

...BUT THIS ISN'T KYLE RICHMOND.
HE'S A SKRULL. WAS.
NOW, ASSUMING THE MYRIAD SENT HIM, I UNDERSTAND WHY HE'D ATTACK. I'VE BEEN UNCOVERING ENOUGH ABOUT THEIR SETUP.
I EVEN GET WHY HE'D USE THE GUISE OF RICHMON
TO THROW ME OFF GUARD.
BUT HOW DID HE KNOW I WAS RAYMOND KANE?
ANSWER'S SIMPLE, IF YOU THINK ABOUT IT. WHO ELSE KNEW MY IDENTITY?
ONE OF OUR OWN BETRAYED US--
WARRIOR WOMAN.
EXACTLY, THUNDRA! AND NOW THE MYRIAD IS HERS TO COMMAND...

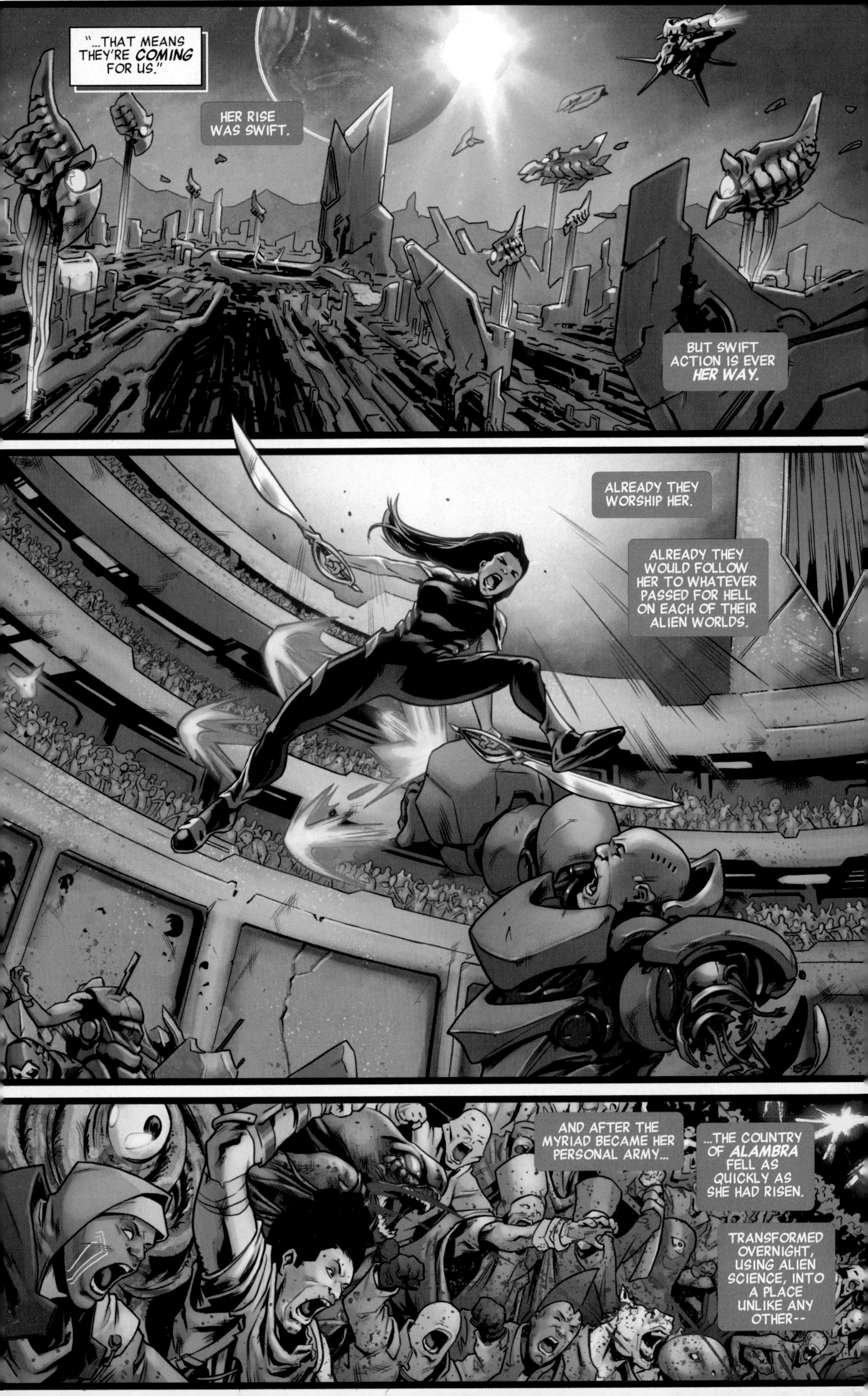

"...THAT MEANS THEY'RE COMING FOR US."
HER RISE WAS SWIFT.
BUT SWIFT ACTION IS EVER HER WAY.
ALREADY THEY WORSHIP HER.
ALREADY THEY WOULD FOLLOW HER TO WHATEVER PASSED FOR HELL ON EACH OF THEIR ALIEN WORLDS.
AND AFTER THE MYRIAD BECAME HER PERSONAL ARMY...
...THE COUNTRY OF ALAMBRA FELL AS QUICKLY AS SHE HAD RISEN.
TRANSFORMED OVERNIGHT, USING ALIEN SCIENCE, INTO A PLACE UNLIKE ANY OTHER--

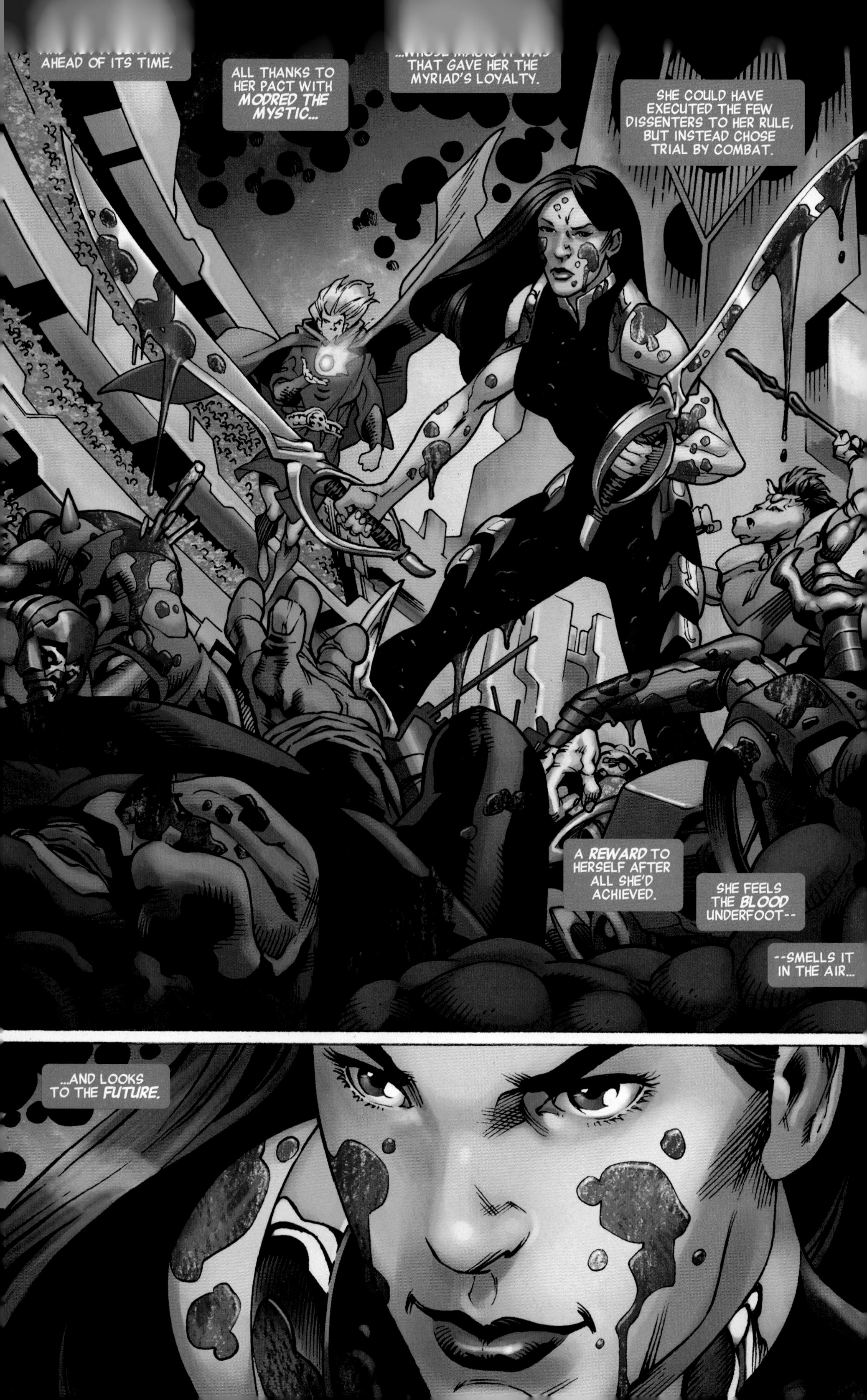
AHEAD OF ITS TIME.
ALL THANKS TO HER PACT WITH MODRED THE MYSTIC...
THAT GAVE HER THE MYRIAD'S LOYALTY.
SHE COULD HAVE EXECUTED THE FEW DISSENTERS TO HER RULE, BUT INSTEAD CHOSE TRIAL BY COMBAT.
A REWARD TO HERSELF AFTER ALL SHE'D ACHIEVED.
SHE FEELS THE BLOOD UNDERFOOT--
--SMELLS IT IN THE AIR...
...AND LOOKS TO THE FUTURE.

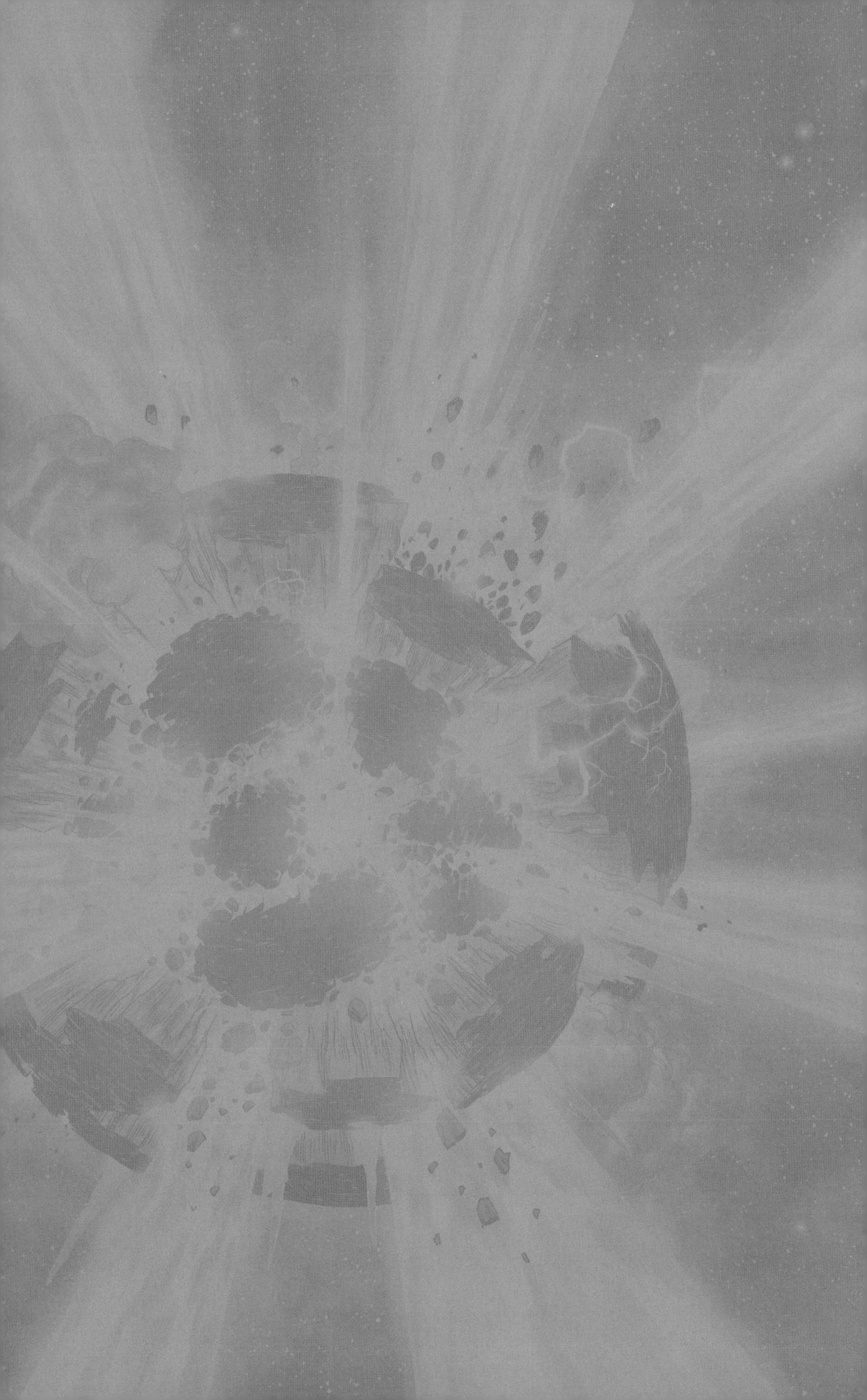

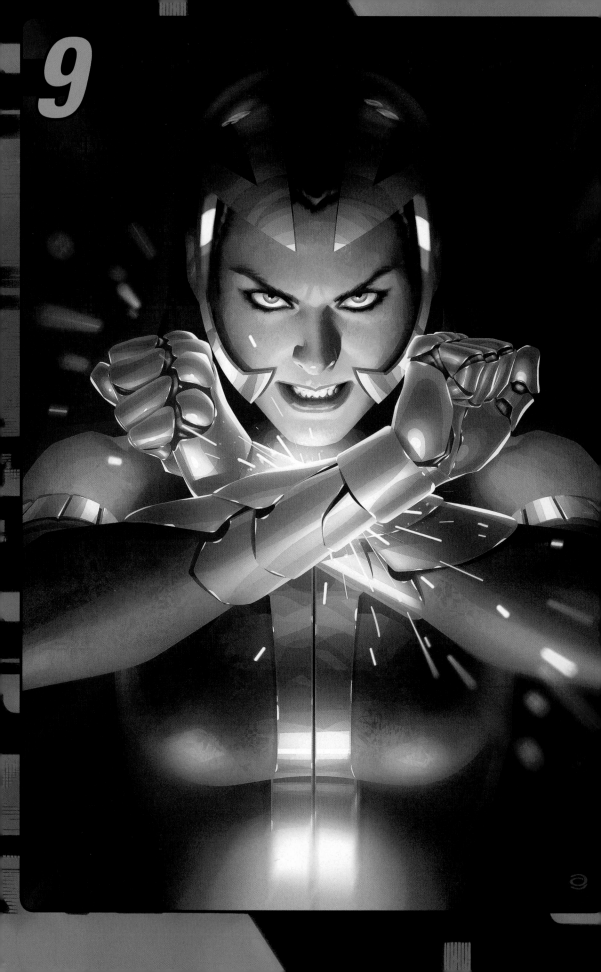

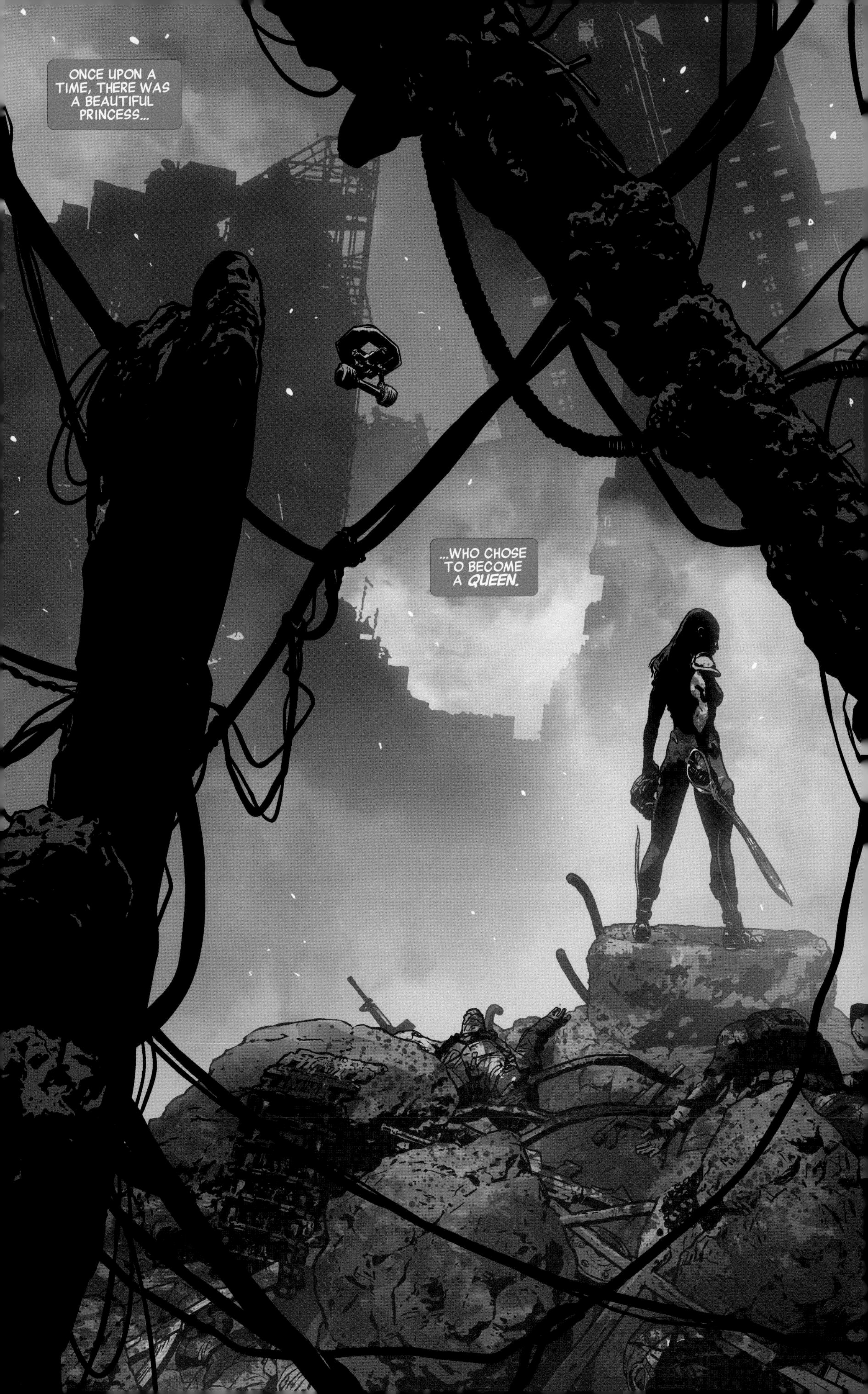
ONCE UPON A TIME, THERE WAS A BEAUTIFUL PRINCESS...
...WHO CHOSE TO BECOME A *QUEEN*.

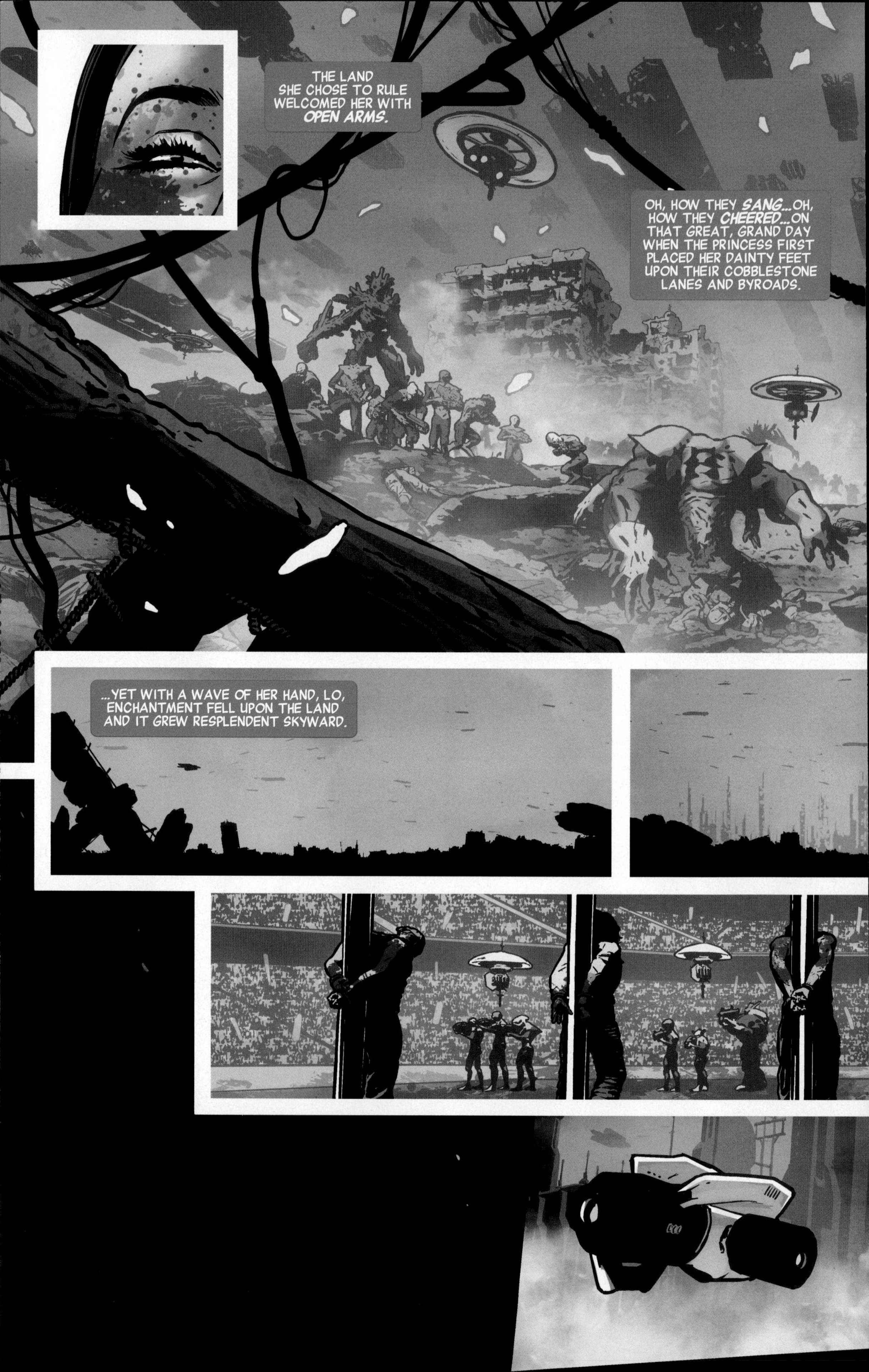
THE LAND SHE CHOSE TO RULE WELCOMED HER WITH OPEN ARMS.
OH, HOW THEY SANG...OH, HOW THEY CHEERED...ON THAT GREAT, GRAND DAY WHEN THE PRINCESS FIRST PLACED HER DAINTY FEET UPON THEIR COBBLESTONE LANES AND BYROADS.
...YET WITH A WAVE OF HER HAND, LO, ENCHANTMENT FELL UPON THE LAND AND IT GREW RESPLENDENT SKYWARD.

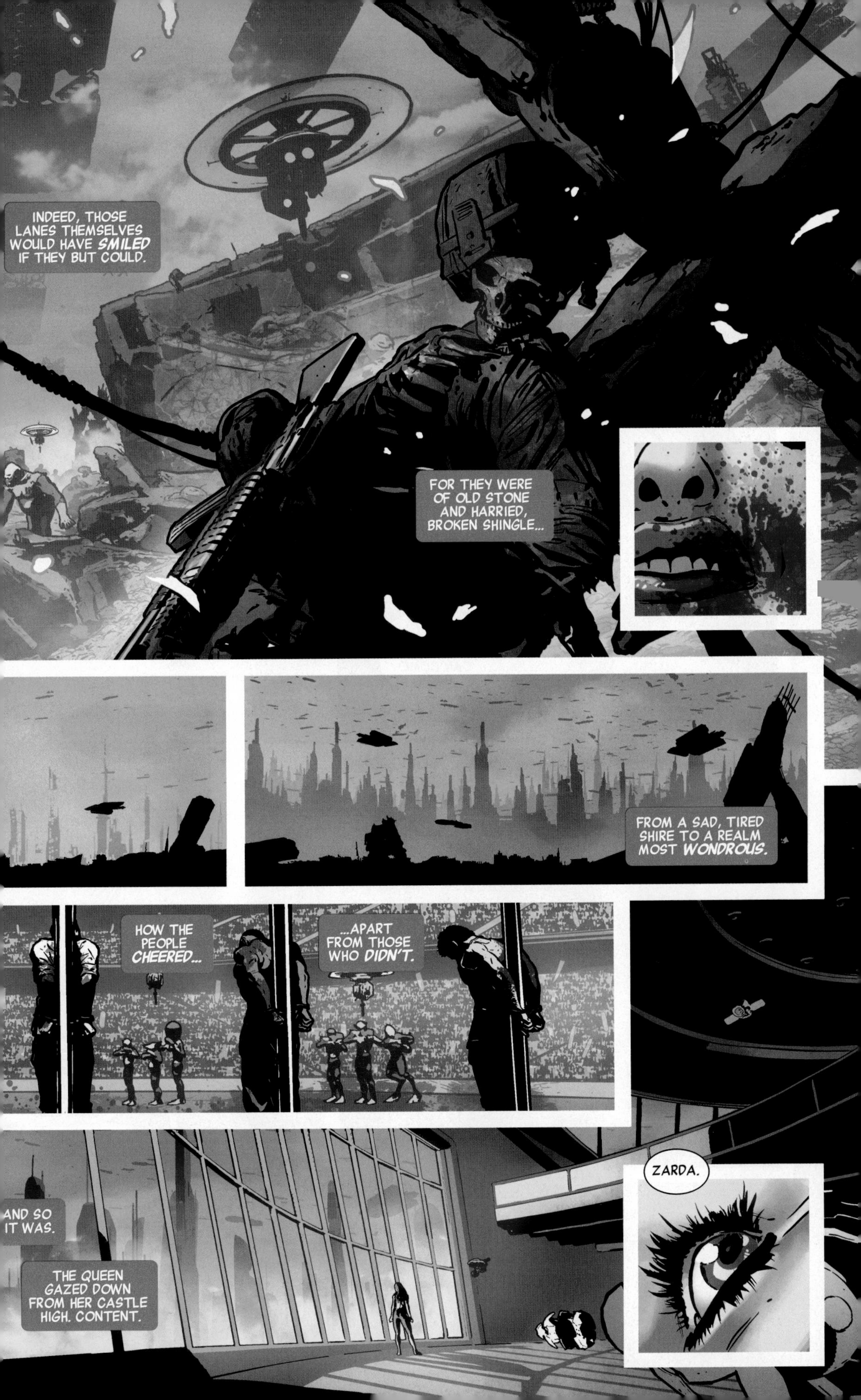
INDEED, THOSE LANES THEMSELVES WOULD HAVE SMILED IF THEY BUT COULD.
FOR THEY WERE OF OLD STONE AND HARRIED, BROKEN SHINGLE...
FROM A SAD, TIRED SHIRE TO A REALM MOST WONDROUS.
HOW THE PEOPLE CHEERED...
...APART FROM THOSE WHO DIDN'T.
AND SO IT WAS.
THE QUEEN GAZED DOWN FROM HER CASTLE HIGH. CONTENT.
ZARDA.

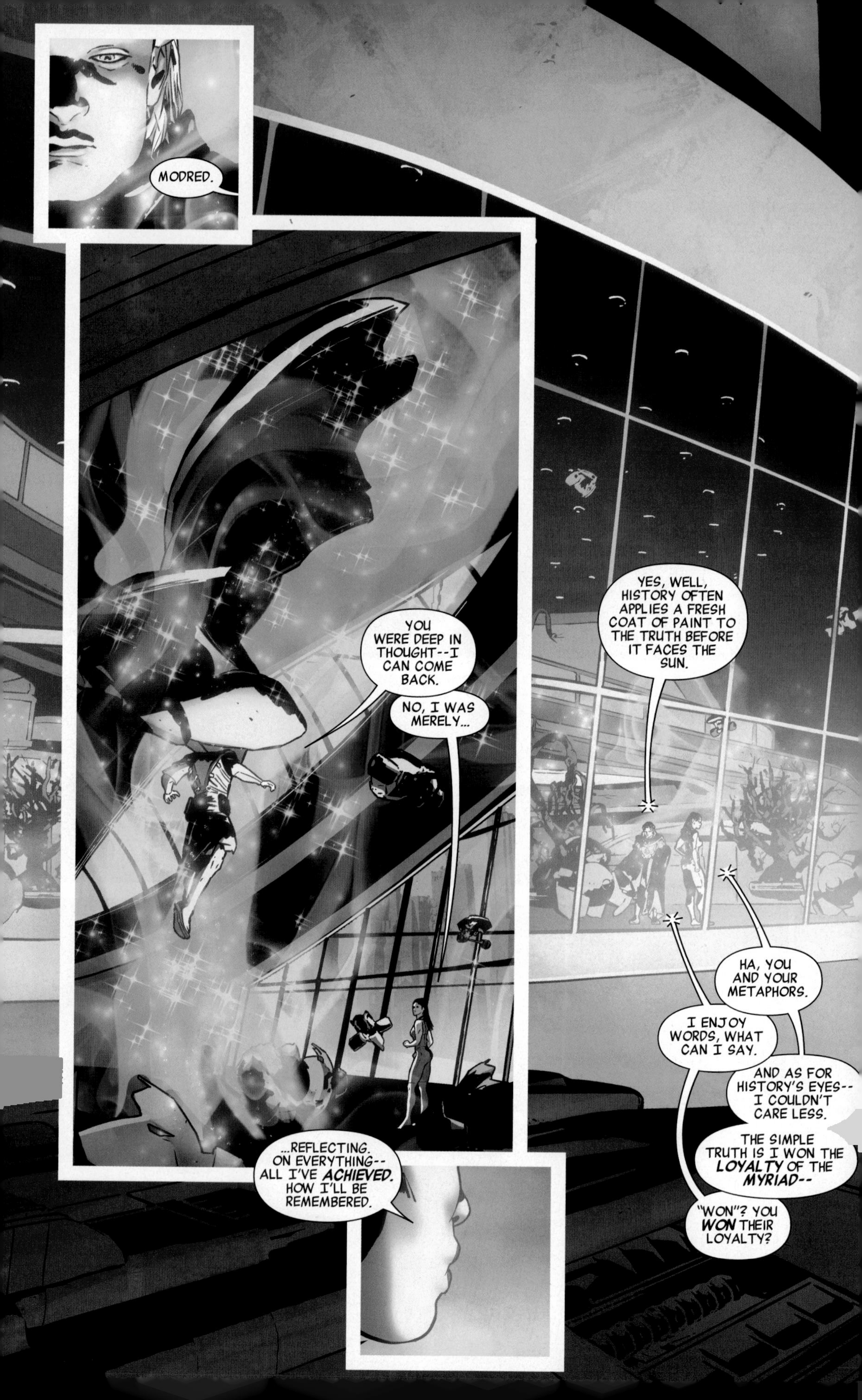
MODRED.
YOU WERE DEEP IN THOUGHT--I CAN COME BACK.
NO, I WAS MERELY...
...REFLECTING. ON EVERYTHING-- ALL I'VE ACHIEVED. HOW I'LL BE REMEMBERED.
YES, WELL, HISTORY OFTEN APPLIES A FRESH COAT OF PAINT TO THE TRUTH BEFORE IT FACES THE SUN.
HA, YOU AND YOUR METAPHORS.
I ENJOY WORDS, WHAT CAN I SAY.
AND AS FOR HISTORY'S EYES-- I COULDN'T CARE LESS.
THE SIMPLE TRUTH IS I WON THE LOYALTY OF THE MYRIAD--
"WON"? YOU WON THEIR LOYALTY?

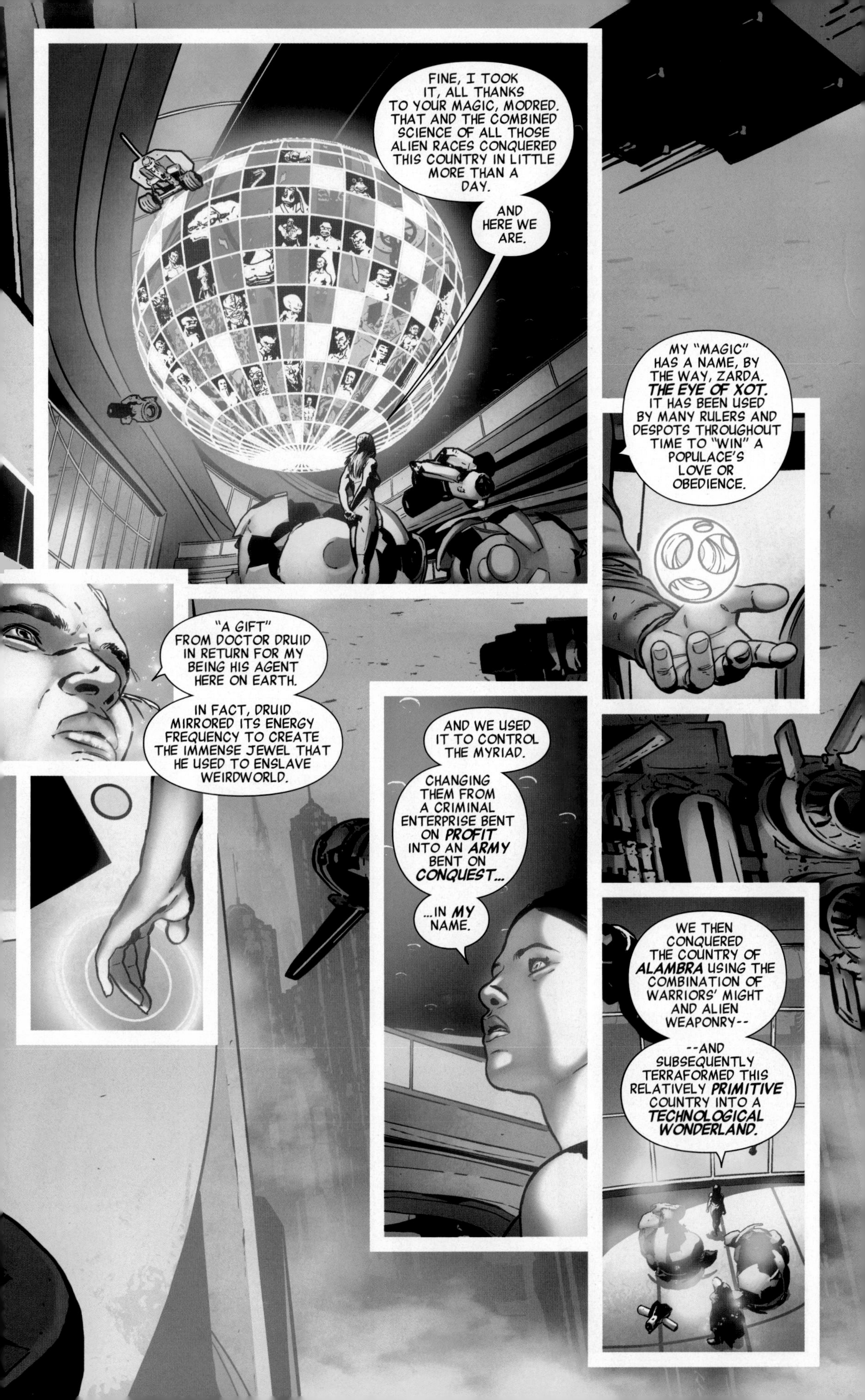
FINE, I TOOK IT, ALL THANKS TO YOUR MAGIC, MODRED. THAT AND THE COMBINED SCIENCE OF ALL THOSE ALIEN RACES CONQUERED THIS COUNTRY IN LITTLE MORE THAN A DAY.
AND HERE WE ARE.
MY "MAGIC" HAS A NAME, BY THE WAY, ZARDA. THE EYE OF XOT. IT HAS BEEN USED BY MANY RULERS AND DESPOTS THROUGHOUT TIME TO "WIN" A POPULACE'S LOVE OR OBEDIENCE.
"A GIFT" FROM DOCTOR DRUID IN RETURN FOR MY BEING HIS AGENT HERE ON EARTH.
IN FACT, DRUID MIRRORED ITS ENERGY FREQUENCY TO CREATE THE IMMENSE JEWEL THAT HE USED TO ENSLAVE WEIRDWORLD.
AND WE USED IT TO CONTROL THE MYRIAD.
CHANGING THEM FROM A CRIMINAL ENTERPRISE BENT ON PROFIT INTO AN ARMY BENT ON CONQUEST...
...IN MY NAME.
WE THEN CONQUERED THE COUNTRY OF ALAMBRA USING THE COMBINATION OF WARRIORS' MIGHT AND ALIEN WEAPONRY--
--AND SUBSEQUENTLY TERRAFORMED THIS RELATIVELY PRIMITIVE COUNTRY INTO A TECHNOLOGICAL WONDERLAND.

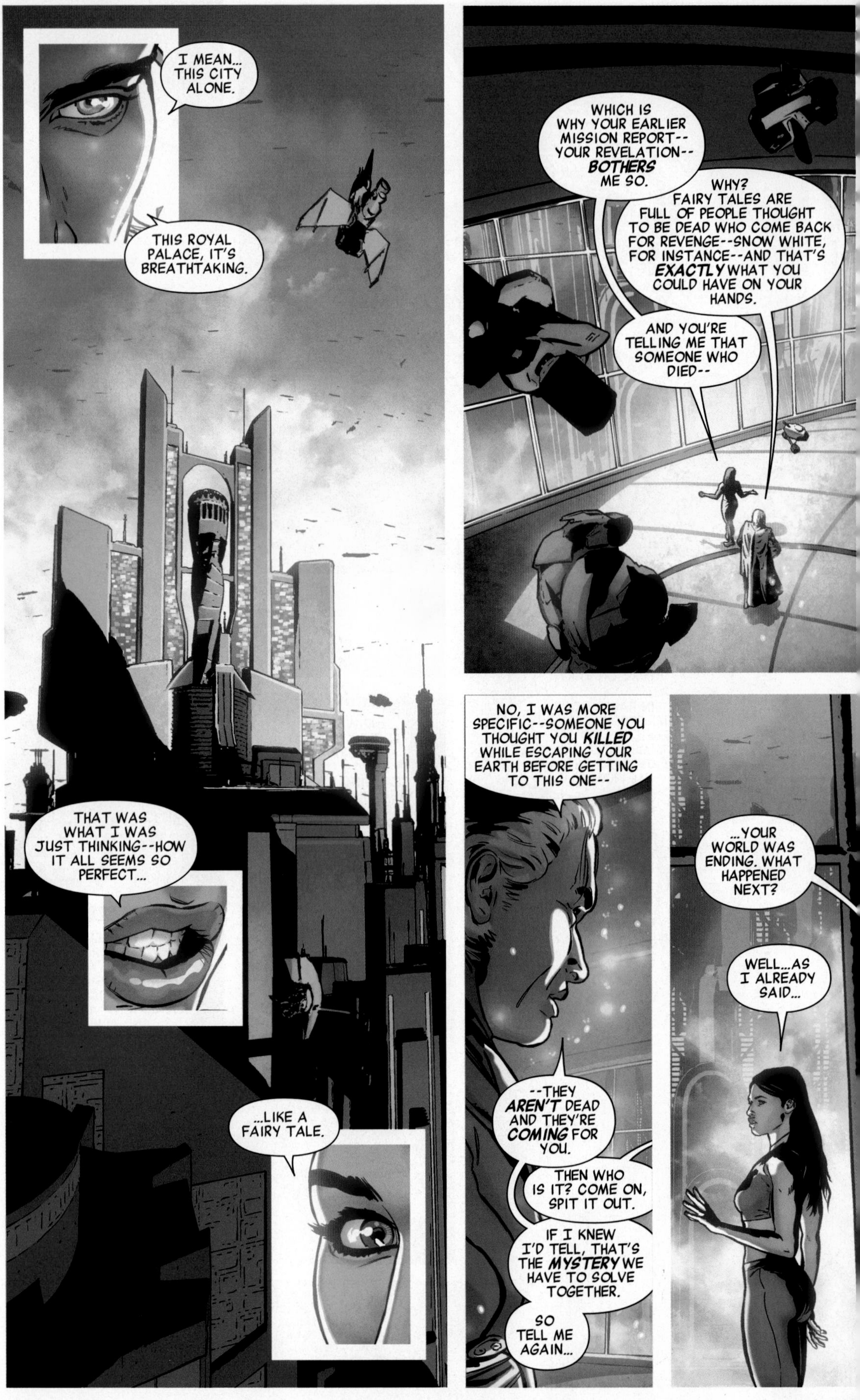

I MEAN... THIS CITY ALONE.
THIS ROYAL PALACE, IT'S BREATHTAKING.
THAT WAS WHAT I WAS JUST THINKING--HOW IT ALL SEEMS SO PERFECT...
...LIKE A FAIRY TALE.
WHICH IS WHY YOUR EARLIER MISSION REPORT-- YOUR REVELATION-- BOTHERS ME SO.
WHY? FAIRY TALES ARE FULL OF PEOPLE THOUGHT TO BE DEAD WHO COME BACK FOR REVENGE--SNOW WHITE, FOR INSTANCE--AND THAT'S EXACTLY WHAT YOU COULD HAVE ON YOUR HANDS.
AND YOU'RE TELLING ME THAT SOMEONE WHO DIED--
NO, I WAS MORE SPECIFIC--SOMEONE YOU THOUGHT YOU KILLED WHILE ESCAPING YOUR EARTH BEFORE GETTING TO THIS ONE--
--THEY AREN'T DEAD AND THEY'RE COMING FOR YOU.
THEN WHO IS IT? COME ON, SPIT IT OUT.
IF I KNEW I'D TELL, THAT'S THE MYSTERY WE HAVE TO SOLVE TOGETHER.
SO TELL ME AGAIN...
...YOUR WORLD WAS ENDING. WHAT HAPPENED NEXT?
WELL...AS I ALREADY SAID...

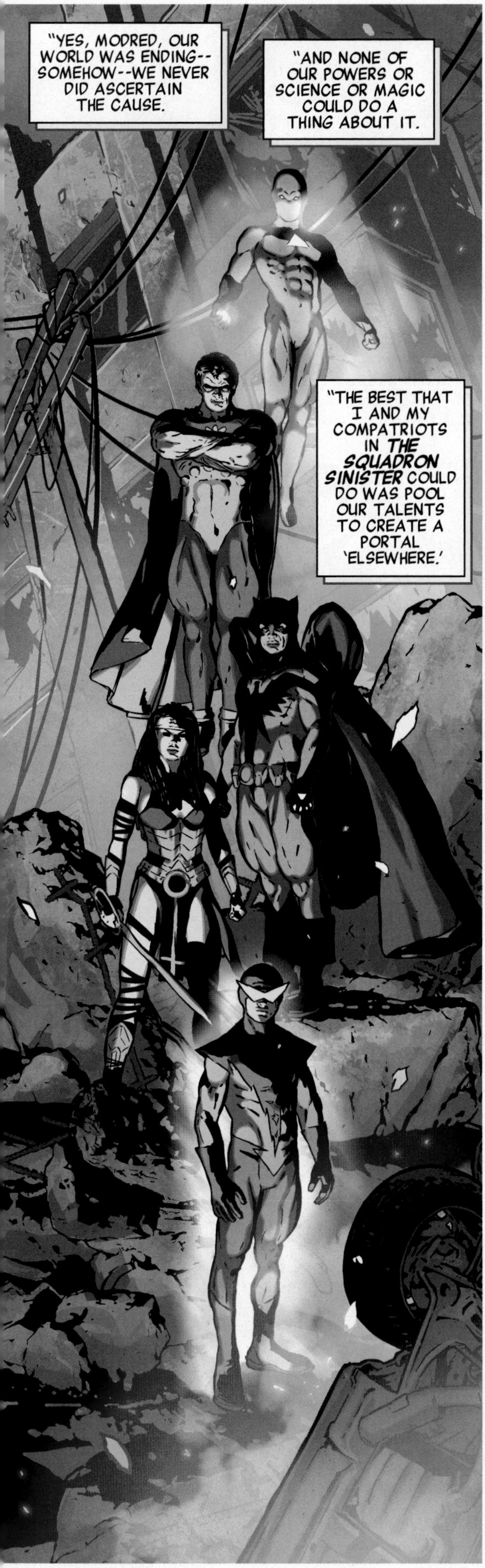
"YES, MODRED, OUR WORLD WAS ENDING--SOMEHOW--WE NEVER DID ASCERTAIN THE CAUSE.
"AND NONE OF OUR POWERS OR SCIENCE OR MAGIC COULD DO A THING ABOUT IT.
"THE BEST THAT I AND MY COMPATRIOTS IN THE SQUADRON SINISTER COULD DO WAS POOL OUR TALENTS TO CREATE A PORTAL 'ELSEWHERE.'
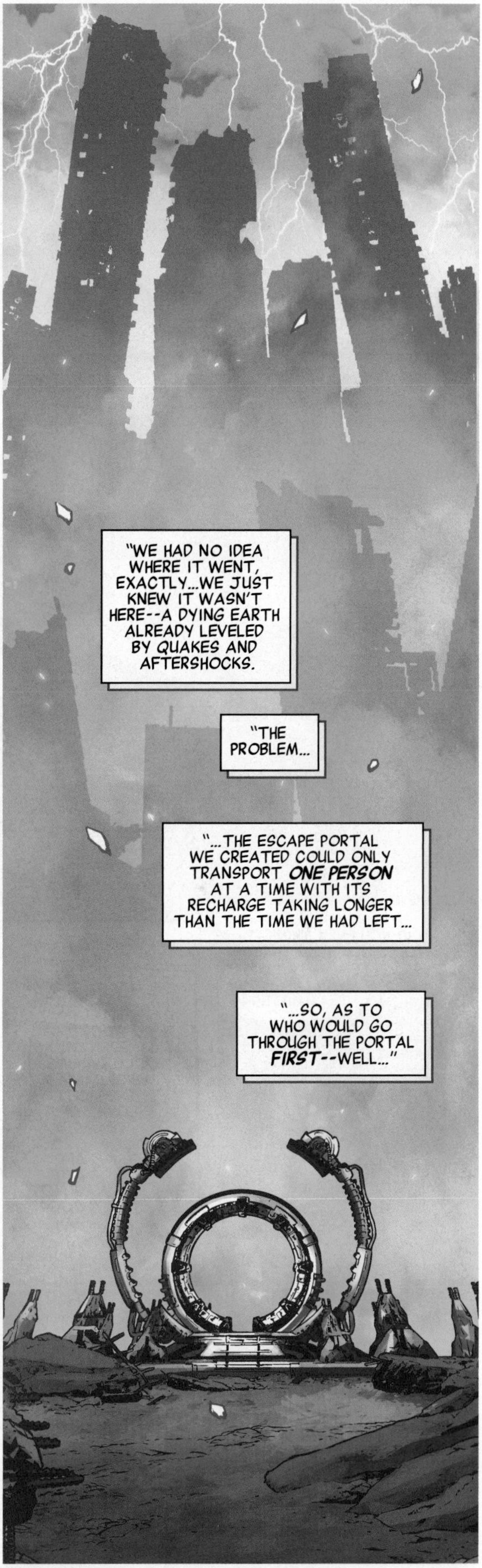
"WE HAD NO IDEA WHERE IT WENT, EXACTLY...WE JUST KNEW IT WASN'T HERE--A DYING EARTH ALREADY LEVELED BY QUAKES AND AFTERSHOCKS.
"THE PROBLEM...
"...THE ESCAPE PORTAL WE CREATED COULD ONLY TRANSPORT ONE PERSON AT A TIME WITH ITS RECHARGE TAKING LONGER THAN THE TIME WE HAD LEFT...
"...SO, AS TO WHO WOULD GO THROUGH THE PORTAL FIRST--WELL..."

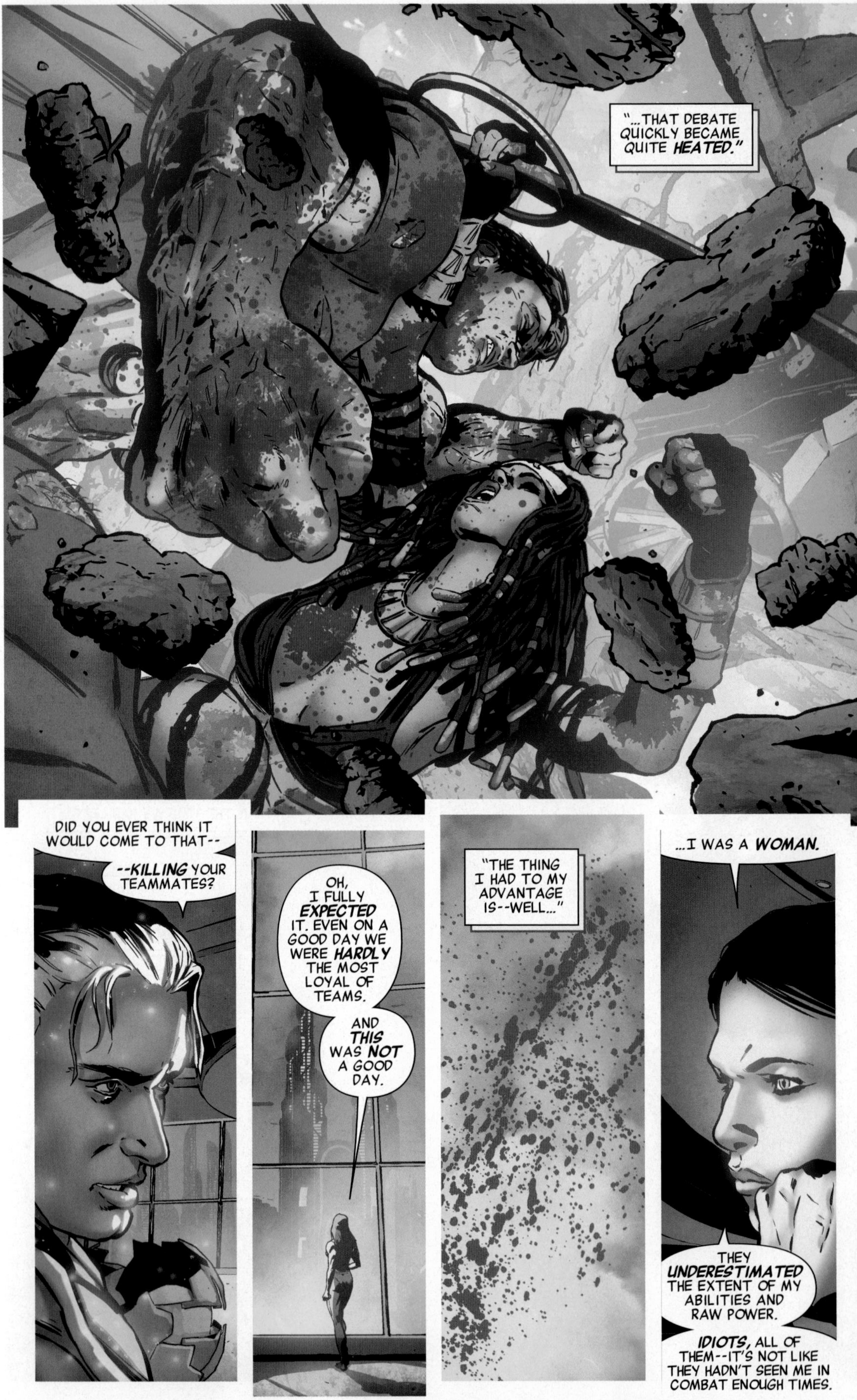
"...THAT DEBATE QUICKLY BECAME QUITE HEATED."
DID YOU EVER THINK IT WOULD COME TO THAT--
--KILLING YOUR TEAMMATES?
OH, I FULLY EXPECTED IT. EVEN ON A GOOD DAY WE WERE HARDLY THE MOST LOYAL OF TEAMS.
AND THIS WAS NOT A GOOD DAY.
"THE THING I HAD TO MY ADVANTAGE IS--WELL..."
...I WAS A WOMAN.
THEY UNDERESTIMATED THE EXTENT OF MY ABILITIES AND RAW POWER.
IDIOTS, ALL OF THEM--IT'S NOT LIKE THEY HADN'T SEEN ME IN COMBAT ENOUGH TIMES.

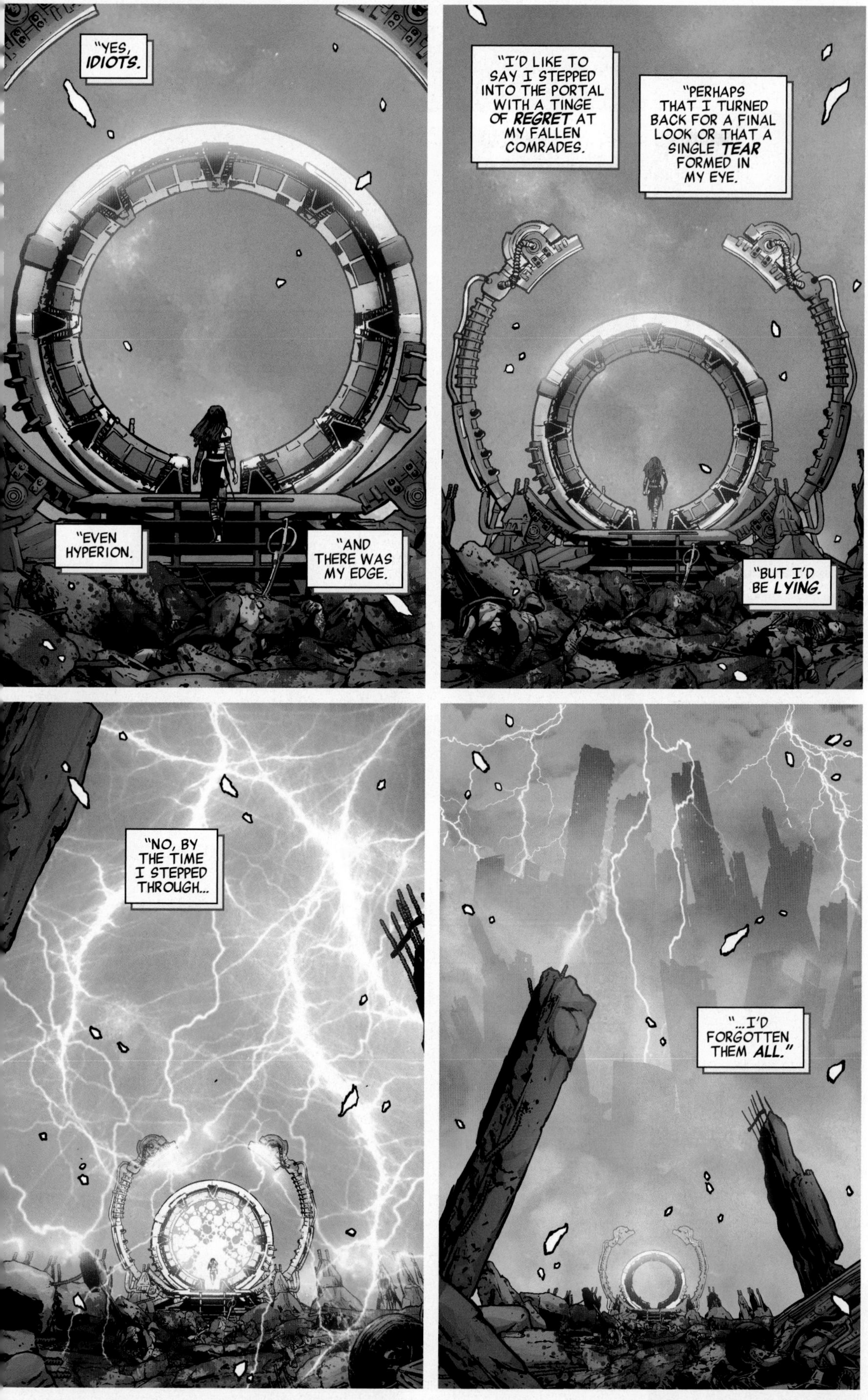
"YES, IDIOTS.
"EVEN HYPERION.
"AND THERE WAS MY EDGE.
"I'D LIKE TO SAY I STEPPED INTO THE PORTAL WITH A TINGE OF REGRET AT MY FALLEN COMRADES.
"PERHAPS THAT I TURNED BACK FOR A FINAL LOOK OR THAT A SINGLE TEAR FORMED IN MY EYE.
"BUT I'D BE LYING.
"NO, BY THE TIME I STEPPED THROUGH...
"...I'D FORGOTTEN THEM ALL."

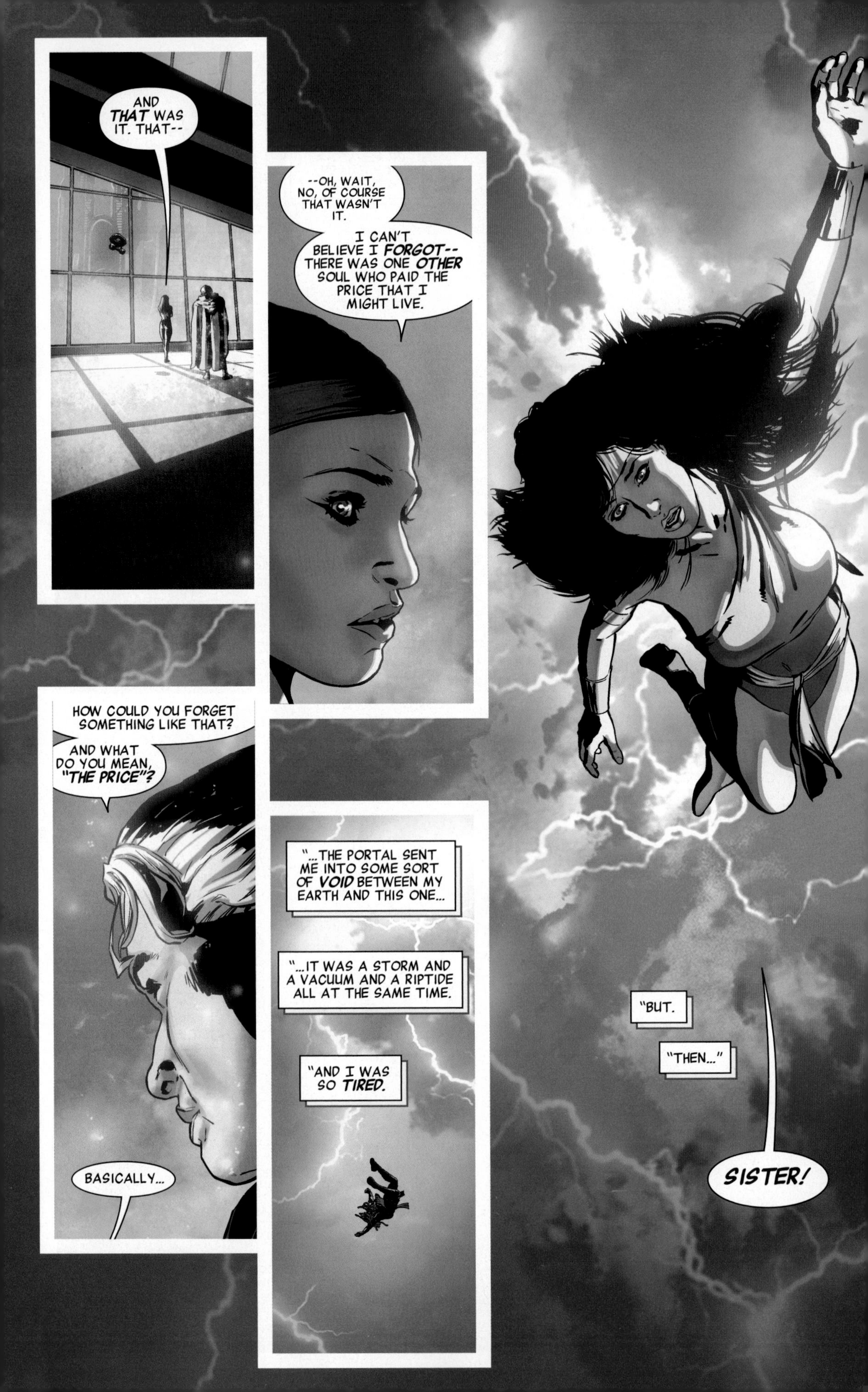
AND THAT WAS IT. THAT--
--OH, WAIT, NO, OF COURSE THAT WASN'T IT.
I CAN'T BELIEVE I FORGOT-- THERE WAS ONE OTHER SOUL WHO PAID THE PRICE THAT I MIGHT LIVE.
HOW COULD YOU FORGET SOMETHING LIKE THAT?
AND WHAT DO YOU MEAN, "THE PRICE"?
BASICALLY...
"...THE PORTAL SENT ME INTO SOME SORT OF VOID BETWEEN MY EARTH AND THIS ONE...
"...IT WAS A STORM AND A VACUUM AND A RIPTIDE ALL AT THE SAME TIME.
"AND I WAS SO TIRED.
"BUT.
"THEN..."
SISTER!

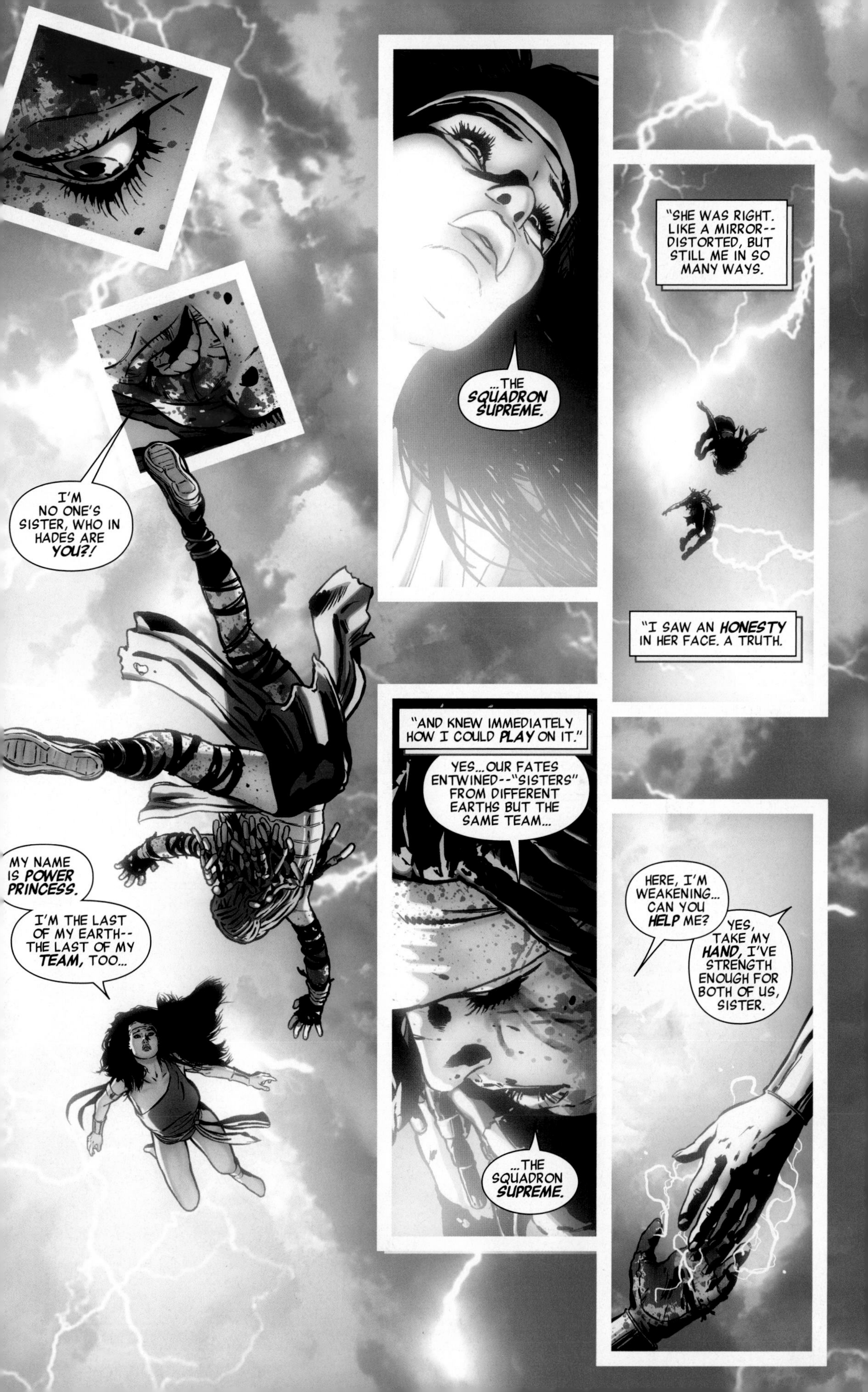
I'M NO ONE'S SISTER, WHO IN HADES ARE YOU?!
MY NAME IS POWER PRINCESS.
I'M THE LAST OF MY EARTH-- THE LAST OF MY TEAM, TOO...
...THE SQUADRON SUPREME.
"SHE WAS RIGHT. LIKE A MIRROR-- DISTORTED, BUT STILL ME IN SO MANY WAYS.
"I SAW AN HONESTY IN HER FACE. A TRUTH.
"AND KNEW IMMEDIATELY HOW I COULD PLAY ON IT."
YES...OUR FATES ENTWINED--"SISTERS" FROM DIFFERENT EARTHS BUT THE SAME TEAM...
...THE SQUADRON SUPREME.
HERE, I'M WEAKENING... CAN YOU HELP ME?
YES, TAKE MY HAND, I'VE STRENGTH ENOUGH FOR BOTH OF US, SISTER.

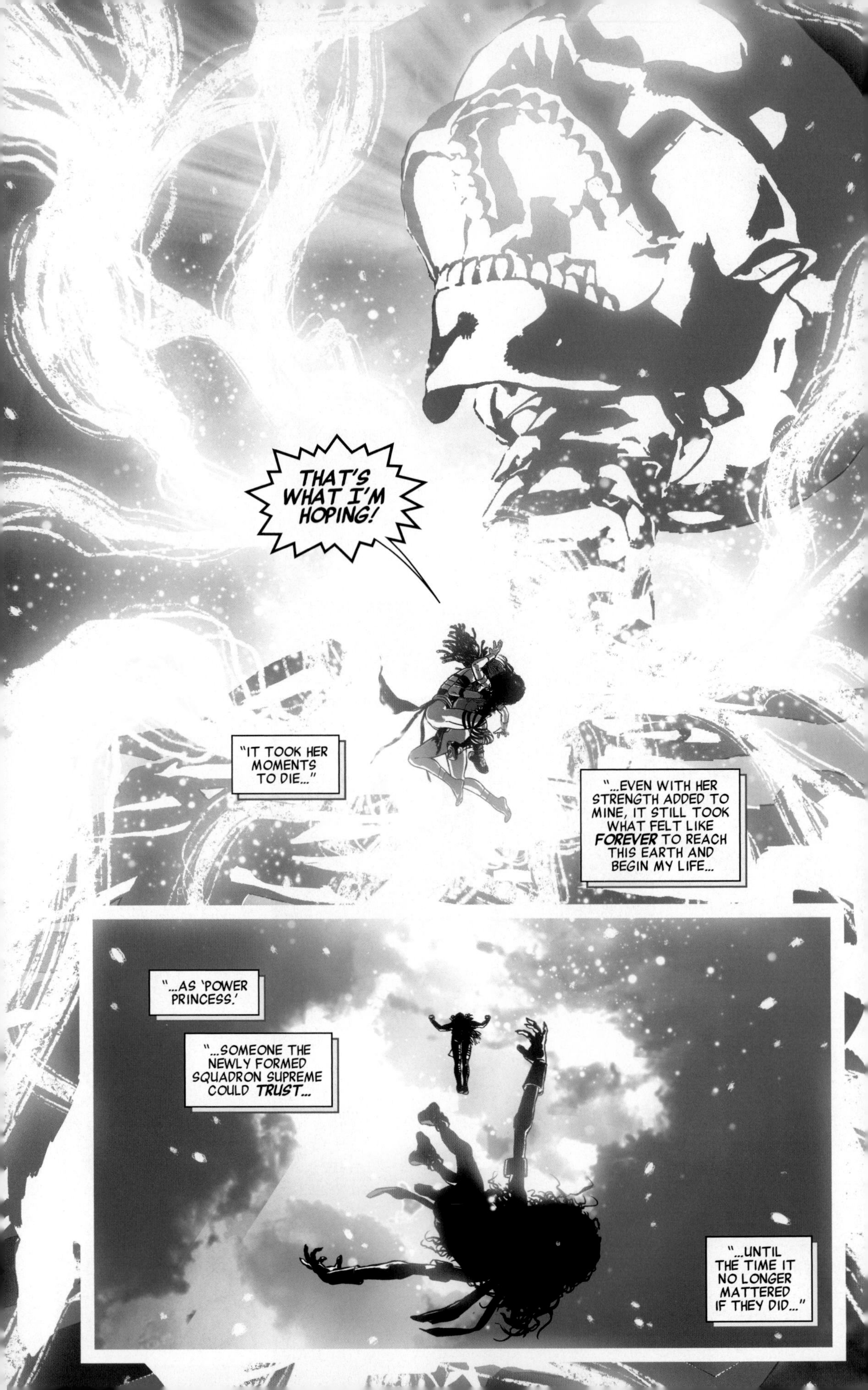
THAT'S WHAT I'M HOPING!
"IT TOOK HER MOMENTS TO DIE..."
"...EVEN WITH HER STRENGTH ADDED TO MINE, IT STILL TOOK WHAT FELT LIKE FOREVER TO REACH THIS EARTH AND BEGIN MY LIFE...
"...AS 'POWER PRINCESS.'
"...SOMEONE THE NEWLY FORMED SQUADRON SUPREME COULD TRUST...
"...UNTIL THE TIME IT NO LONGER MATTERED IF THEY DID..."

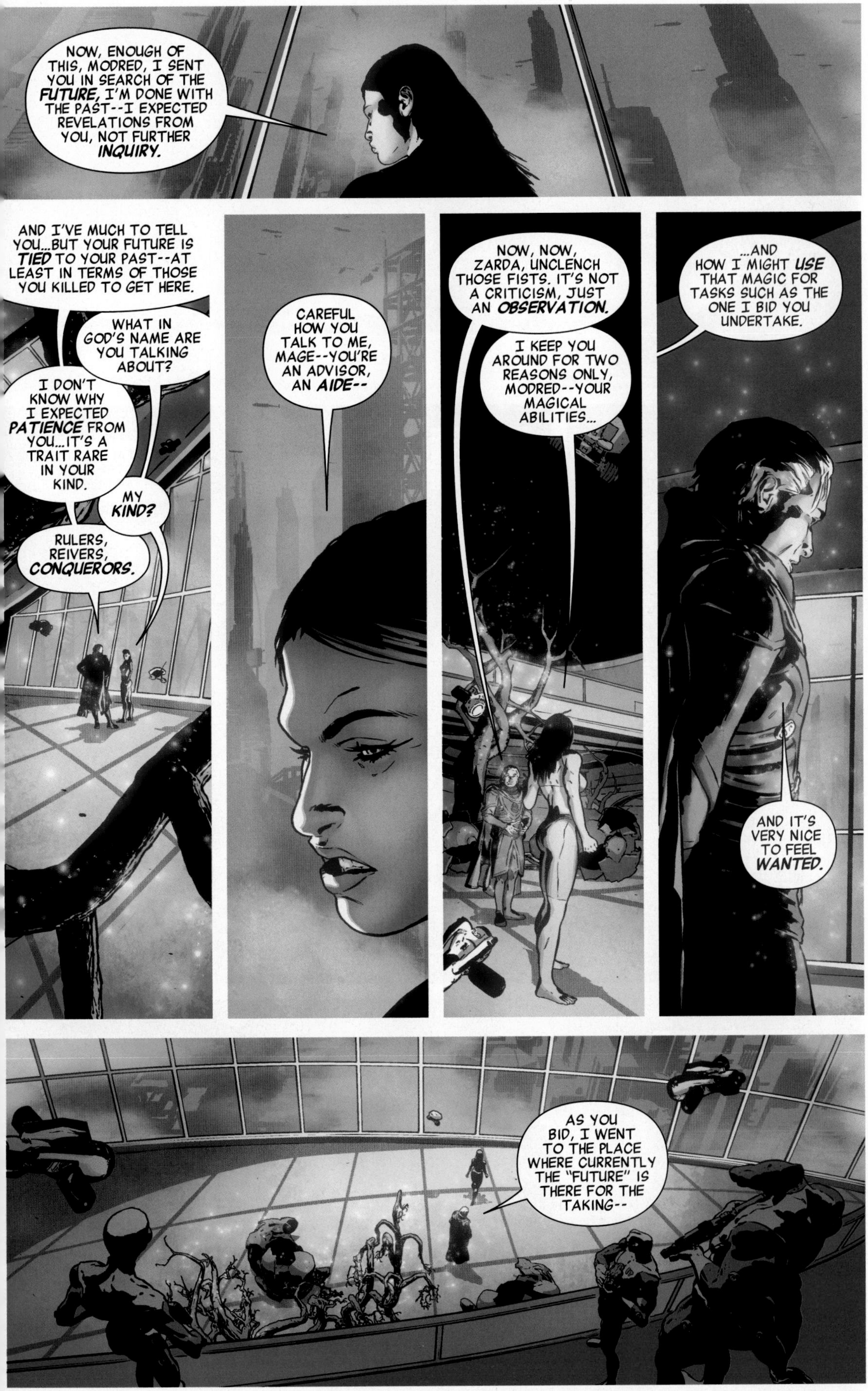
NOW, ENOUGH OF THIS, MODRED, I SENT YOU IN SEARCH OF THE FUTURE, I'M DONE WITH THE PAST--I EXPECTED REVELATIONS FROM YOU, NOT FURTHER INQUIRY.
AND I'VE MUCH TO TELL YOU...BUT YOUR FUTURE IS TIED TO YOUR PAST--AT LEAST IN TERMS OF THOSE YOU KILLED TO GET HERE.
WHAT IN GOD'S NAME ARE YOU TALKING ABOUT?
I DON'T KNOW WHY I EXPECTED PATIENCE FROM YOU...IT'S A TRAIT RARE IN YOUR KIND.
MY KIND?
RULERS, REIVERS, CONQUERORS.
CAREFUL HOW YOU TALK TO ME, MAGE--YOU'RE AN ADVISOR, AN AIDE--
NOW, NOW, ZARDA, UNCLENCH THOSE FISTS. IT'S NOT A CRITICISM, JUST AN OBSERVATION.
I KEEP YOU AROUND FOR TWO REASONS ONLY, MODRED--YOUR MAGICAL ABILITIES...
...AND HOW I MIGHT USE THAT MAGIC FOR TASKS SUCH AS THE ONE I BID YOU UNDERTAKE.
AND IT'S VERY NICE TO FEEL WANTED.
AS YOU BID, I WENT TO THE PLACE WHERE CURRENTLY THE "FUTURE" IS THERE FOR THE TAKING--

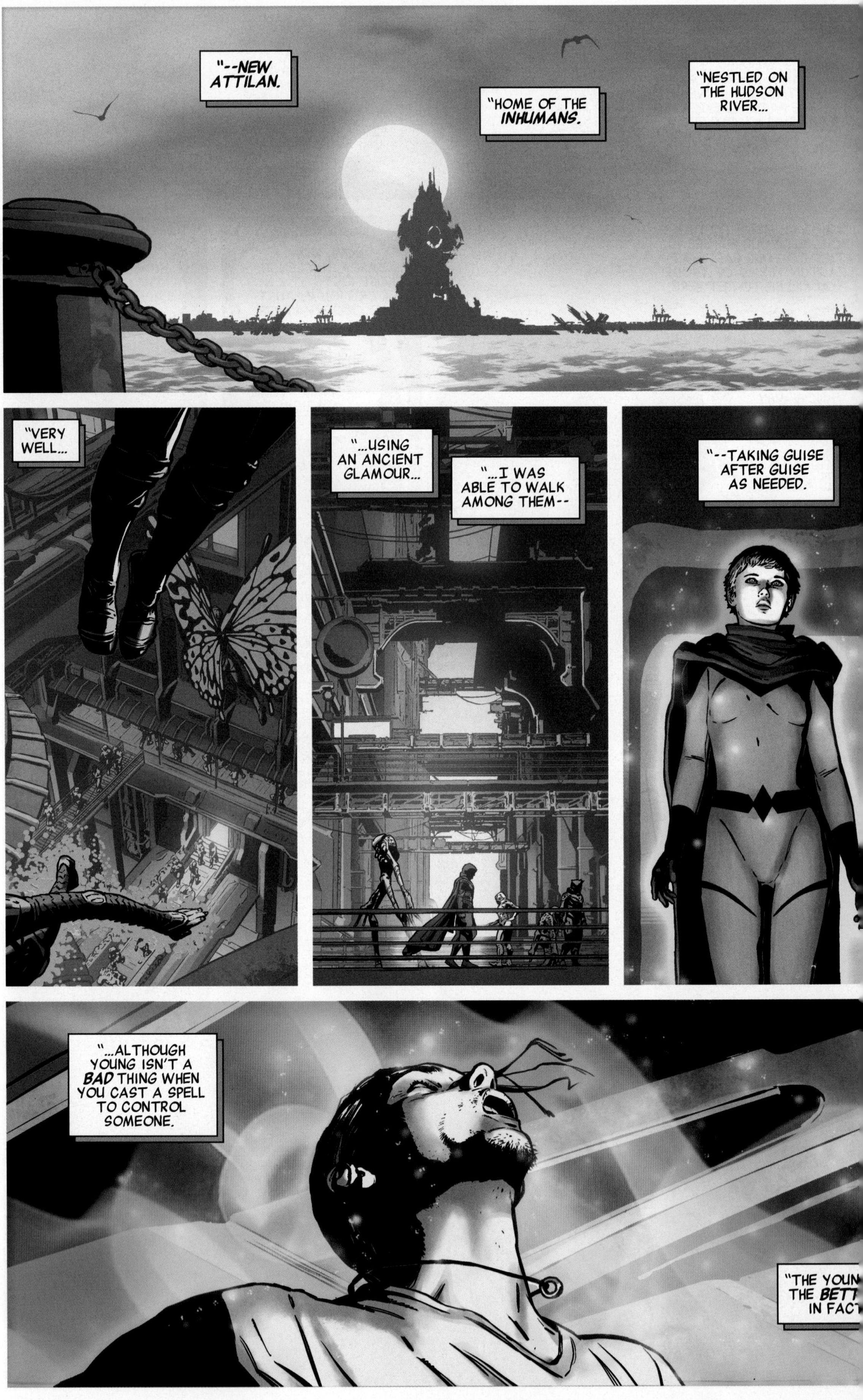
"--NEW ATTILAN.
"HOME OF THE INHUMANS.
"NESTLED ON THE HUDSON RIVER...
"VERY WELL...
"...USING AN ANCIENT GLAMOUR...
"...I WAS ABLE TO WALK AMONG THEM--
"--TAKING GUISE AFTER GUISE AS NEEDED.
"...ALTHOUGH YOUNG ISN'T A BAD THING WHEN YOU CAST A SPELL TO CONTROL SOMEONE.
"THE YOUN THE BETT IN FACT

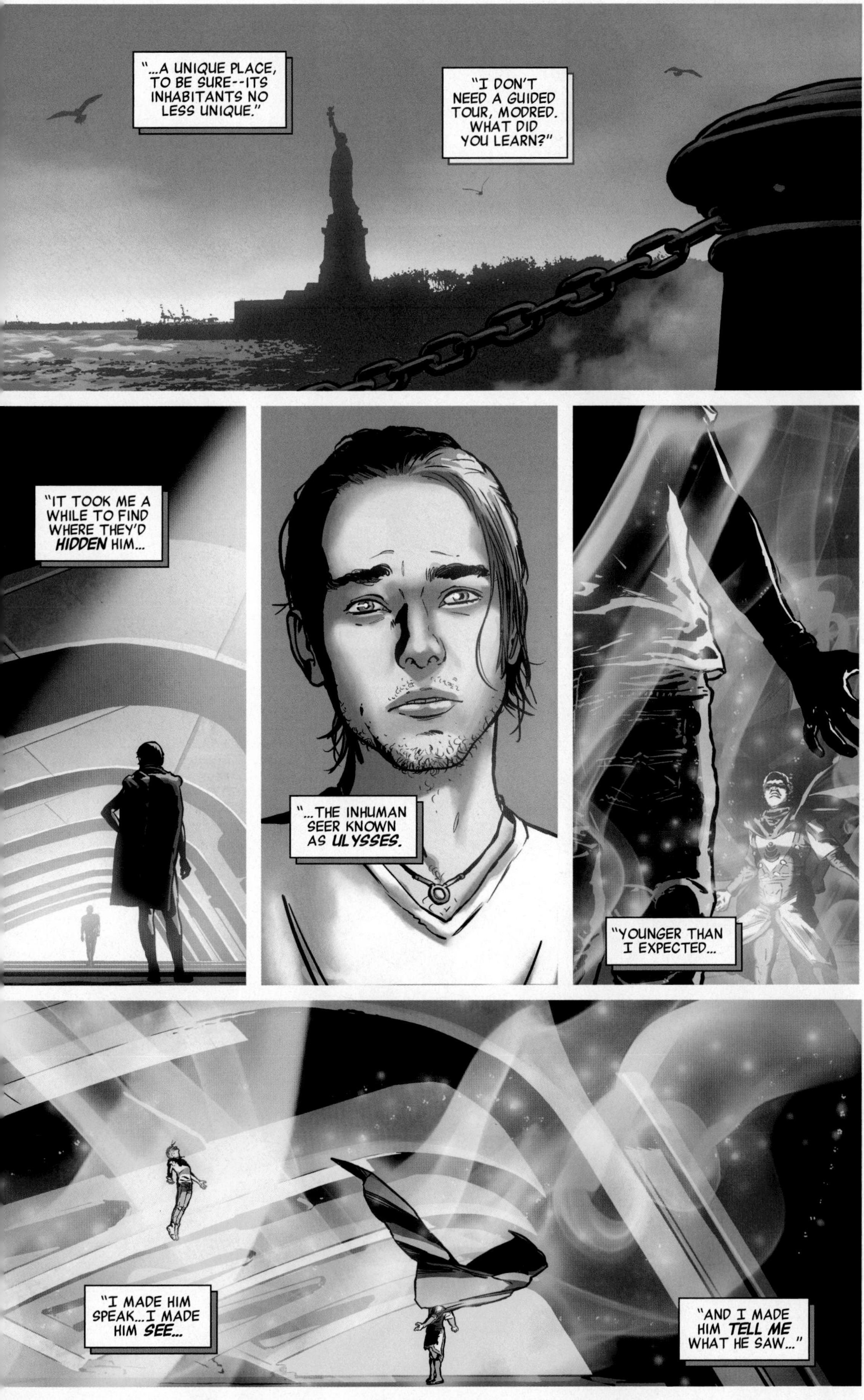
"...A UNIQUE PLACE, TO BE SURE--ITS INHABITANTS NO LESS UNIQUE."
"I DON'T NEED A GUIDED TOUR, MODRED. WHAT DID YOU LEARN?"
"IT TOOK ME A WHILE TO FIND WHERE THEY'D HIDDEN HIM...
"...THE INHUMAN SEER KNOWN AS ULYSSES.
"YOUNGER THAN I EXPECTED...
"I MADE HIM SPEAK...I MADE HIM SEE...
"AND I MADE HIM TELL ME WHAT HE SAW..."

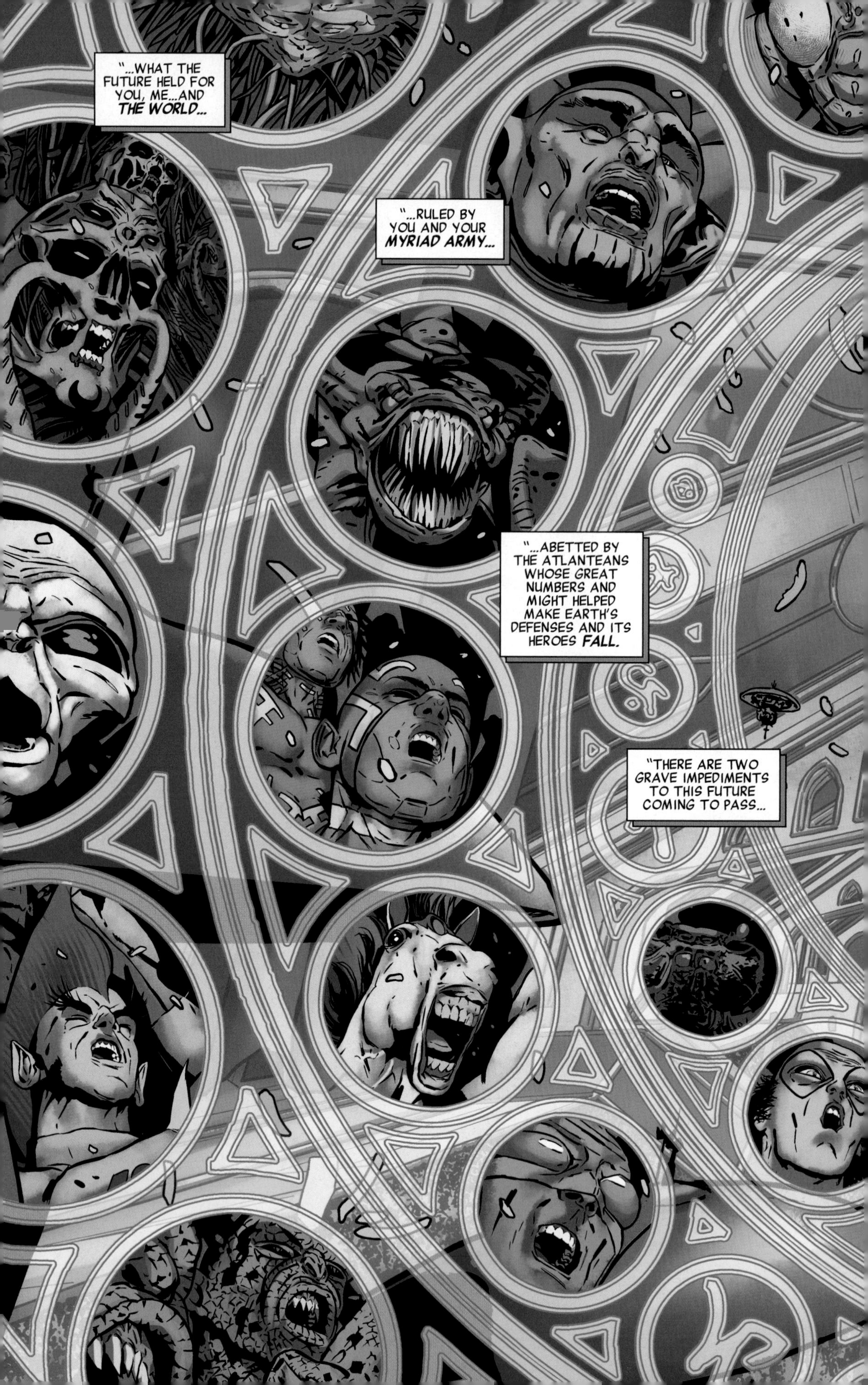
"...WHAT THE FUTURE HELD FOR YOU, ME...AND *THE WORLD*...
"...RULED BY YOU AND YOUR *MYRIAD ARMY*...
"...ABETTED BY THE ATLANTEANS WHOSE GREAT NUMBERS AND MIGHT HELPED MAKE EARTH'S DEFENSES AND ITS HEROES *FALL*.
"THERE ARE TWO GRAVE IMPEDIMENTS TO THIS FUTURE COMING TO PASS...

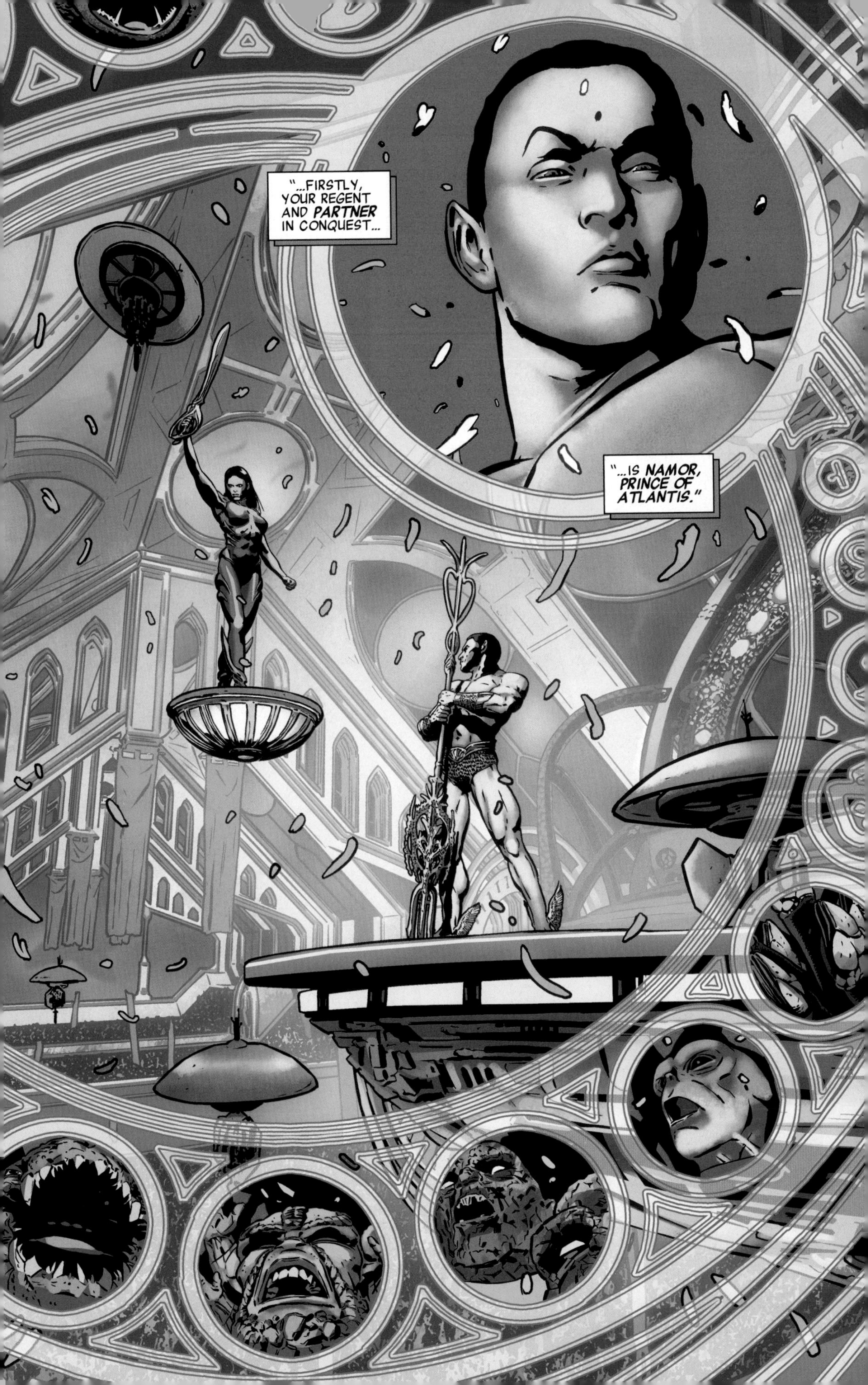
"...FIRSTLY, YOUR REGENT AND PARTNER IN CONQUEST...
"...IS NAMOR, PRINCE OF ATLANTIS."

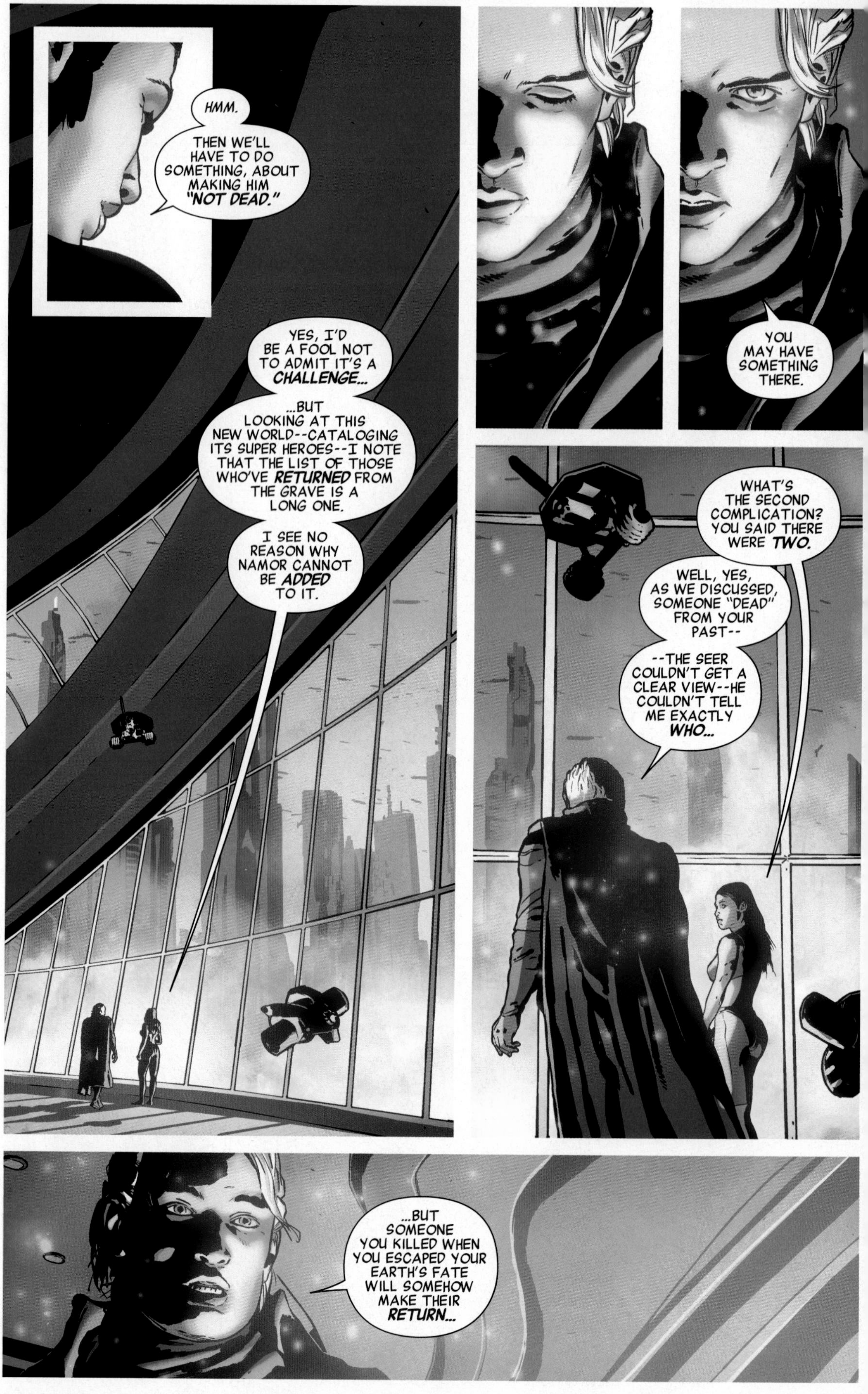
HMM.
THEN WE'LL HAVE TO DO SOMETHING, ABOUT MAKING HIM "NOT DEAD."
YOU MAY HAVE SOMETHING THERE.
YES, I'D BE A FOOL NOT TO ADMIT IT'S A CHALLENGE...
...BUT LOOKING AT THIS NEW WORLD--CATALOGING ITS SUPER HEROES--I NOTE THAT THE LIST OF THOSE WHO'VE RETURNED FROM THE GRAVE IS A LONG ONE.
I SEE NO REASON WHY NAMOR CANNOT BE ADDED TO IT.
WHAT'S THE SECOND COMPLICATION? YOU SAID THERE WERE TWO.
WELL, YES, AS WE DISCUSSED, SOMEONE "DEAD" FROM YOUR PAST--
--THE SEER COULDN'T GET A CLEAR VIEW--HE COULDN'T TELL ME EXACTLY WHO...
...BUT SOMEONE YOU KILLED WHEN YOU ESCAPED YOUR EARTH'S FATE WILL SOMEHOW MAKE THEIR RETURN...

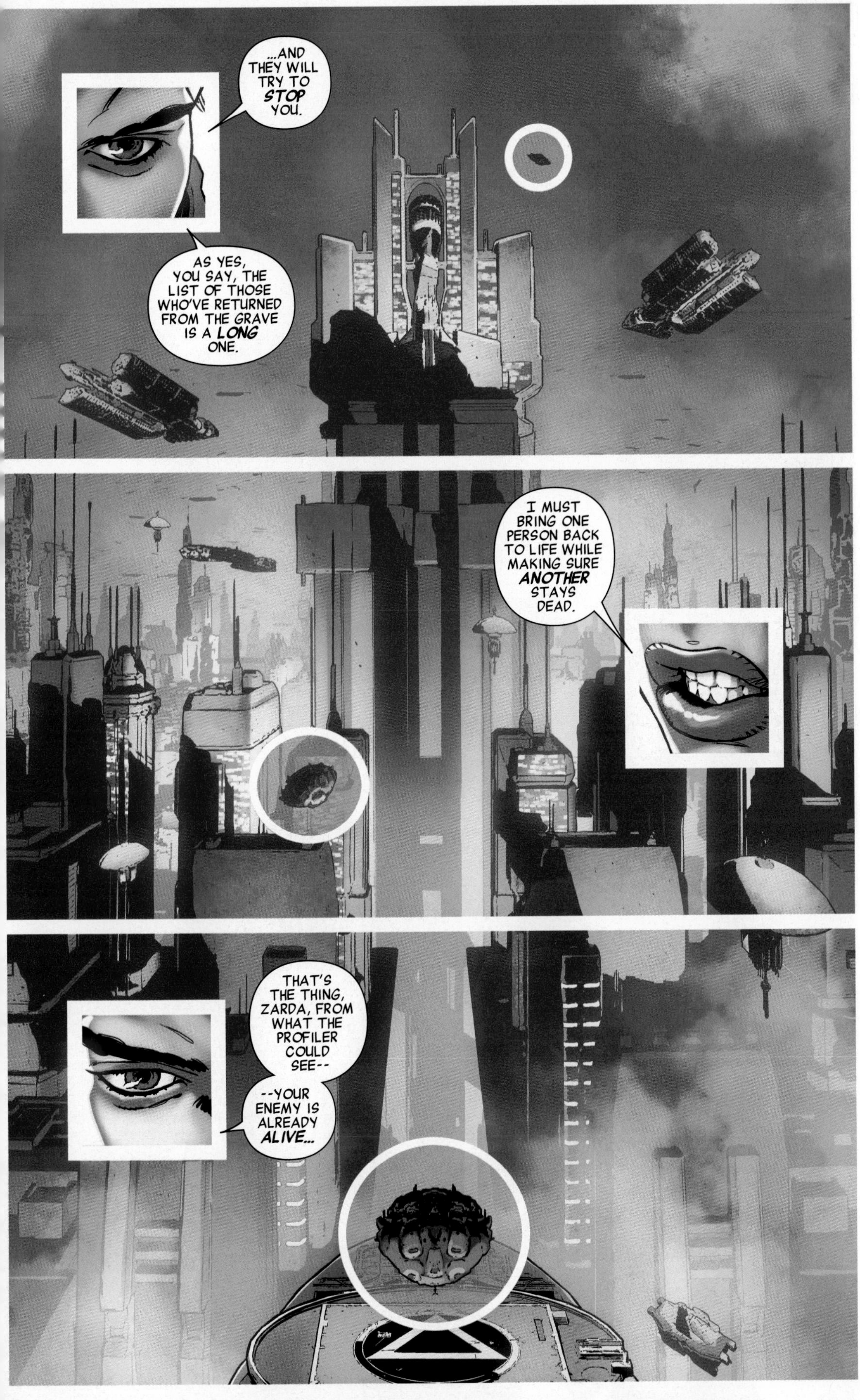
...AND THEY WILL TRY TO STOP YOU.
AS YES, YOU SAY, THE LIST OF THOSE WHO'VE RETURNED FROM THE GRAVE IS A LONG ONE.
I MUST BRING ONE PERSON BACK TO LIFE WHILE MAKING SURE ANOTHER STAYS DEAD.
THAT'S THE THING, ZARDA, FROM WHAT THE PROFILER COULD SEE--
--YOUR ENEMY IS ALREADY ALIVE...

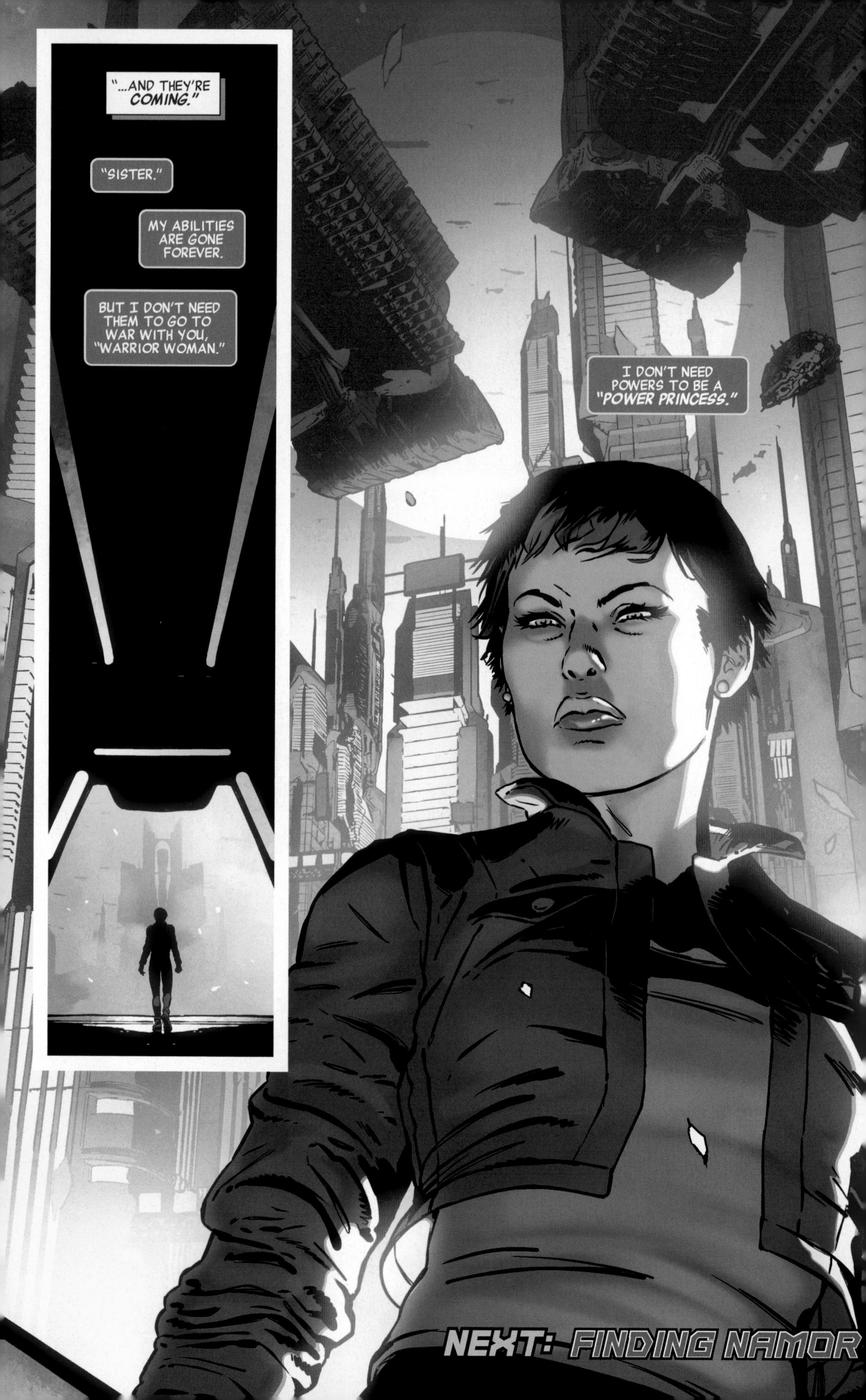
"...AND THEY'RE *COMING.*"
"SISTER."
MY ABILITIES ARE GONE FOREVER.
BUT I DON'T NEED THEM TO GO TO WAR WITH YOU, "WARRIOR WOMAN."
I DON'T NEED POWERS TO BE A "*POWER PRINCESS.*"
NEXT: FINDING NAMOR

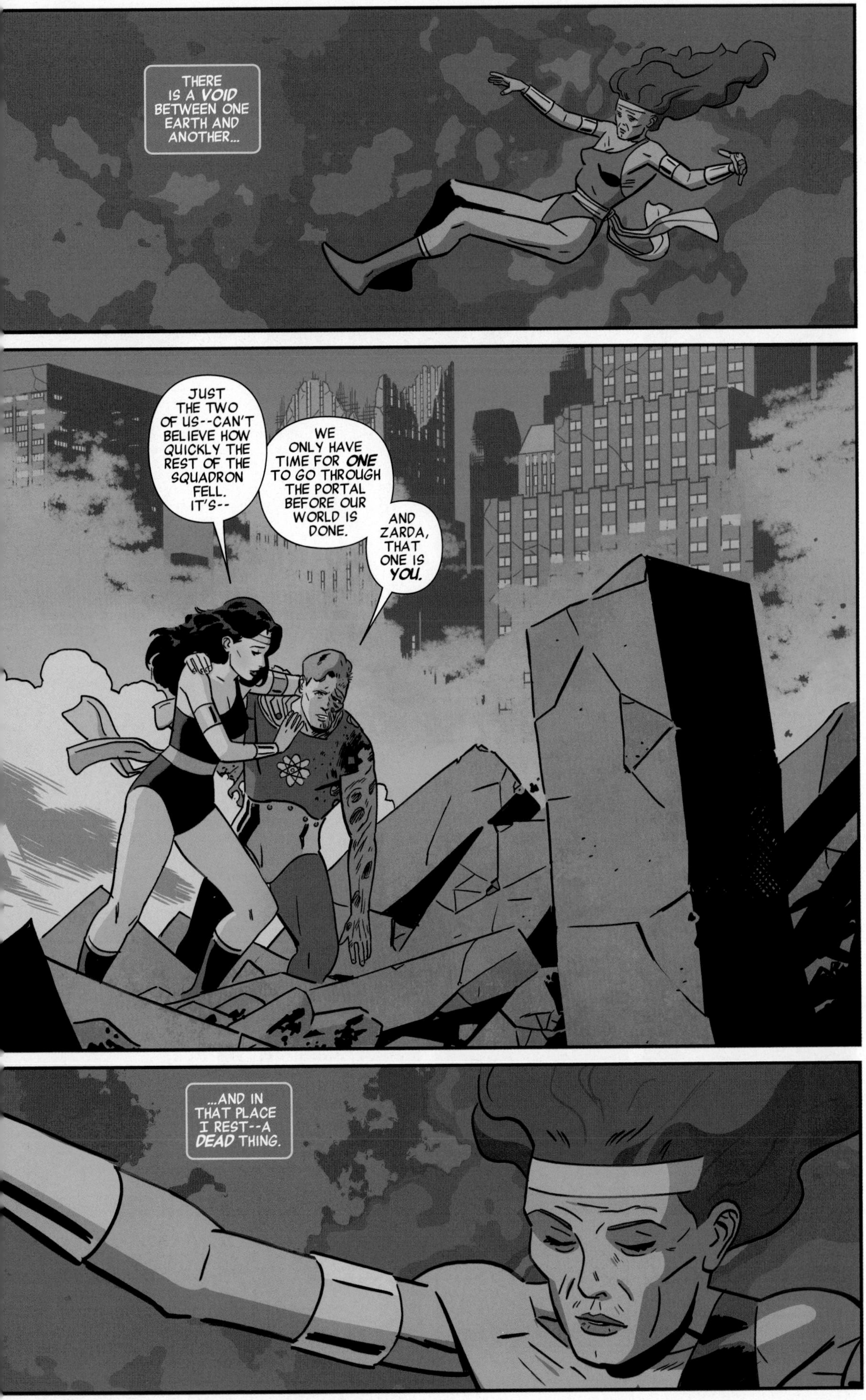
THERE IS A VOID BETWEEN ONE EARTH AND ANOTHER...
JUST THE TWO OF US--CAN'T BELIEVE HOW QUICKLY THE REST OF THE SQUADRON FELL. IT'S--
WE ONLY HAVE TIME FOR ONE TO GO THROUGH THE PORTAL BEFORE OUR WORLD IS DONE.
AND ZARDA, THAT ONE IS YOU.
...AND IN THAT PLACE I REST--A DEAD THING.

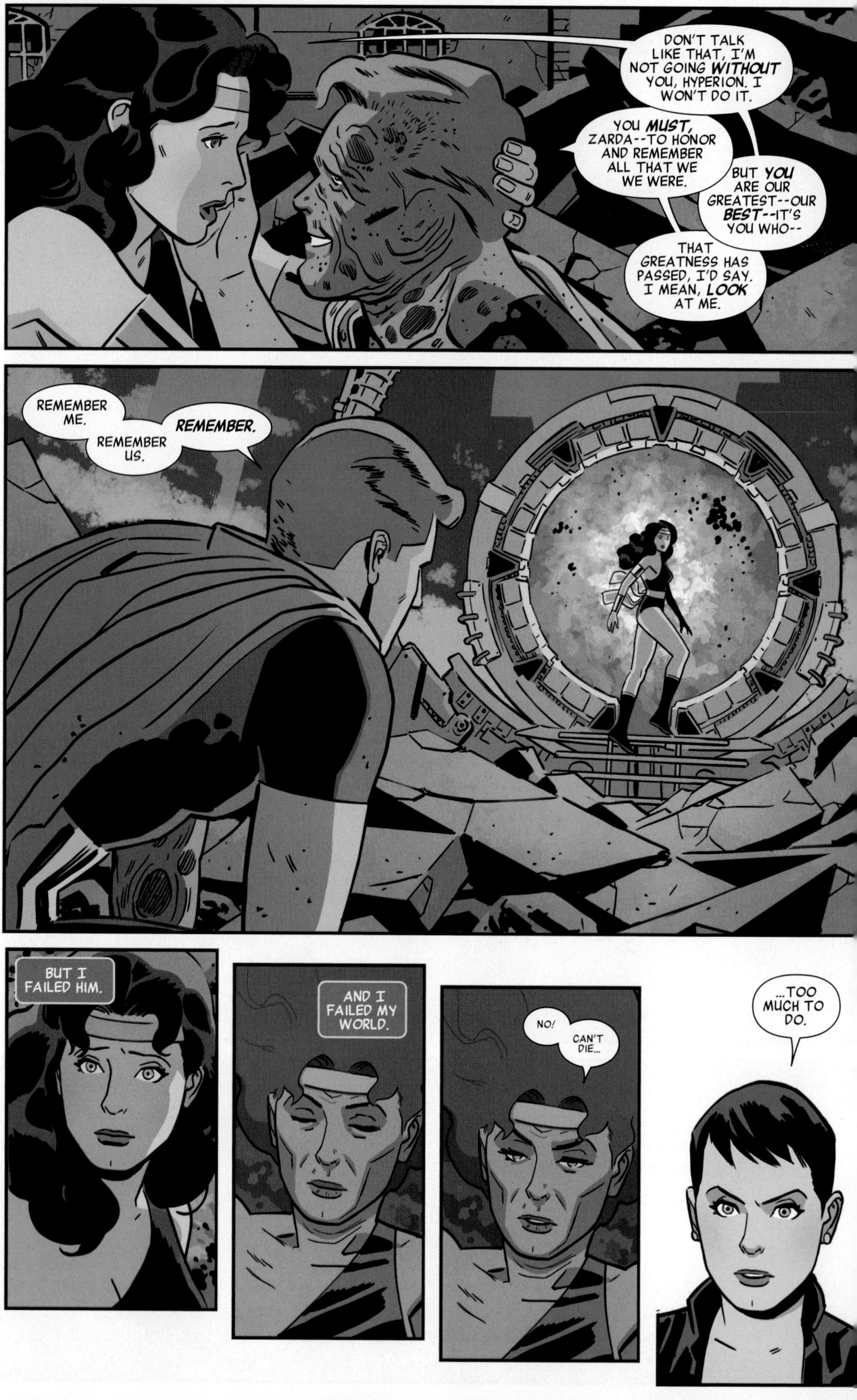
DON'T TALK LIKE THAT, I'M NOT GOING WITHOUT YOU, HYPERION. I WON'T DO IT.
YOU MUST, ZARDA--TO HONOR AND REMEMBER ALL THAT WE WE WERE.
BUT YOU ARE OUR GREATEST--OUR BEST--IT'S YOU WHO--
THAT GREATNESS HAS PASSED, I'D SAY. I MEAN, LOOK AT ME.
REMEMBER ME.
REMEMBER US.
REMEMBER.
BUT I FAILED HIM.
AND I FAILED MY WORLD.
NO!
CAN'T DIE...
...TOO MUCH TO DO.

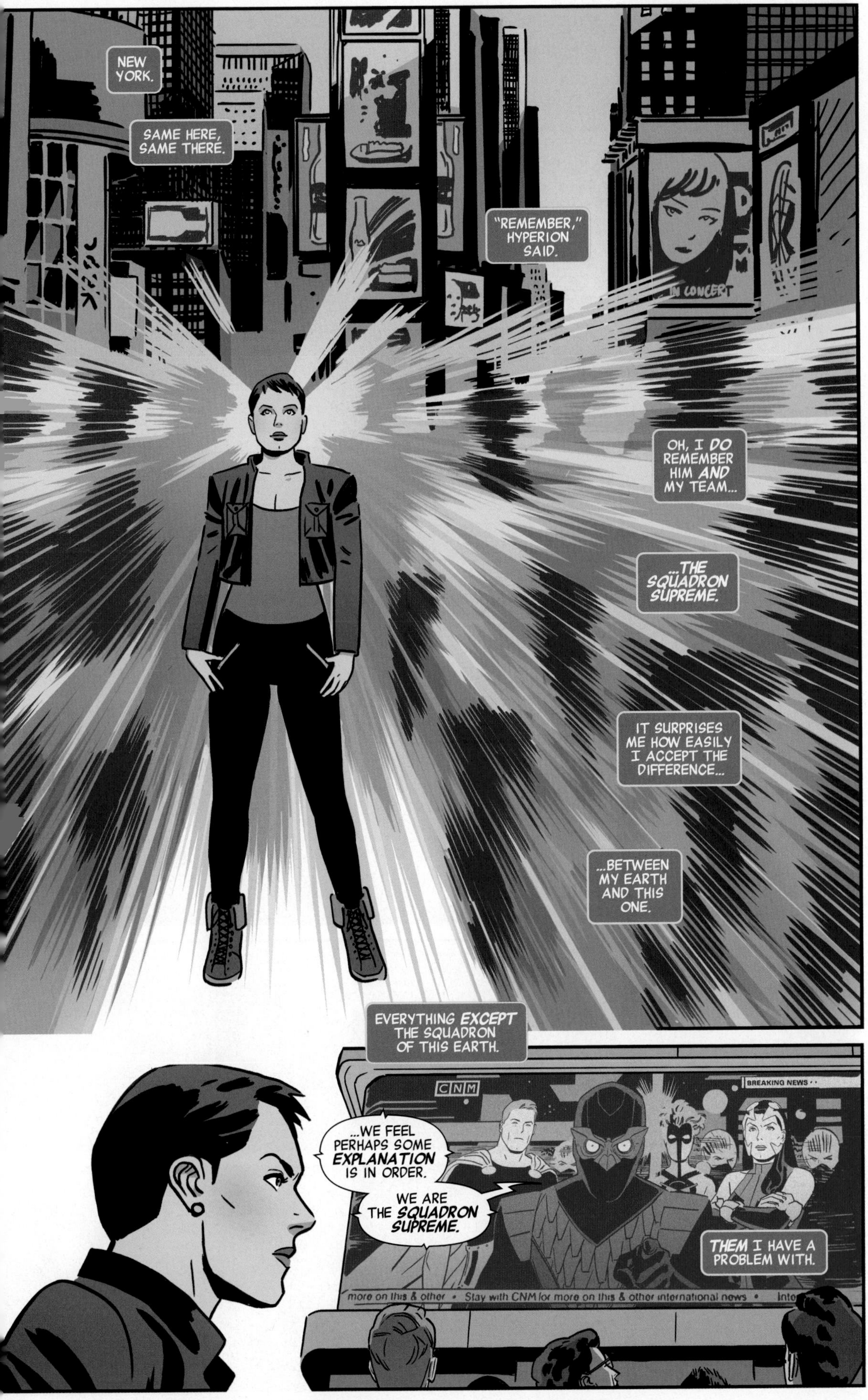
NEW YORK.
SAME HERE, SAME THERE.
"REMEMBER," HYPERION SAID.
IN CONCERT
OH, I DO REMEMBER HIM AND MY TEAM...
...THE SQUADRON SUPREME.
IT SURPRISES ME HOW EASILY I ACCEPT THE DIFFERENCE...
...BETWEEN MY EARTH AND THIS ONE.
EVERYTHING EXCEPT THE SQUADRON OF THIS EARTH.
CNM
BREAKING NEWS
...WE FEEL PERHAPS SOME EXPLANATION IS IN ORDER.
WE ARE THE SQUADRON SUPREME.
THEM I HAVE A PROBLEM WITH.
more on this & other • Stay with CNM for more on this & other international news •

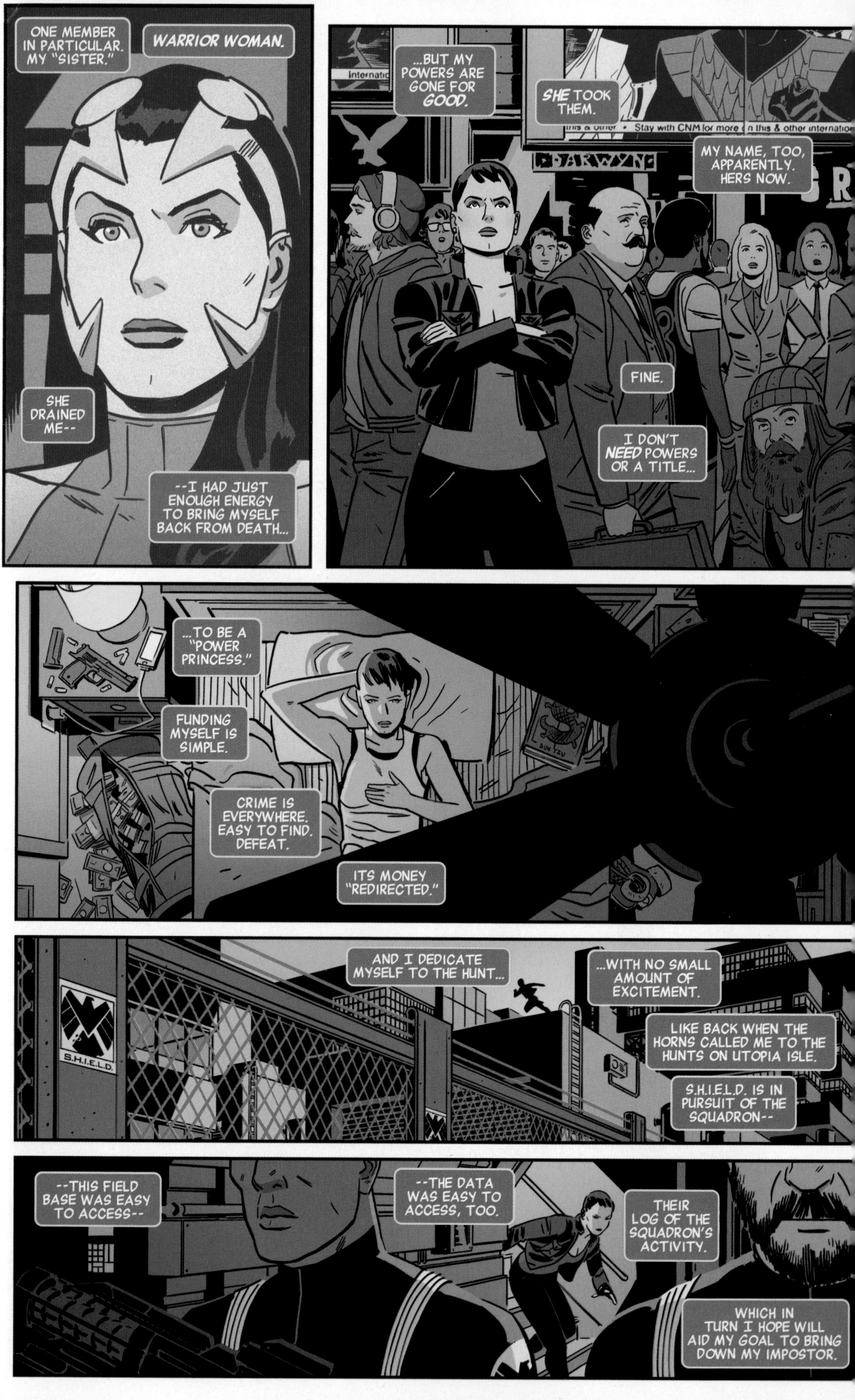

ONE MEMBER IN PARTICULAR. MY "SISTER."
WARRIOR WOMAN.
SHE DRAINED ME--
--I HAD JUST ENOUGH ENERGY TO BRING MYSELF BACK FROM DEATH...
...BUT MY POWERS ARE GONE FOR GOOD.
SHE TOOK THEM.
Stay with CNM for more on this & other internatio
DARWYN
MY NAME, TOO, APPARENTLY. HERS NOW.
FINE.
I DON'T NEED POWERS OR A TITLE...
...TO BE A "POWER PRINCESS."
FUNDING MYSELF IS SIMPLE.
SUN TZU
CRIME IS EVERYWHERE. EASY TO FIND. DEFEAT.
ITS MONEY "REDIRECTED."
S.H.I.E.L.D.
AND I DEDICATE MYSELF TO THE HUNT...
...WITH NO SMALL AMOUNT OF EXCITEMENT.
LIKE BACK WHEN THE HORNS CALLED ME TO THE HUNTS ON UTOPIA ISLE.
S.H.I.E.L.D. IS IN PURSUIT OF THE SQUADRON--
--THIS FIELD BASE WAS EASY TO ACCESS--
--THE DATA WAS EASY TO ACCESS, TOO.
THEIR LOG OF THE SQUADRON'S ACTIVITY.
WHICH IN TURN I HOPE WILL AID MY GOAL TO BRING DOWN MY IMPOSTOR.

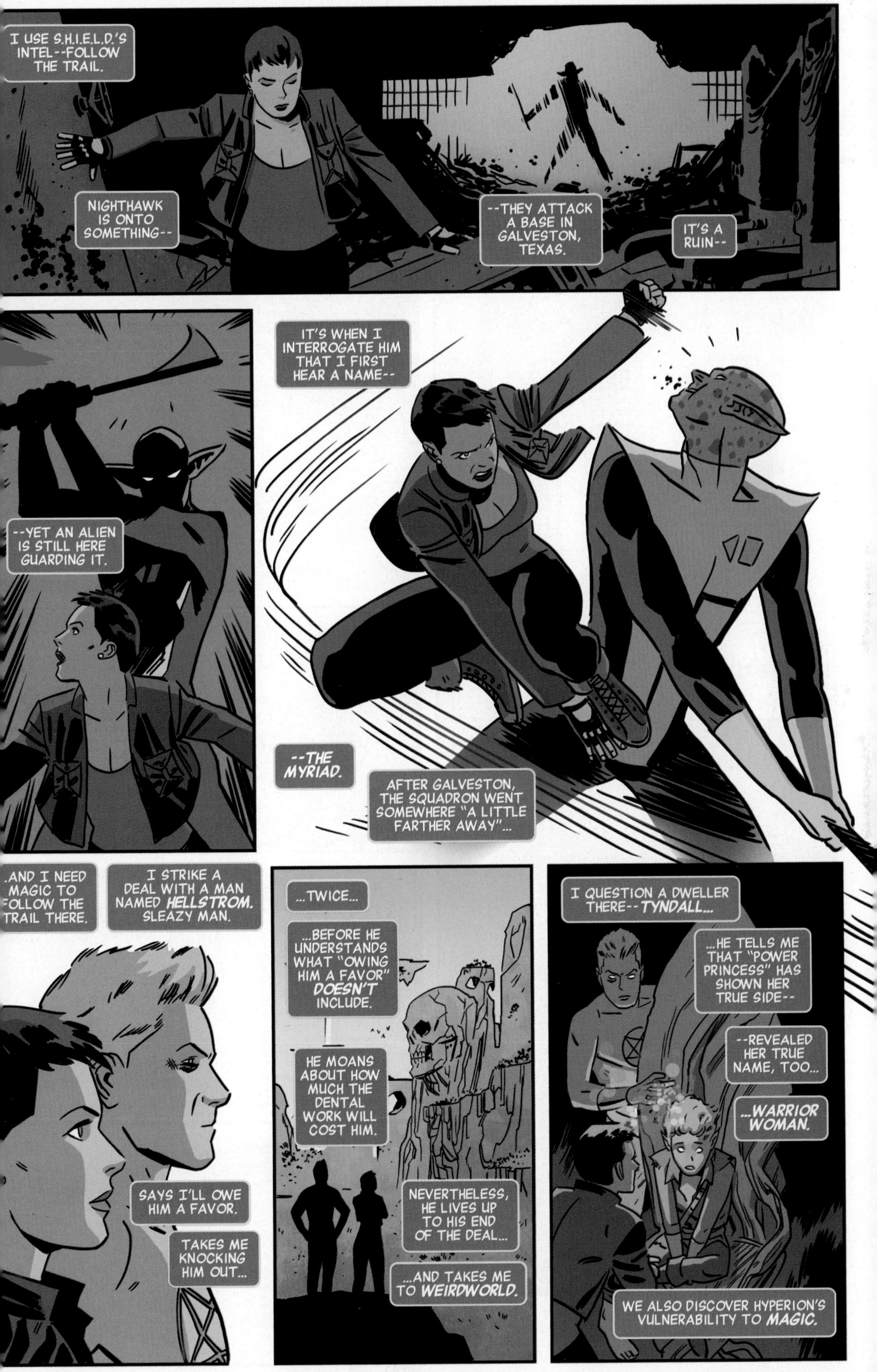
I USE S.H.I.E.L.D.'S INTEL--FOLLOW THE TRAIL.
NIGHTHAWK IS ONTO SOMETHING--
--THEY ATTACK A BASE IN GALVESTON, TEXAS.
IT'S A RUIN--
--YET AN ALIEN IS STILL HERE GUARDING IT.
IT'S WHEN I INTERROGATE HIM THAT I FIRST HEAR A NAME--
--THE MYRIAD.
AFTER GALVESTON, THE SQUADRON WENT SOMEWHERE "A LITTLE FARTHER AWAY"...
.AND I NEED MAGIC TO FOLLOW THE TRAIL THERE.
I STRIKE A DEAL WITH A MAN NAMED HELLSTROM. SLEAZY MAN.
SAYS I'LL OWE HIM A FAVOR.
TAKES ME KNOCKING HIM OUT...
...TWICE...
...BEFORE HE UNDERSTANDS WHAT "OWING HIM A FAVOR" DOESN'T INCLUDE.
HE MOANS ABOUT HOW MUCH THE DENTAL WORK WILL COST HIM.
NEVERTHELESS, HE LIVES UP TO HIS END OF THE DEAL...
...AND TAKES ME TO WEIRDWORLD.
I QUESTION A DWELLER THERE--TYNDALL...
...HE TELLS ME THAT "POWER PRINCESS" HAS SHOWN HER TRUE SIDE--
--REVEALED HER TRUE NAME, TOO...
...WARRIOR WOMAN.
WE ALSO DISCOVER HYPERION'S VULNERABILITY TO MAGIC.

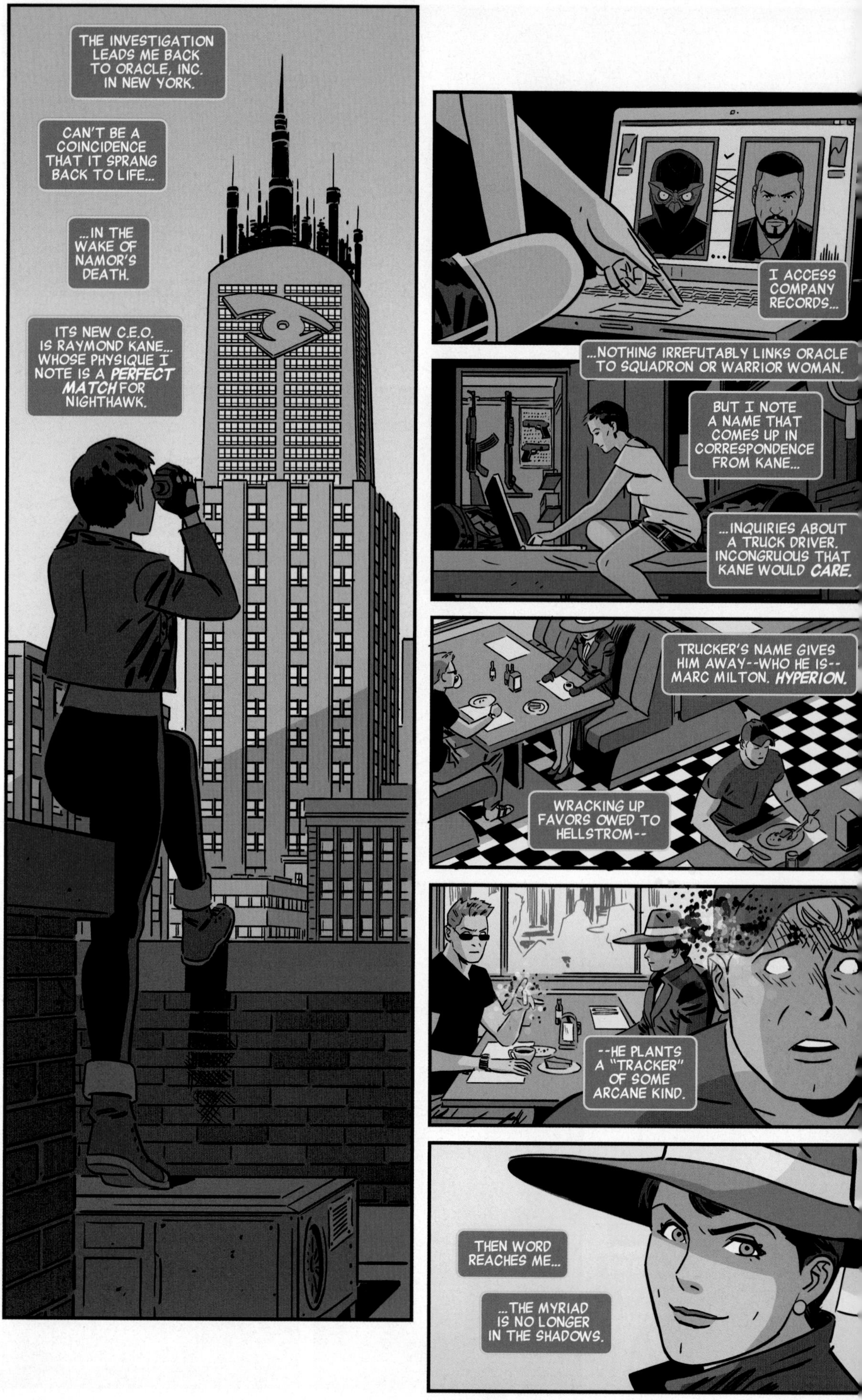
THE INVESTIGATION LEADS ME BACK TO ORACLE, INC. IN NEW YORK.
CAN'T BE A COINCIDENCE THAT IT SPRANG BACK TO LIFE...
...IN THE WAKE OF NAMOR'S DEATH.
ITS NEW C.E.O. IS RAYMOND KANE... WHOSE PHYSIQUE I NOTE IS A PERFECT MATCH FOR NIGHTHAWK.
I ACCESS COMPANY RECORDS...
...NOTHING IRREFUTABLY LINKS ORACLE TO SQUADRON OR WARRIOR WOMAN.
BUT I NOTE A NAME THAT COMES UP IN CORRESPONDENCE FROM KANE...
...INQUIRIES ABOUT A TRUCK DRIVER. INCONGRUOUS THAT KANE WOULD CARE.
TRUCKER'S NAME GIVES HIM AWAY--WHO HE IS--MARC MILTON. HYPERION.
WRACKING UP FAVORS OWED TO HELLSTROM--
--HE PLANTS A "TRACKER" OF SOME ARCANE KIND.
THEN WORD REACHES ME...
...THE MYRIAD IS NO LONGER IN THE SHADOWS.

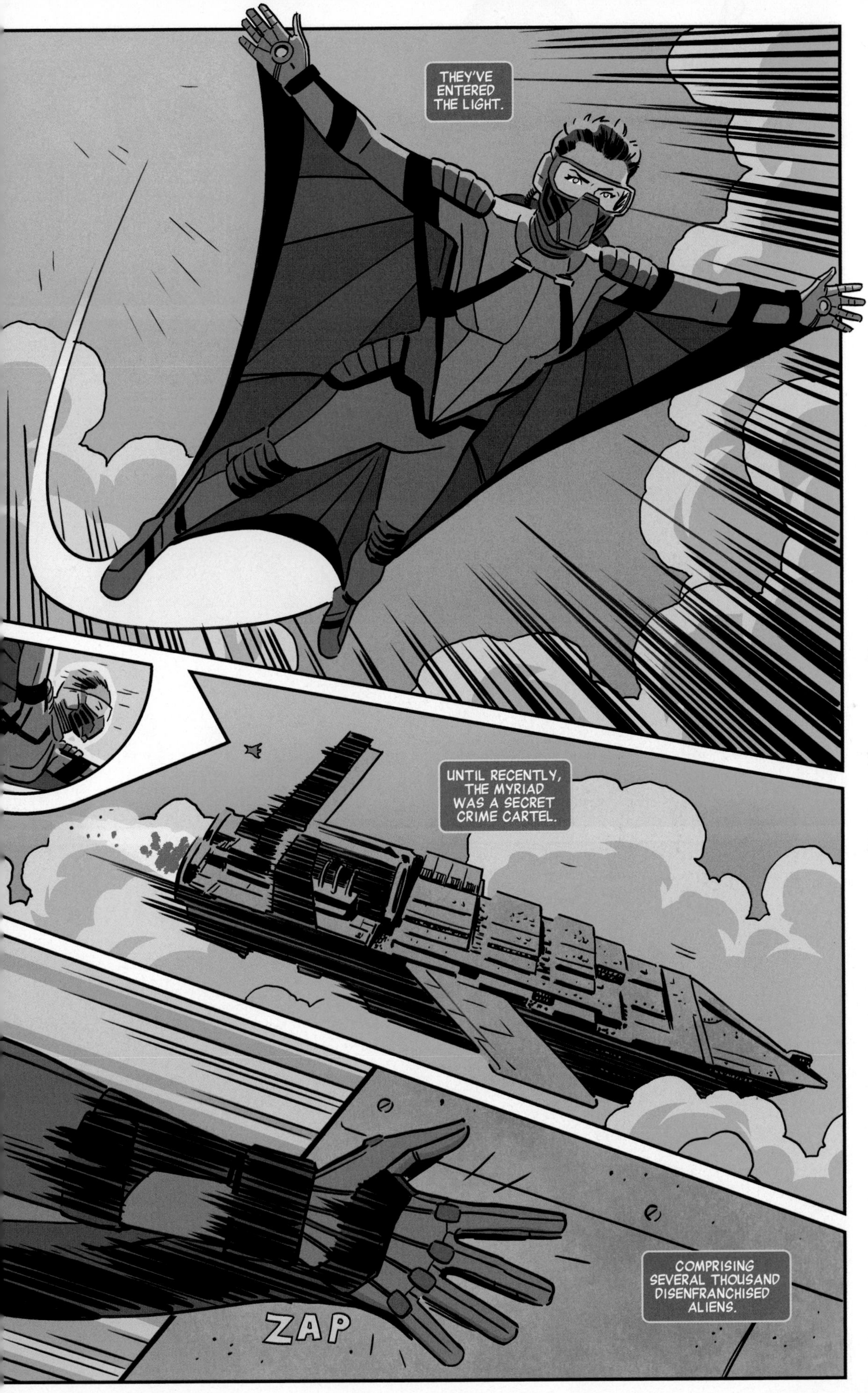
THEY'VE ENTERED THE LIGHT.
UNTIL RECENTLY, THE MYRIAD WAS A SECRET CRIME CARTEL.
COMPRISING SEVERAL THOUSAND DISENFRANCHISED ALIENS.
ZAP

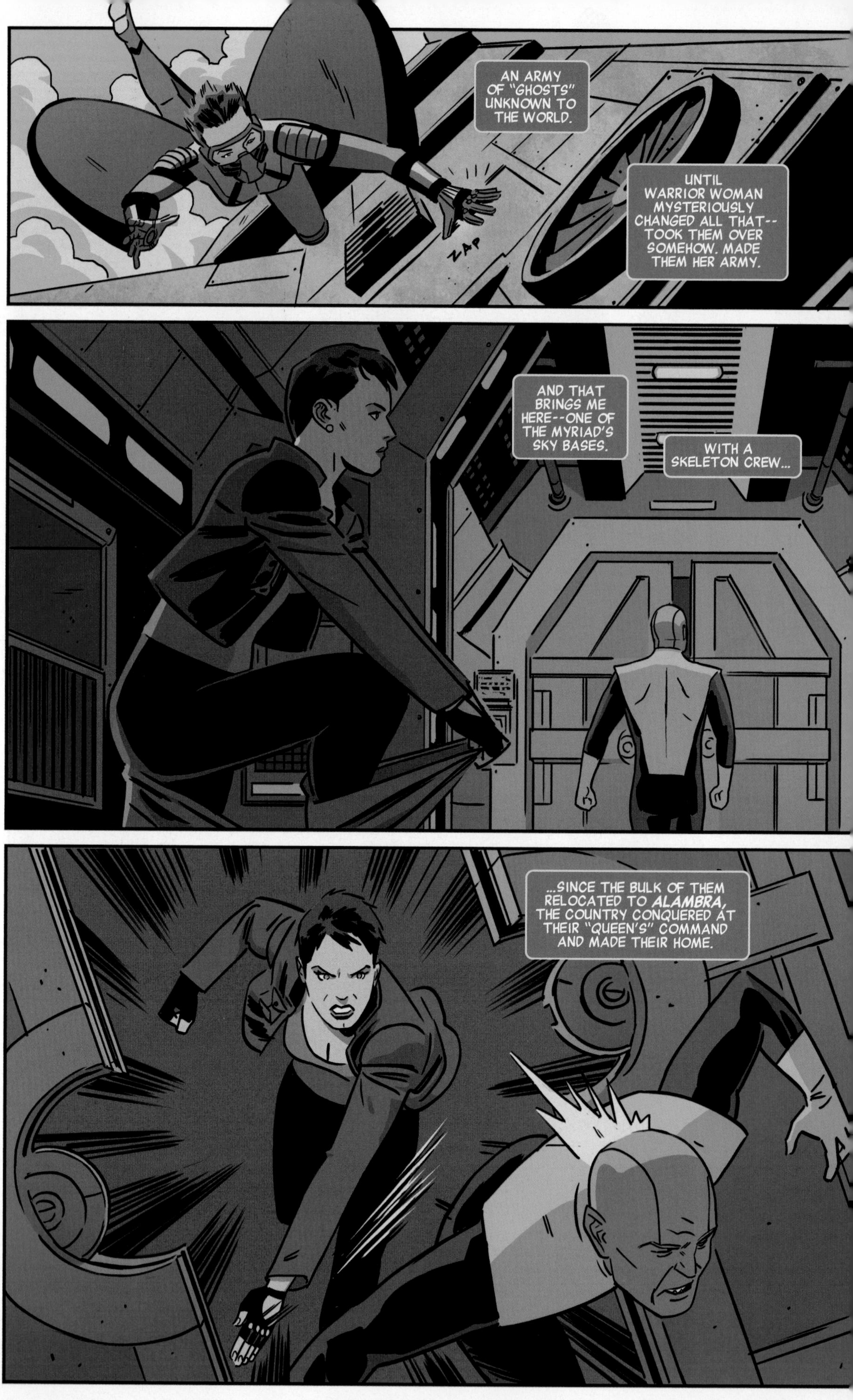
AN ARMY OF "GHOSTS" UNKNOWN TO THE WORLD.
UNTIL WARRIOR WOMAN MYSTERIOUSLY CHANGED ALL THAT--TOOK THEM OVER SOMEHOW. MADE THEM HER ARMY.
ZAP
AND THAT BRINGS ME HERE--ONE OF THE MYRIAD'S SKY BASES.
WITH A SKELETON CREW...
...SINCE THE BULK OF THEM RELOCATED TO ALAMBRA, THE COUNTRY CONQUERED AT THEIR "QUEEN'S" COMMAND AND MADE THEIR HOME.

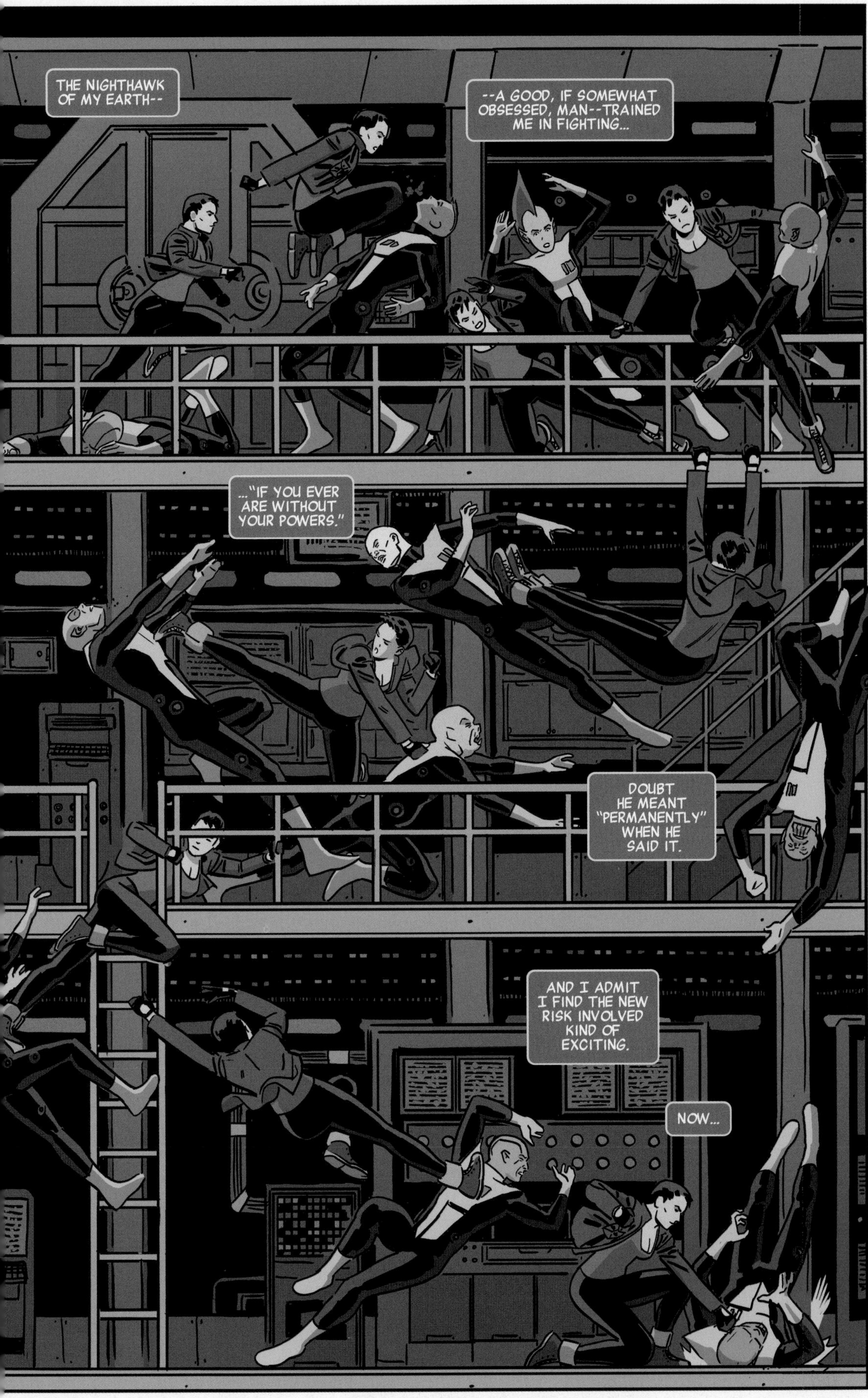
THE NIGHTHAWK OF MY EARTH--
--A GOOD, IF SOMEWHAT OBSESSED, MAN--TRAINED ME IN FIGHTING...
..."IF YOU EVER ARE WITHOUT YOUR POWERS."
DOUBT HE MEANT "PERMANENTLY" WHEN HE SAID IT.
AND I ADMIT I FIND THE NEW RISK INVOLVED KIND OF EXCITING.
NOW...

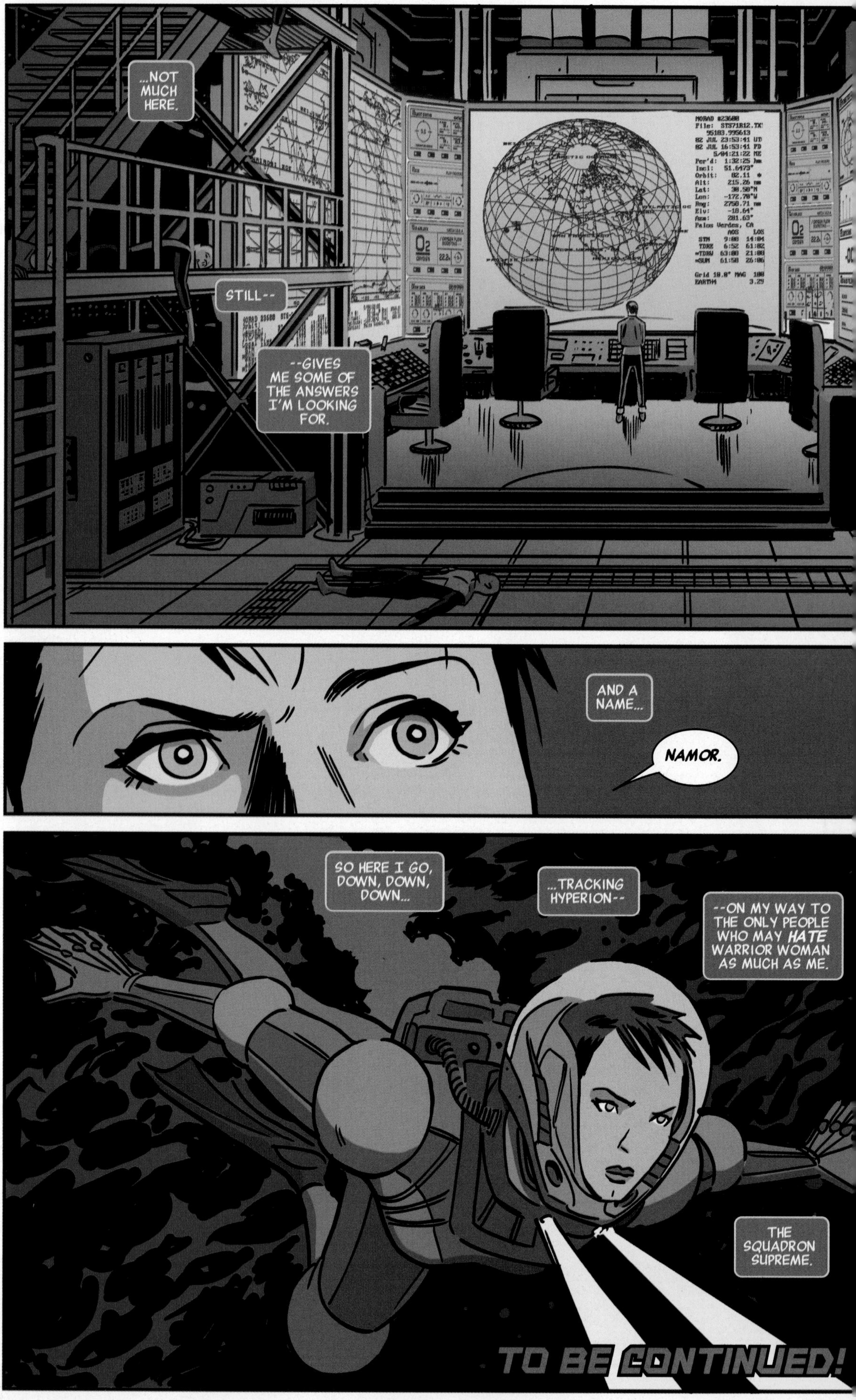
...NOT MUCH HERE.
STILL--
--GIVES ME SOME OF THE ANSWERS I'M LOOKING FOR.
AND A NAME...
NAMOR.
SO HERE I GO, DOWN, DOWN, DOWN...
...TRACKING HYPERION--
--ON MY WAY TO THE ONLY PEOPLE WHO MAY HATE WARRIOR WOMAN AS MUCH AS ME.
THE SQUADRON SUPREME.
TO BE CONTINUED!

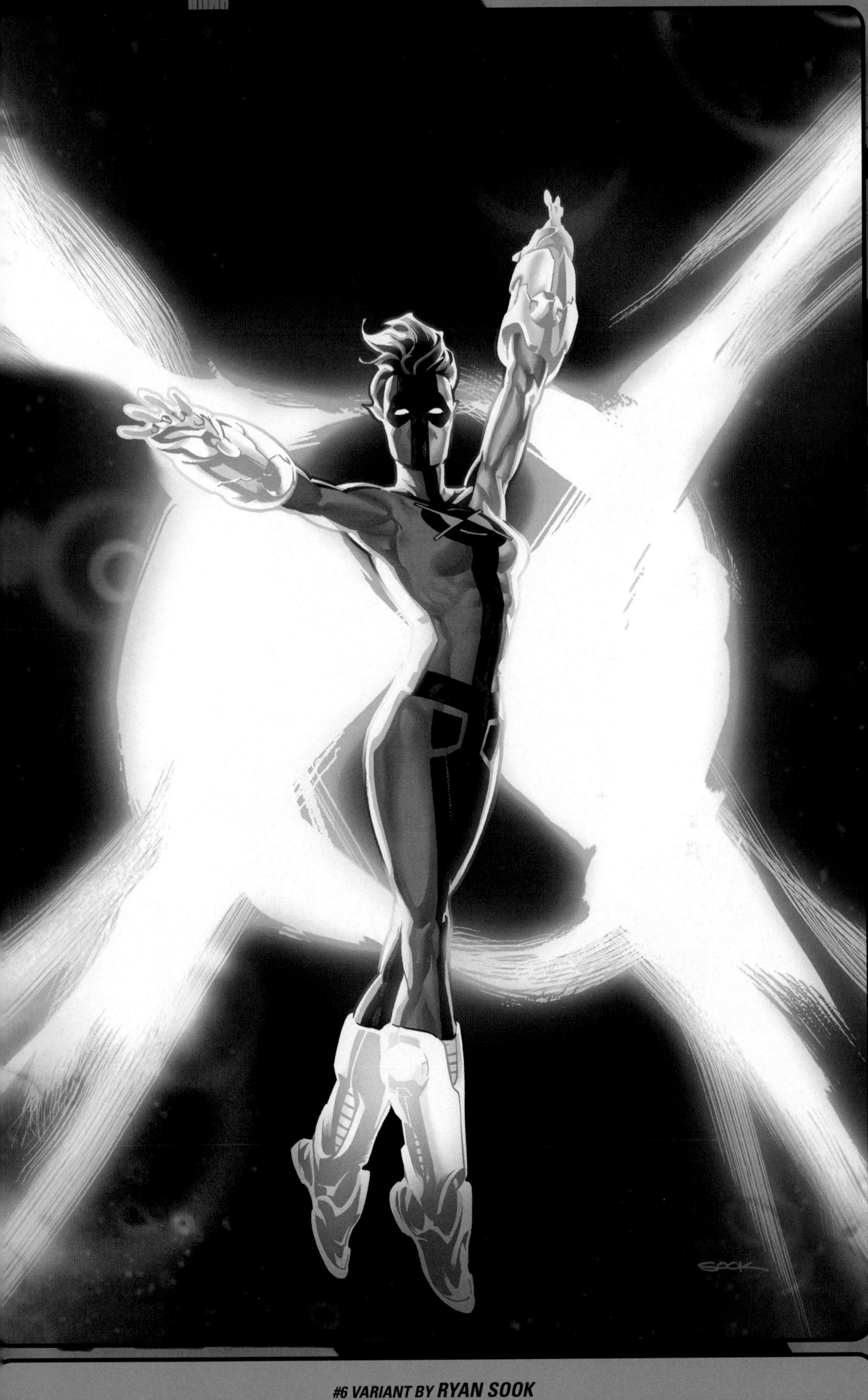
SOOK
#6 VARIANT BY **RYAN SOOK**

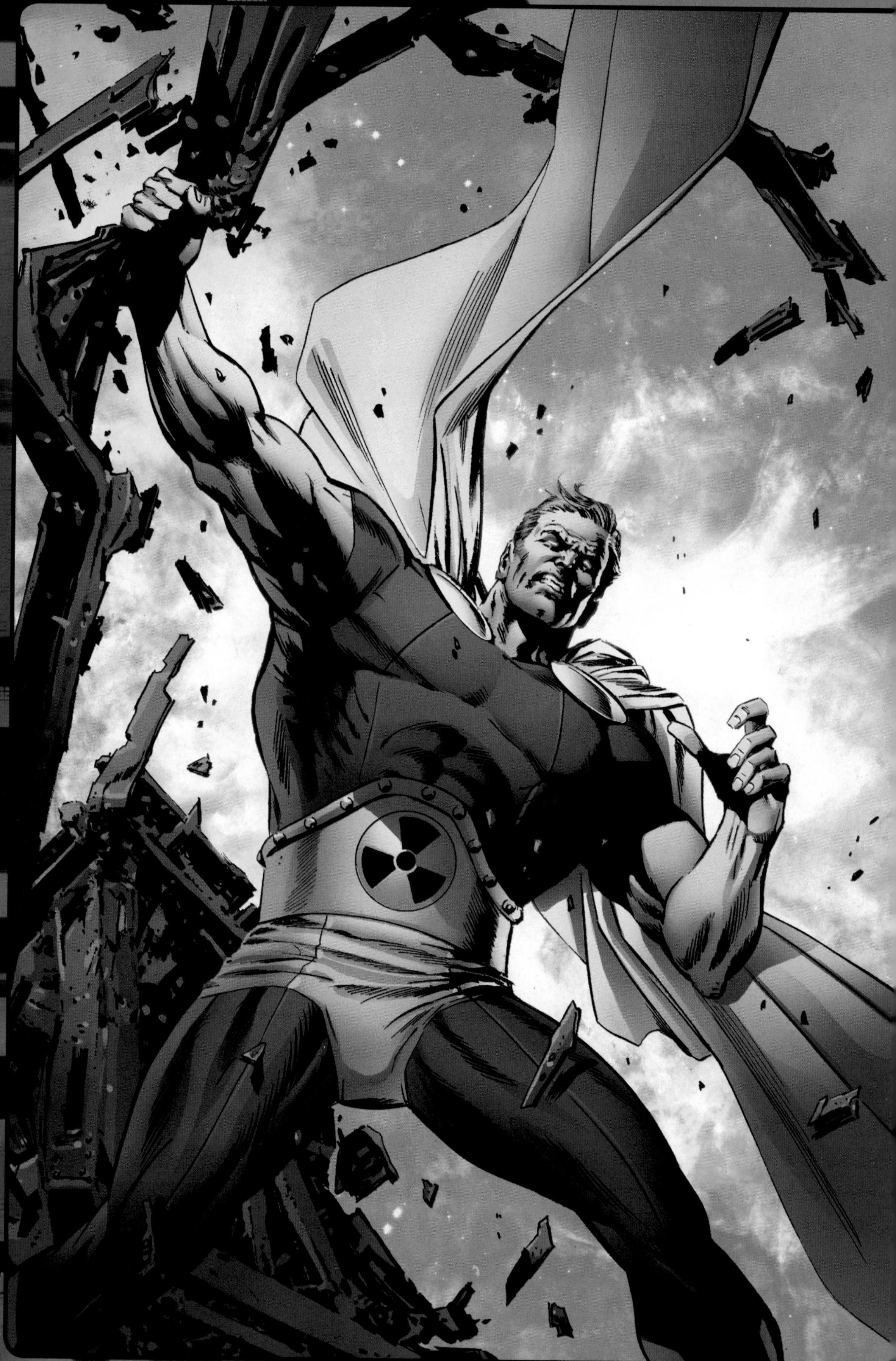

#6 VARIANT BY **BUTCH GUICE** & **FRANK D'ARMATA**

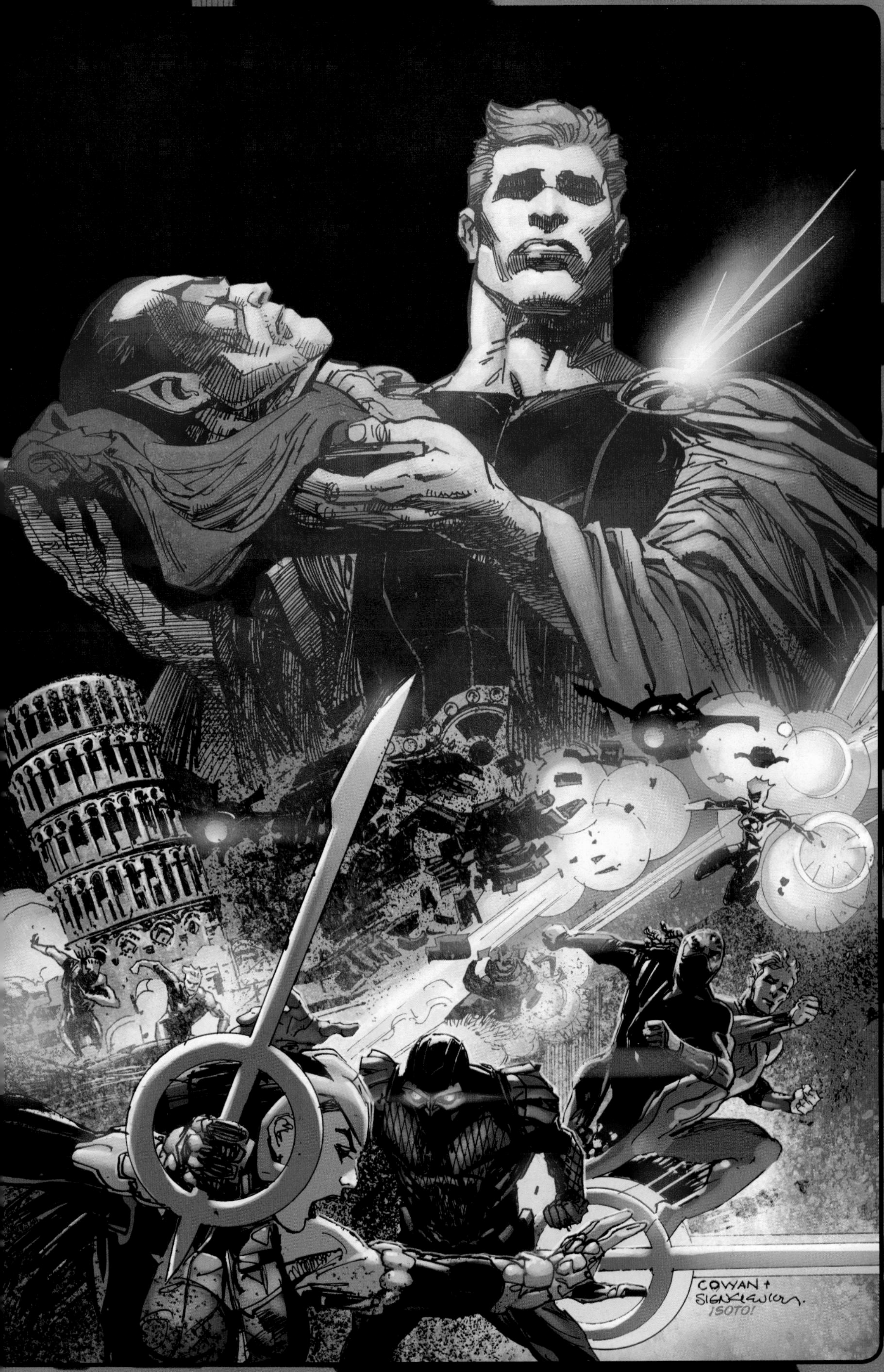
COWAN +
SIENKIEWICZ
¡SOTO!

#6 STORY THUS FAR VARIANT BY **DENYS COWAN, BILL SIENKIEWICZ & CHRIS SOTOMAYOR**

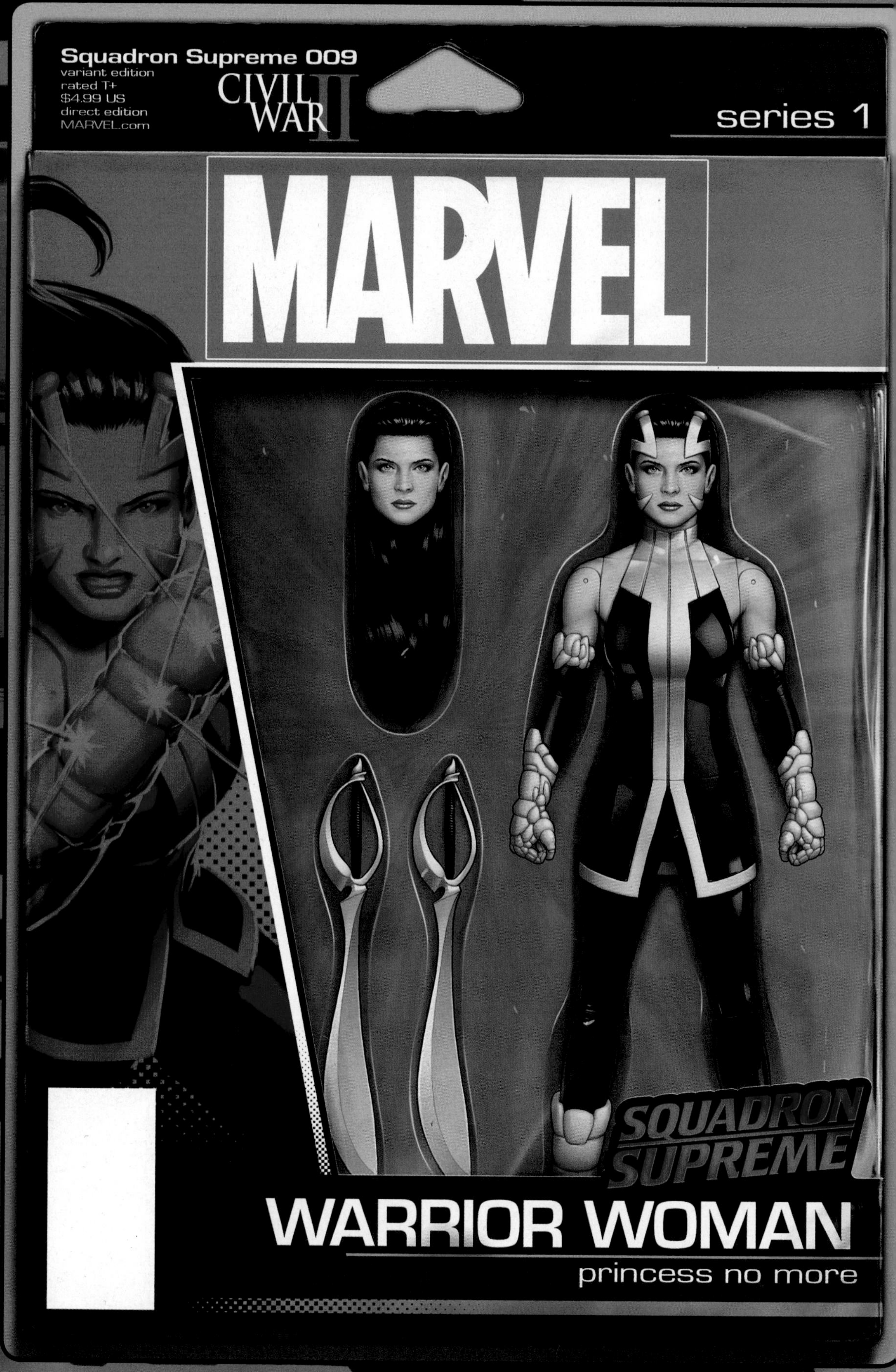
Squadron Supreme 009
variant edition
rated T+
$4.99 US
direct edition
MARVEL.com
CIVIL WAR II
series 1
MARVEL
SQUADRON SUPREME
WARRIOR WOMAN
princess no more

#9 ACTION FIGURE VARIANT BY JOHN TYLER CHRISTOPHER

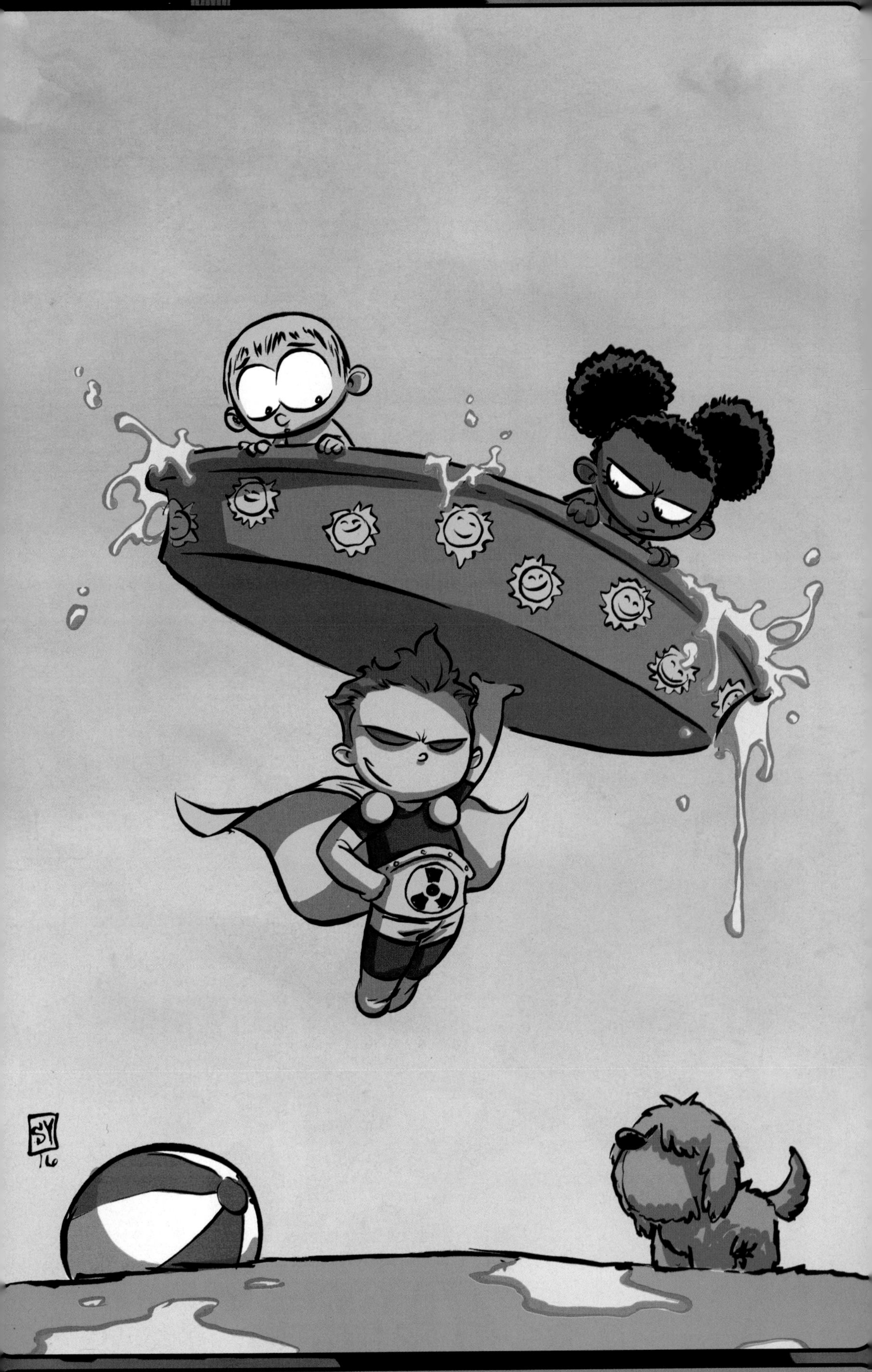

**#9 VARIANT BY SKOTTIE YOUNG**

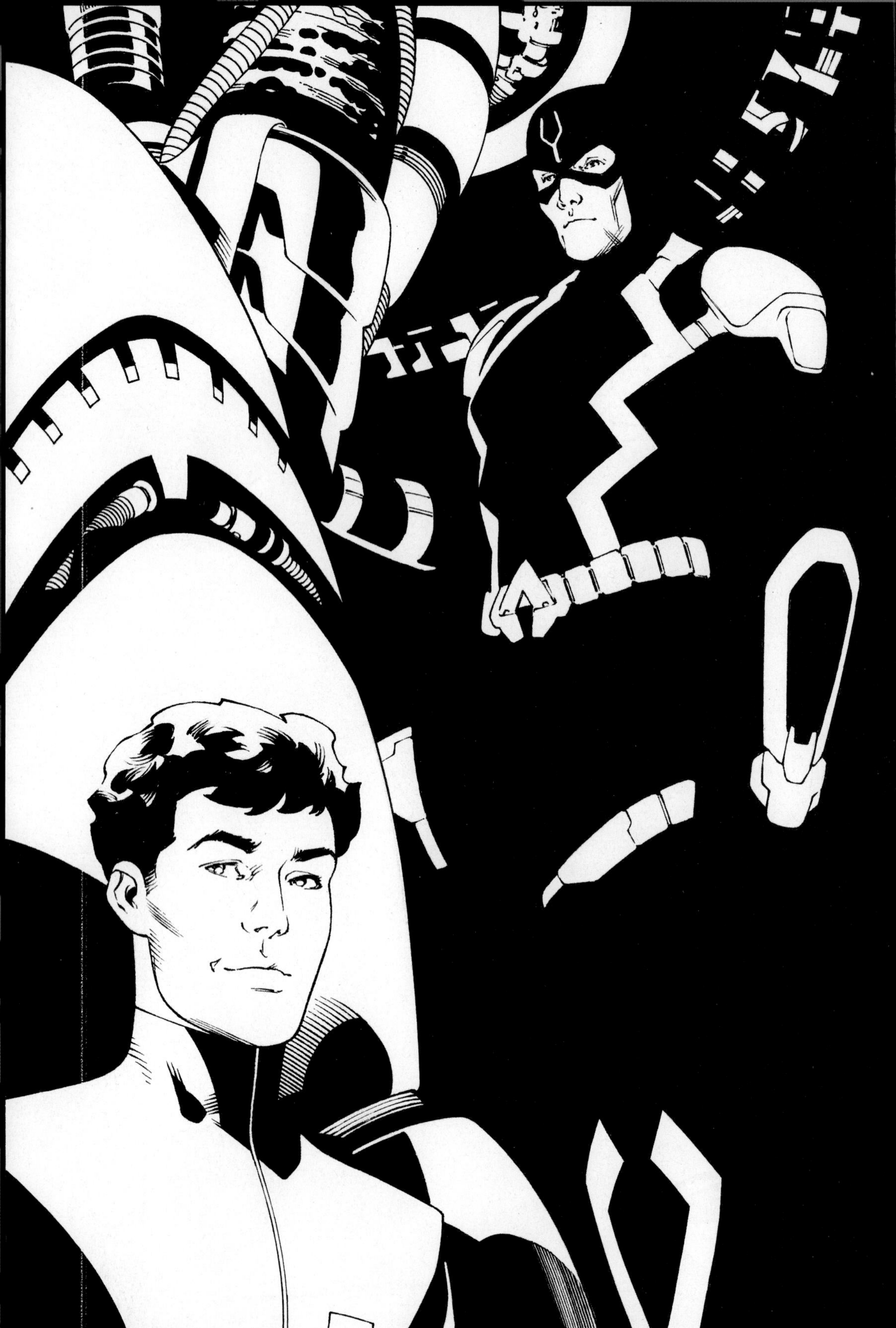

#6, PAGE 21 ART BY **LEONARD KIRK & PAUL NEARY**

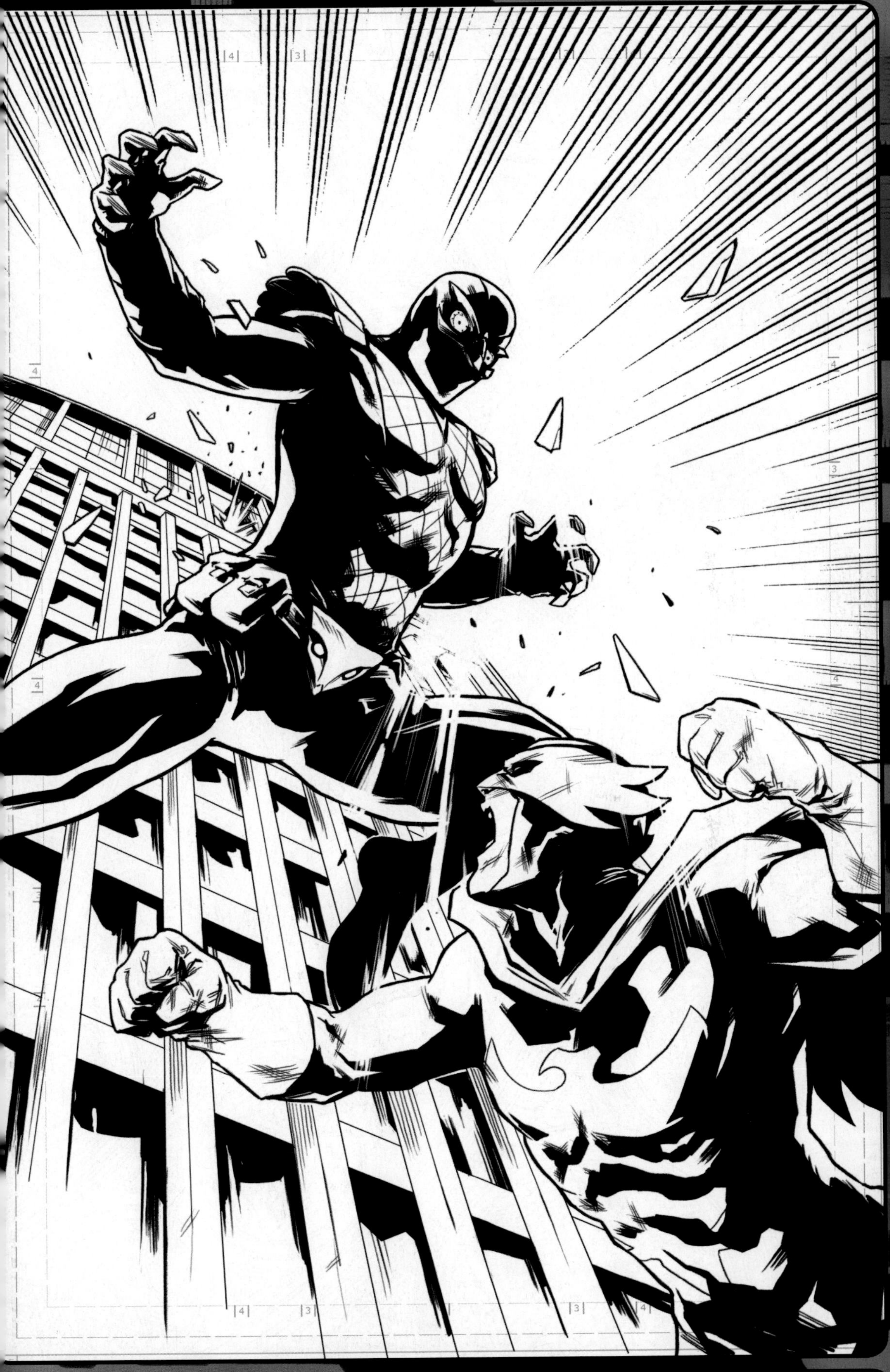

*#7, PAGE 20 ART BY* **PAOLO VILLANELLI**

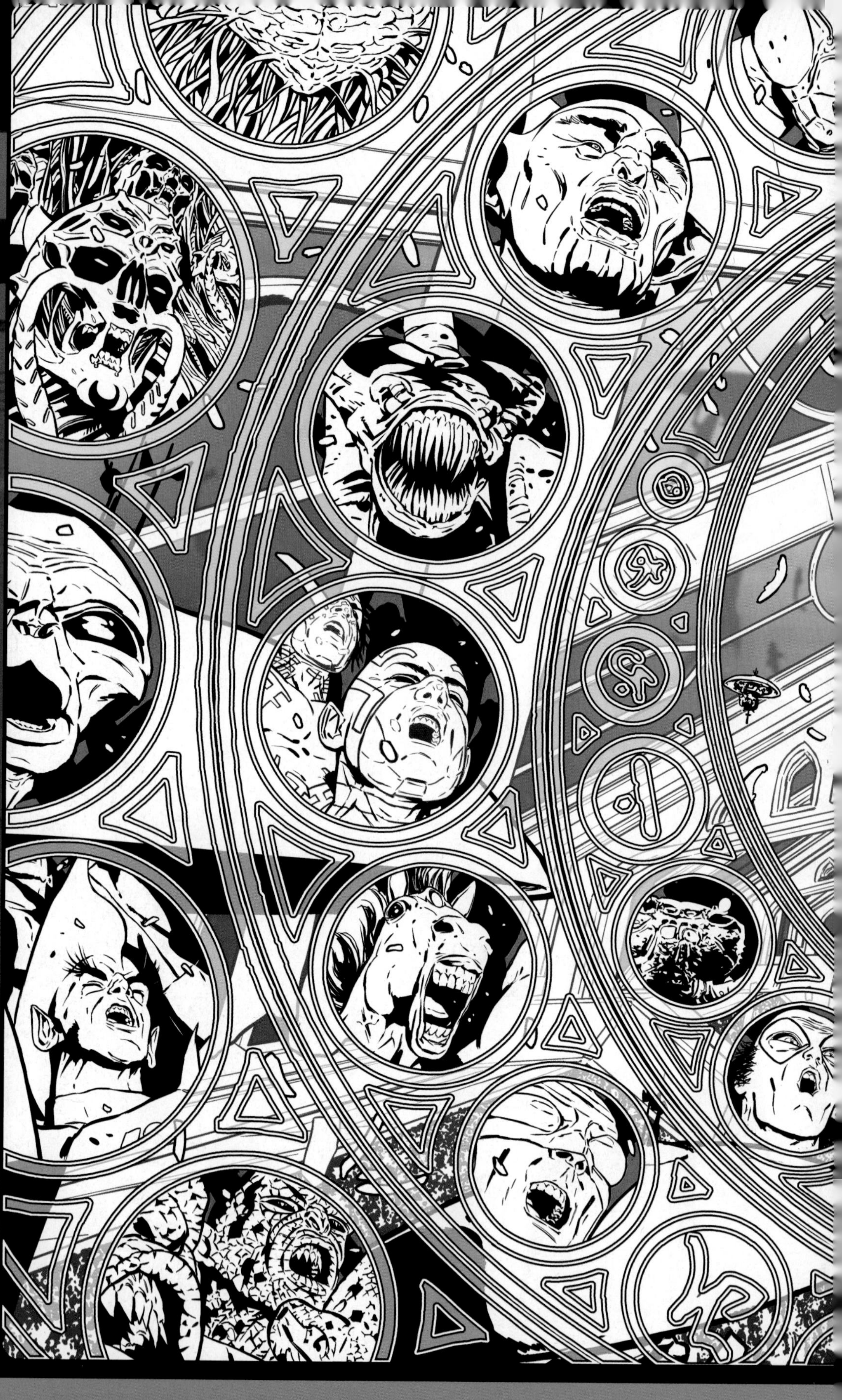

#9, PAGES 16-17 ART BY ACO

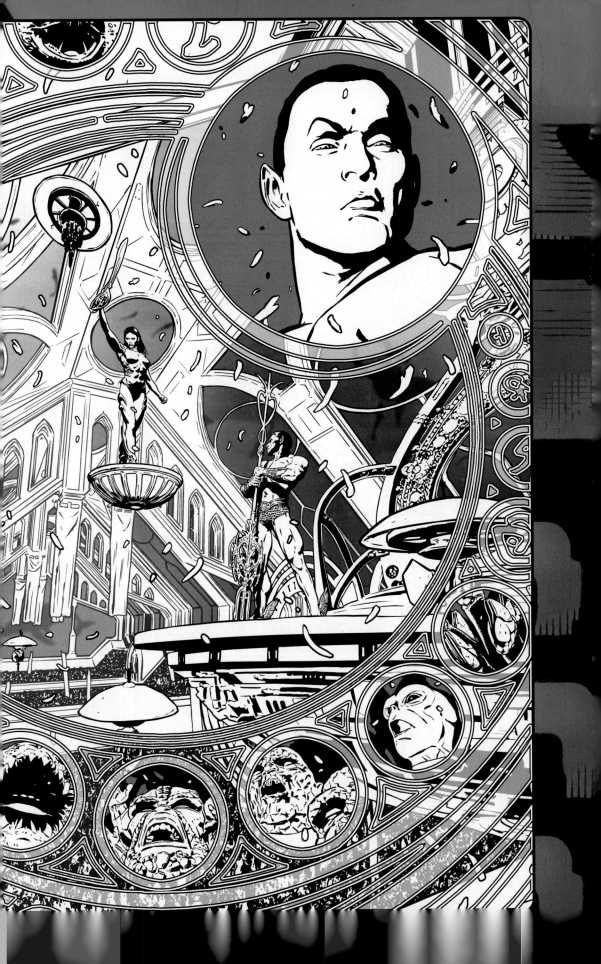

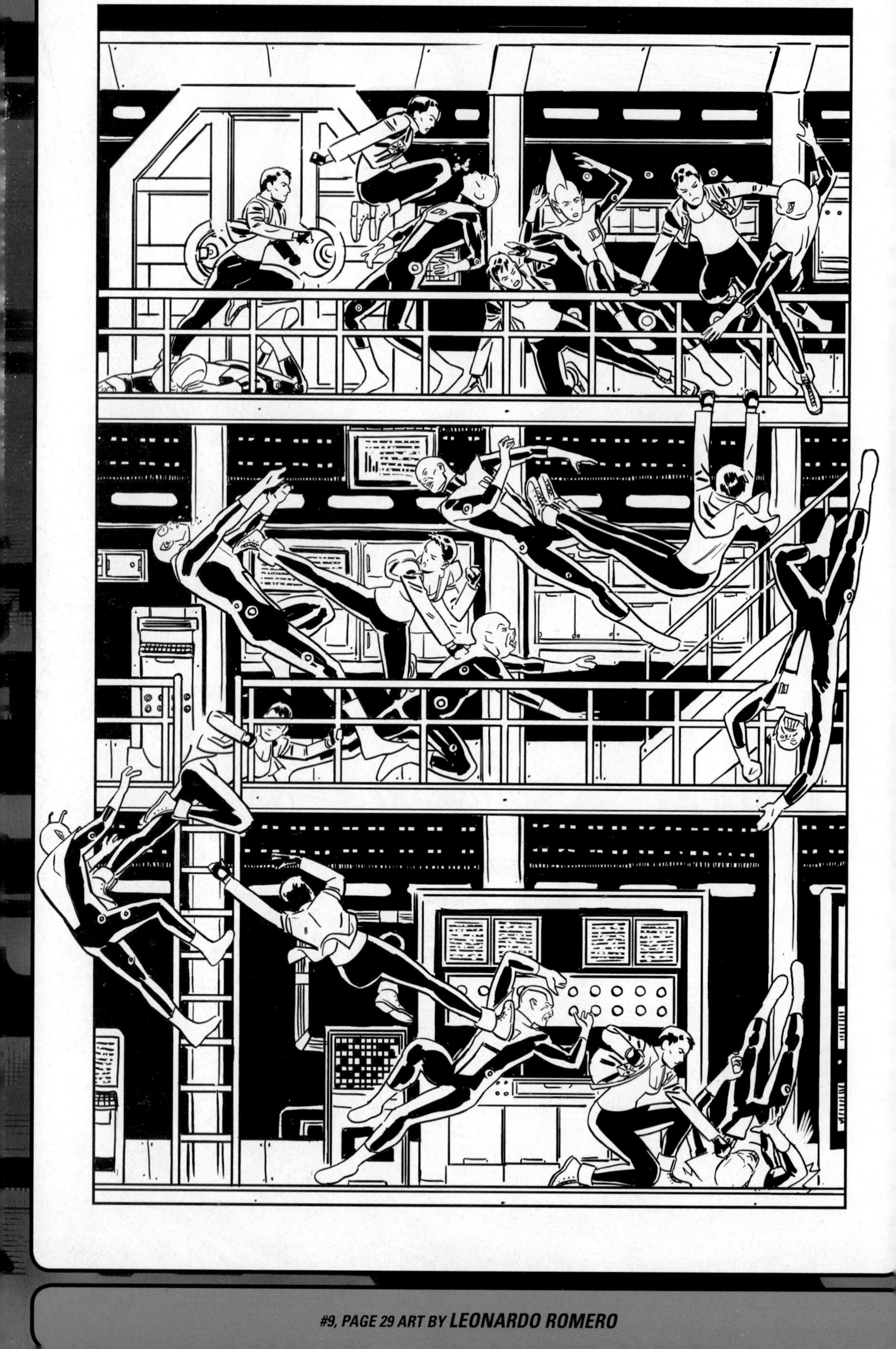

#9, PAGE 29 ART BY **LEONARDO ROMERO**